C000253493

FICTION

COLLECTIVE LIFE

In this book the author argues that the distinctive forms of modern popular culture can only be understood through the ways we dramatise public life, and that in the dramatic 'fictions' of collective experience we represent the terms of social order. The argument is richly illustrated with chapters on the theoretical character of performance in modernity; photography as the first means of mass representation; the nature of public discourse in mass democracy; and the elaboration of space for theatrical performance; and the marketing of culture and communication through mass systems of distribution.

The book aims to provide a framework within which any of the popular cultural forms of modernity can be understood. Drawing upon and adapting the extensive literature of cultural studies the author offers a distinctive and original sociological perspective on the relationship between individual and community in popular culture. The author also sets out the distinctive features of change in late-modern and postmodern culture. *Fictions of Collective Life* will be of interest to all those working in the field of the sociology of culture and cultural studies.

David Chaney is Senior Lecturer in Sociology at the University of Durham and has been working in the field of cultural and communication studies throughout his career.

FICTIONS OF COLLECTIVE LIFE

Public drama in late modern culture

David Chaney

London and New York

First published 1993
by Routledge
11 New Fetter Lane, London EC4P 4EE

Simultaneously published in the USA and Canada
by Routledge
29 West 35th Street, New York, NY 10001

© David Chaney 1993

Typeset in Garamond by LaserScript, Mitcham, Surrey

Printed and bound in Great Britain by
TJ Press (Padstow) Ltd, Padstow, Cornwall

All rights reserved. No part of this book may be reprinted or
reproduced or utilized in any form or by any electronic,
mechanical, or other means, now known or hereafter
invented, including photocopying and recording, or in any
information storage or retrieval system, without permission in
writing from the publishers.

British Library Cataloguing in Publication Data

A catalogue record for this book is available from the British Library

Library of Congress Cataloging in Publication Data

Chaney, David C.
Fictions of collective life: public drama in late modern culture/David
Chaney.
p. cm.
Includes bibliographical references and index.
1. Culture. 2. Communication and culture. 3. Popular culture.
I. Title.
HM101.C46 1993
306–dc20 92-40460
CIP
ISBN 0–415–03233–4
0–415–09319–8 (pbk)

I dedicate the book
to the memory of my parents
who both died while the book
was being planned and written

CONTENTS

Acknowledgements   ix
Introduction   1

1 SPECTACULAR SOCIETY/SOCIETY OF
  SPECTACLE   12
  Order and change   12
  Social dramas   16
  Two forms of spectacular social order   23
  Social order in a society of the spectacle   31
  Spectacular drama   39

2 DRAMATISING CHANGE: THEATRICALITY
  AND SPECTACLE IN NINETEENTH CENTURY
  BRITAIN   45
  Staged dramas   45
  Becoming the theatre   50
  Urban landscape and popular culture   59
  Spectacular entertainment   71

3 PHOTOGRAPHIC PICTURES   81
  Popular photography   81
  Public memory   86
  Conventions of looking   93
  Ritual and reflexivity   105

4 DISCOURSES OF PUBLIC LIFE   113
  The public sphere   113
  Addressing the public   120
  The discourse of actuality   130
  Public figures   140

5 MARKETING CULTURE   148
   The abstract crowd   148
   Mass communication and mass consumerism   154
   Leisure and the theatre of shopping   162
   Utopian intimations   170
   Traversing a fictive landscape   180

6 CONCLUSION: POPULAR AND CULTURE   189

   References   199
   Name index   214
   Subject index   219

ACKNOWLEDGEMENTS

While writing the book I have greatly enjoyed the friendship of members, both staff and students, of the Department of Sociology and Social Policy at Durham. It would be invidious to name individuals but the company of Bob and his mates has consistently been something I have valued and appreciated.

I have also spent two periods at McGill University, Montreal, the first as part of a research leave and the second giving an intensive lecture series on popular culture. I would like to acknowledge my appreciation of the friendship I received there and in particular the very real friendship and constant intellectual stimulation of Marike Finlay.

I would also like to acknowledge the help of Chris Stanbury in encouraging me to have sufficient faith to risk trusting in myself.

Connoisseurs of Acknowledgements sections, and particularly those prefacing books in sociology published by Routledge, will by now be familiar with tributes to the help authors have received from Chris Rojek. I cannot think of an original way of reiterating their remarks, so I must simply echo my predecessors and say that his help and encouragement have been invaluable.

Above all, the love, sympathy and encouragement of Sophie and Karina, in their different ways, have given the work of authorship a personal purpose and meaning.

INTRODUCTION

The fact is, living permanently in a well-ordered State has an out-and-out spectral aspect: one cannot step into the street or drink a glass of water or get into a tram without touching the perfectly balanced levers of a gigantic apparatus of laws and relations, setting them in motion or letting them maintain one in the peace and quiet of one's existence. One hardly knows any of these levers, which extend deep into the inner workings and on the other side are lost in a network the entire constitution of which has never been disentangled by any living being. Hence one denies their existence, just as the common man denies the existence of the air, insisting that it is mere emptiness; but it seems that precisely this is what lends life a certain spectral quality – the fact that everything that is denied reality, everything that is colourless, odourless, tasteless, imponderable and non-moral, like water, air, space, money and the passing of time, is in reality what is most important.

R. Musil (1953): *The Man Without Qualities*

Sociation is the form (realised in innumerably different ways) in which individuals grow together into a unity and within which their interests are realised. . . . If, therefore, there is to be a science whose subject matter is society and nothing else, it must exclusively investigate these interactions, these kinds and forms of sociation.

G. Simmel (1971): *The Problem of Sociology*, pp. 24–5

My intentions in this book can be summarised under two headings. I shall seek to show, first, the relevance of a vocabulary of drama to describe how our sense of collective experience is expressed. I shall show that this sense of collectivity enacts a type of social order and,

1

secondly, that we can use features of the ways we dramatise our-selves to delineate the main characteristics of modernity. I shall use the general term public drama or public culture to refer to dramatisations of ourselves, and I will show that in modernity certain features, we can provisionally refer to here by the label of spectacular theatricality, have come to be dominant. I will therefore use aspects of public drama to illuminate the social order of modernity. In this Introduction I will explain what I mean by these terms and describe how the book is organised. What is distinctive to my work here is that in exploring the institutional forms of modern sociation, the ways in which the culture of an urban-industrial society has changed should become clearer – so that much of what we can take for granted as features of mass culture can be seen in a different light. This in turn will help to clarify the distinctiveness of much that is claimed to mark transitions between modernity and post-modernity.

I believe that any attempt to explore the non-phenomenal must work at least initially through metaphor. The key metaphor in this study will be the idea that the relations of dramatic performance can be used to describe or characterise interactional forms. By relations of dramatic performance, I mean the structural organisation that underlies the experience of a dramatisation of social action. The relations are understood to be common to the huge variety of types of dramatic performance cross-culturally. The relations will be con-cretised in particular cases through a vocabulary such as notions of a stage, perspective, audience, address and frame (the metaphoric relevance to social order will be illustrated in succeeding chapters).

These are structural features of the making of the human enter-prise of a drama. They can be used without any commitment or reference to what is being performed, whether it is a play or some other scripted enterprise (such as a political speech) or a more traditional mode of performance such as a ceremony or a ritual. The relations of dramatic performance as structural relationships can be used as a means to bring into consciousness our expectations for collective forms of interaction. The metaphor of dramatisation is a way of talking about Musil's invisible levers or expectations; it is a separate and distinct project to describe particular forms of inter-action – those that we can call performances.

Following this distinction between expectations and perform-ance I should note that the metaphor of dramatic relations does not have to be illustrated through those social occasions that we might

2

normally call dramatic. As examples of social drama I can point to the ceremonies through which organisations imbue their identity and purposes with tradition and dignity, or the ways in which institutionalised authority, be it political, military, legal or monarchical, attempts to display its legitimacy. These are the sorts of public events that Handelman (1990) has studied as either models or mirrors of themes of social order; I shall discuss further aspects of Handelman's work on public events in subsequent chapters. The ceremonies of the modern nation-state are obviously a major genre of public drama but I shall only touch upon them in passing.

One of the more provocative attempts to use a dramatic occasion – the practice of cock-fighting in the island of Bali – as a model for social concerns, is provided in Clifford Geertz' (1972) famous paper. In a frequently cited passage Geertz talks about forms of perform-ance as a way of talking about ourselves: 'What sets the cockfight apart from the ordinary course of life . . . [is that] it provides a metasocial commentary upon the whole matter of assorting human beings into fixed hierarchical ranks and then organizing the major part of collective existence around that assortment. Its function, if you want to call it that, is interpretive: it is a Balinese reading of Balinese experience; a story they tell themselves about themselves' (op. cit. p. 26). The cockfight involves playing between men through the medium of animals and signifying their investment of status through gambling so that it becomes a piece of 'deep play'. Geertz renders the play through a metaphor of story, a bridge towards theories of narrative which has been very influential (although the authority of Geertz' text as a reading of 'their' texts has been questioned, see the discussion in Crapanzo 1986; I have attempted to use concepts of narrative in relation to the anonymous entertainment of mass society in a previous book, Chaney (1979)).

Two further aspects of Geertz' account of reading a dramatic performance should be noted at this stage as they underlie my approach in succeeding chapters. The first is that the dramatic metaphor in a form of play works because it is *a form of play*: 'the cockfight renders ordinary, everyday experience comprehensible by presenting it in terms of acts and objects which have had their practical consequences removed and been reduced (or, if you prefer raised) to *the level of sheer appearances*' (op. cit. p. 22, emphasis added). There is a recurrently tempting pun between play, as form of interaction, and a play as a staged enterprise. Discussing forms of dramatisation I focus upon the significance of the ways in

3

which we routinely play with social forms rather than the content of particular plays.

The second point I want to emphasise at this stage is that the meanings or subjective intensity of the relations of dramatic performance in the cock-fight are not a shadow of some prior and more substantial reality. Rather, the play of dramatic performance in and through its being enacted constitutes the being-in-the-world it represents or articulates: 'art forms generate and regenerate the very subjectivity they pretend only to display. Quartets, still-lifes, and cockfights are not merely reflections of a preexisting sensibility analogically represented; they are positive agents in the creation and maintenance of such a sensibility' (op. cit. p. 28). This is not to say that resources for the production of meaning are universally available – in cultural industries they clearly are not. It is rather that both personal experience and institutional form are being made up (constituted) through the process of enactment (performance).

The theme of this study will be that, without restricting ourselves to theatrical drama or to the highly charged dramatic occasion of instances of deep play, we can use the relations of dramatic performance to talk about ourselves. Or, more complexly, we can use any one of the forms of self-reflection available in everyday life (forms of dramatisation) as an analytic resource to talk about how we tell ourselves about ourselves. The word 'ourselves' is a convenient shorthand for an only imperfectly understood sense of membership. But the term 'ourselves' is misleading if it is taken to connote a collection of individuals – it should be understood to point to networks of relationships, forms of interaction. The relations of dramatic performance articulate what provides a tangible feeling of shared forms of perception and understanding. The self as personal identity is counterpointed by an enormous range of affiliations to more-or-less demanding collectivities of family, gender, race and religion, etc. It is in the dialogic interaction between our identities that a distinctive style of life is played out.

It is at this point that we can begin to sense the limitations of metaphors of telling and talking. Geertz' formulation leads, as I have noted, to rendering occasions of deep play as texts. I see the metaphor of text as a limitation because texts are not apprehended sensually and because a text implies that something has been completed. A text may be engrossing but it is a disembodied engrossment. It is the performative character of dramatic performance that I wish to stress. It is in the enaction of performance, all the ways in

4

which we participate in apprehending experience (the density of inter-action), that we get caught up in the this-ness of the here-and-now. The relations of dramatic performance are a generative metaphor for our sense of communal experience because they are literally engrossing in that they are the fabric out of which we weave the forms and styles of social life. The framing of performance is necessarily permeable and frequently ironic.

I have emphasised that a dramatic vocabulary is metaphorical. To say this is not just to nod towards the conventional use of dramatic metaphor and dramatic irony. The nature of a metaphor is that in the image an impossible conjunction is made possible. Two or more words from incompatible domains are combined (as in 'the chattering train') in order to create an arbitrary illusion. Although a tremendous amount has now been published on the nature of metaphor a very clear account of the sociological promise of metaphor is in Brown (1977 especially Chapter 4); see also Lakoff and Johnson (1980). A semiotic reality or a truth of the imagination is created by metaphor in order to capture something elusive beyond the immediately given. In this way metaphors are fundamental to any imaginative account and equally to social theory (the title of this book is taken from Clifford's (1988 p. 10) discussion of the project of ethnographic narratives).

I cannot pretend that the chapters that follow are an exhaustive or authoritative account. They are more like a travelogue or a documentary in which I attempt to assemble some notes on journeys. I can only report on observations and readings which are necessarily partial and selective; this is the data of contemporary cultural history. They have been collected through a metaphoric leap in order to give a semblance of order.

The consequence I wish to draw out is that, regardless of our attitude to the relationship between culture as theory and culture as practice in native cultures, we cannot pretend that cultural models of public events in our own culture are merely interpretive resources. Tools of that trade that is everyday life so to speak. The media of apprehension have to be seen as prescriptive in their dominating force. They provide for the orderliness of mundane experience. In the first chapter I will discuss in greater detail my understanding of some aspects of the dramatisation of social order.

At this point in the Introduction I want to emphasise that metaphors for forms of interaction, or more generally the ways we talk about ourselves (the discourses of popular experience), entail relations of power. By this I mean that differences in access to and use of cultural resources are legitimated and naturalised so that the disadvantaged have little means of redress or repair (or even frequently of appreciating their disadvantage). A sensitivity to the interdependence of knowledge and power is of course inseparable from the body of work by Michel Foucault and those strongly influenced by him (see in particular the essays in Foucault 1980; and the critical discussions in Hoy 1986). This book is not, however, situated within his concerns except to the extent that all work in the dying years of the century cannot escape issues raised in his account of discursive practices.

My approach here is centrally concerned with the institutionalisation of a reflexive metaphor. If a social institution is a set of characteristic habits and understandings clustering around interdependent roles, then the relations of dramatic performance act as structuring roles in this case. My understanding of how an interpretive resource such as the notion of an institution could be seen to have effects on how we think, perceive and understand has been greatly helped by the work of Mary Douglas (in particular 1987). Another way of phrasing a concern with institutionalisation is to ask how, in ways that have been powerfully generative, our dim sense of ourselves as particular sorts of social actors has been inflected in forms of entertainment.

In the first chapter I explore the metaphor of drama in greater depth. In addition to more general points about the meaning of drama I introduce the notion of spectacle as a form of drama that is particularly appropriate as a characterisation of interactional forms in mass culture. This is not a new idea. Indeed the claim of a spectacular society has become a central slogan for certain strands of post-modern posturing (see for example Kroker *et al.* 1989). In this chapter, however, I argue that the terms of spectacular dramatisation can be used with comparable legitimacy as a characterisation of the social order of both early modern and post-modern Europe. This paradox forces us to develop a more sensitive account of the spectacular as a form of drama, a more troubled appreciation of the relationships between form of drama and community, and a closer concern with the logic of dramatisation in mass culture. Such major themes are only sketched in such a relatively short chapter but a set of concerns which will inform succeeding chapters are introduced.

In the second chapter the issue of theatricality is more explicitly addressed. In the first chapter I draw a distinction between drama and theatre; now I argue that in the course of the nineteenth century, theatre became a popular cultural form. Forms of dramatic entertainment had of course been popular before, but the theatre had principally been an élite cultural form. It became a defining feature of modernisation that the new audiences of urbanising Britain sought out entertainment in a variety of new theatres and in a variety of new theatrical genres. The central reason for my concern with this strand of cultural history is that I want to use the form of the theatre, as a changing type of place or social space as a template for the social language of urban-industrial society.

The essence of this argument lies in the changing meanings of spectacular entertainment. Theatres, as part of a re-staging of city centres (and urban life) became spectacular sites, and, in a progression that is consistent with the changing theatre, the form of performance became characterised by an attempt to combine spectacular artifice with pictorial naturalism. I argue that it is through what I describe as the conventions of pictorial naturalism, that we have learnt to imagine the often unimaginable city; and, inseparable from that task, the new social entities of the metropolis – the proletariat and their popular culture. The nature of theatricality introduces us therefore to themes of pictorialism and ways of perceiving forms of social life.

The centrality of the implied order of ways of seeing to the staging of processes of social intercourse in modernity is engaged more closely in the third chapter on the cultural form of photographic pictures. Popular photography is a mode of representation in which technological innovation has been used to facilitate what has quickly become an unremarkable resource for a language of social experience. In this chapter themes such as the definition of a cultural form, the nature of popular entertainment and the reflexivity of picturing intertwine in a discussion of the sorts of things we take photographs of. The history of popular photography also provides an important illustration of the interdependence of dramatic order as resource for representation and dramatic order as a form of social control discussed earlier. In the several genres of photographic practice we seem to have a way of looking at the representation of performance on the borders of public and private experience. In the transparency and artlessness of most modes of popular photography there is buried an intriguing form of spectacular dramatisation.

The most obviously apparent way of talking about ourselves as a multiplicity of collectivities is the ever-expanding compilation of written and broadcast reports on public life. In the fourth chapter this profusion of reports is characterised as a discourse of public and publics which shapes mass democratic politics. The initial theme is that as this discourse is constitutive as well as descriptive, the analogy of voice or address is necessary as a key illustration of how the politics of mass culture are staged and articulated. The theme of calling into being is used in a discussion of the transformation of publics in mass politics; the centrality of the imagined community of the nation in the public discourse of mass communication; the ritual character of news as a form of drama; and the perenially interesting question of the status of the cast of figures who people the stage of public events. All these are the common subject matter of studies in mass communication and studies of power and authority in advanced industrial societies (see for example Thompson 1990). In this chapter, and the book in general, focussing on the character of publics as a form of collectivity interrelates with the more persistent theme of the constitutive forms of popular experience.

It is apparent that in theoretical discussions the character of public discourse is most frequently criticised because of the man-ipulation of consciousness. That is, that those who are the audience for this discourse might have their appreciation of social and cultural realities significantly influenced. This theme of disciplining audiences through controlling knowledge is taken up more directly in the fifth chapter. Although here the central theme is less con-straint through textual restrictions, and more that the cultural space for audience-ing (the forms of participation available to audiences) entails forms of order which are constraining and restrictive. And yet simultaneously in those forms of participation in dramatic scenarios there has come to seem for the popular audience scope for im-provisation and elaboration on a previously unprecedented scale.

This contradiction, which has been a perennial theme in accounts of mass culture, is addressed in the fifth chapter through aspects of the marketing of cultural forms, as well as the organi-sation of marketing itself as a cultural form. It will be argued that popular cultural forms are inherently commercial entertainments and in their vocabulary of pleasure can be found the practical forms of what we have seen as metaphor. The pleasures of consumer culture are usually taken to be the illusions of exploitation and paradigmatic of industries of mass entertainment (the 'bread and circuses' of which intellectuals despair, see Brantlinger 1983). In my account of the interdependencies of market and entertainment I shall pay particular attention to the associated activities of tourism, leisure and fashions as adaptations of popular drama for everyday life.

There is a persistent strain of idealisation in the commercial pragmatism of popular entertainment. It has been tempting but not very enlightening to see the need for idealisation as a functional response to the mundane tedium and exploitation of everyday life. The limitation of this view is that all forms of 'the sacred' are forced into the mechanical mould of functionalism. As an alternative I shall explore in the fifth chapter how in the cultural forms of mass entertainment, the space framed in dramaturgy has been transformed so that the landscape of our social environment is fictionalised. The salience of utopian forms in modernism and in popular entertainment is that they provide a secular normative order for modernity. In design, style and structure I argue that there is a language or set of resources for negotiating a fictive landscape. Although the forms available are generally spectacular illusions they also offer the promise of capturing the resources (or language of ritual) for dramatisation.

The material in the fifth chapter raises more forcibly than in some others sociological issues concerning the character of representation. I said earlier in this Introduction that I want to broaden the idea that cultural representations are ways in which we are able to talk about ourselves. I have developed a new account of the concept of a cultural form (Chaney 1990A and in the chapters of this book) in order to make the notion of representation more complexly adequate. I also use the root metaphor of the relations of dramatic performance to amplify the notion of 'talking about'. If we make talk into a more encompassing notion of performance, the relations of dramatic action can be seen to be both marked off from and buried within the quotidian. It is in engaging with the forms of commonsense that I find myself, somewhat to my surprise, reprising the project that Berger and Luckmann (1967) described some years ago as the study of everything that passes for knowledge.

The limitations of commonsense, as the self-evident knowings of the man or woman in the street, are that because it can be taken for granted, that which the knowledge trades upon and which makes it possible is frequently hidden from view. One illustration of such a commonsensical presupposition in this chapter is that I have taken 'ourselves' as self-evidently available. But it is precisely the ambiguities, overlappings, contradictions and duplicities of such memberships that in urban culture become written (inscribed) into normality. (Thereby creating an anomie of ambiguity and uncertainty which has generated the documentary literature of ethnographic narratives; see for example Plummer 1983 and Atkinson 1990). It is in the stagings and playings of interactional forms, and the modes of dramatisation discussed in this book, that the possibilities for who ourselves are become articulated and available. The relations of dramatic performance are therefore reflexive accounts of collective experience (the notion of reflexivity is returned to in the following chapters, the main source for how it is being used here is Garfinkel 1967).

Cultural studies embraces those cross-disciplinary concerns with the social organisation and significance of different forms of expressive rather than instrumental activities. There is such a range of types of action, from art forms to cock-fights to ethnographies, that the general term representation has become common. Representation is convenient and it is consistent with a vocabulary of signs and significations but like the latter terms it does imply a relationship of standing for an independent reality. While I continue to use the term representation I do so as convenient shorthand for a socially organised complex of activities which generate a particular form of narrative and are institutionalised as an occasion. In my previous discussion of representation in popular culture (Chaney 1979), I tried to develop a methodology based on a combination of the production of culture approach of American sociologists with the constructivist formalism of Mayakovsky and Brecht. In this study I have taken the metaphor of construction further and use it to 'de-construct' the social organisation of dramatisation.

Re-thinking representation has in its turn implications for our account of culture. The concept of culture has been used in arguments to act as a type of conceptual screen, behind it activities by members of a group or community can be shown to make sense, although equivalently incomprehensible to those beyond the screen. This has lead to a type of cultural reification which has been an important political strategy for groups seeking to assert a distinctive identity; but it mistakes the nature of culture as an interpretive resource. I shall argue that culture is more usefully understood as a style. By this I mean a recognisable and distinctive set of practices which are forms of knowledge. The consistency of a style has also to accommodate variations, inflections and contradictions. This is why in the Conclusion I have chosen to focus on the consequences of the arguments in this book for our understanding of popular culture. The recurrent theme of the ways in which we use the term popular especially in relation to culture provides an appropriate focus to pull together the wide-ranging discussion of the main chapters.

The term 'popular' is usually used to refer to either a particular type of cultural activity or entertainment, or with different forms of political discourse (a repertoire that is more fully discussed in Chaney 1990B). While these uses are illuminating they do seem restrictive; popular is being treated almost as a qualification, a variant on an implied norm. I shall argue that the development of a notion of the popular should also be understood as the gradual recognition of a changing cultural formation. The vocabulary of ourselves has patently been forcibly rewritten (while retaining many of the same terms) in the course of modernisation. The popular is therefore more than a claim for a particular type of collective identity (although it is often that). The popular implies a stance or form of engagement with the invisible mechanisms of sociation. The popular is modernity's recognition of its own spectral quality; it is therefore the ironic recognition at the heart of modern dramatisation.

1

SPECTACULAR SOCIETY/SOCIETY OF SPECTACLE

ORDER AND CHANGE

At a casual glance the phrases bracketed together in the title of this chapter duplicate each other. They are, however, in this context going to be used as polar contrasts. They refer to ideal-typical forms of social order. Not, that is, the relations of social order directly but the cultural imagery and more particularly the forms of dramatisation through which types of social order are staged. The two phrases are used to mark out the terms of cultural change. In a later part of this chapter I will specify the differences in dramatisation between these forms of social order in order to show how the dynamics of meaning and gratification in personal experience have been radically transformed.

In order to elucidate how I can use the contrast between spectacular society and society of spectacle in this way I need first to make some preliminary notes on what I mean by key terms. In this first part of the chapter I shall discuss the interdependent concepts of social order, cultural imagery and cultural change. I hope that by making clearer how they are being used in this context, an introduction to the more general argument will be provided.

The concept of social order refers to the predictable, indeed the prescribed, character of everyday life. It is not just that any one individual may have an orderly routine, more that the others with whom they interact will also conform to predictable expectations so that while we are capable of creative autonomy, everyday life is not normally full of uncertainty. The orderliness of routinisation may be experienced as oppressive, and there are of course many different occasions when shocks and ruptures tear the fabric of conventional expectations; but in general the predictability of order is what we mean when we say we live in society rather than a random collection of individuals. (Sociology as a meta-discourse of common-sense, is inevitably susceptible to the charge of merely replicating normality; both as a way of evading that charge and transcending the recuperative inertia of the everyday, it may be that our most productive sociology (has and) will develop from concentrating upon moments of disorder but this does not undercut the primary significance of forms of order.)

It is apparent that order, if it is to assuage our uncertainties, may need to be imposed as well as more voluntarily agreed upon. It seems reasonable to postulate that there will be different forms of order distinguishable by the ways they command assent. I shall mention three types. The first can be called formal order and is articulated in the rules and laws of social organisation. This in contemporary society is principally those clustered under the heading of the state – a form of order which is both explicit and is often enforced by the specification of penalties which will be applied to those who do not conform. In contrast, a second form of order is normative or moral rather than bureaucratic. The obligations may be equally or more binding than the criminal code but are rarely expressed as explicitly, and sanctions for nonconformity usually involve degrees and types of social ostracism. Thirdly, there are a multitude of expectations in everyday life which constitute the institutionalised normality of particular settings and occasions. In this sense the order will still be generally prescriptive but implicit and contextualised with a wide variety of sanctions for nonconformity.

The reason for making these very obvious distinctions is that they provide a framework within which we can mark out differences in the character of consensus. Thus they provide a descriptive resource for the ways in which the social order of a pre-industrial village will be different from that of a metropolitan city. If we use a set of references to features such as the nature of others' expectations, the language of obligations, the means and manner of negotiating non-conformity, and the types of sanctions that are – or can be – invoked in relation to nonconformity, we will have a more precise framework for specifying types of social order. In the following chapters I will not be concerned to describe a structure of social order but will use the scope for independence open to social actors as a guide to the dynamics of social life. The reason is that underlying this framework, the forms of social order also mark out ways in which we understand distinctions between individual and collectivity. The social entities of individual and collectivity are not self-evident – although they will be experienced as such in any particular setting – and their mutual interdependence will be charted in the lineaments of social order. It is a premise of my approach that it cannot be assumed that there are a collection of individuals who exist prior to and independently of a collectivity displayed through a form of order. Rather it is that the web of expectations and understanding and incoherence provides for a particular type of individuality or social consciousness (an approach that has been particularly influenced by the work of Norbert Elias 1978 and 1982).

The notion of social order is reflexive in that it makes sense of, or legitimates, its own necessity. While it provides for the possibility of particular modes of interaction it also institutionalises differences in degree of access to the interpretation of the practical meaning of order. That is to say, a form of order will be symbolically bound up with structured forms of differentiation in which differences in status between groups will mark differences in the autonomy and authority, etc. of members of those groups. Forms of social order therefore work to inscribe structural differences in power between groups such as those that organise gender relationships in all modes of interaction. The predictable character of order means both that normal interaction is not threatening and that the 'normal' in any particular setting is both predictable and, indeed, may well seem inevitable. The aspects of order which entail institutionalised constraint will be masked or even possibly celebrated as naturally justified.

The salience of a concept of power in social thought in recent years has stemmed from a realisation that the force of power is, in addition to the ability to enforce, or even more than its naturalisation in inscribed order, also declamatory. Power bellows forth its own majesty sometimes in the rituals of force and authority but more commonly in the insidious whisper of ways of imag(in)ing forms of pleasure and entertainment. While the concept of order is of course an abstraction, it is accessible in the courtesies of everyday interaction as much as the pronouncements of judges. And if we search for the reflexive legitimacy of social order it is more accessible in the presuppositions of practical consciousness. I shall argue that the institutionalisation of modernity (here used to refer to a social process that entails characteristic ways of being in the world) has involved a distinctive re-staging of collective consciousness – in particular that forms of popular culture have become embedded in everyday life principally through the organisation and labelling of social space.

The imagery of a particular culture is, then, the ways in which the conventions through which the normality of social order are represented to its inhabitants. To take a straightforward example, the conventions governing posing in the various types of domestic snapshot represent relations of family, gender and biographical order, amongst others. It is precisely everything we take for granted in perceiving and recognising 'normal reality' that provides a form of life: 'Cultural production and reproduction concern not only the shifting cosmetic surface, but the underlying foundation which any society proposes and assumes as its Reality' (Bryson 1983 p. 5 *sic*).

Cultural conventions are distinctive forms of symbolic imagination embodied in material practices, aspects of the institutionalisation of a more-or-less coherent sense of order. It is important to stress here that the connections between imagery and order being made should not be understood to be suggesting that imagery is solely or dominantly regulatory. There is an inextricable dialogia (as an intertwining of voices) between order and jouissance in the dramas of collective experience.

If the idea of an imagery of order is understood literally it could be thought of as a series of exhortatory stories, as for example in the fairy-tales of childhood socialisation. Not only would this not be appropriate for the elements of festive transgression that we have already noted, it is also too restricting in using imagery as illustration. The delineation of meaning is a process of *performance* in which all the elements of the material world (usually currently at hand) are treated as means of signification. As in a performance which is more self-consciously staged, the whole is necessary in order to ground any individual part, and therefore interpretation is contingent and infinitely capable of reconsideration.

It follows that the progress of performance is constructed through being enacted (the pretensions of social thought should never obscure the ways in which we make performances up as we go along). The conventions of a cultural repertoire may function as something analogous to a script but they are more usefully seen as a competence upon which our performance is infinitely creative. The recognition that interpretation is a social practice politicises the constitutive significance of cultural imagery rather than atomising

15

meaning (points made well in Pratt 1986). If a form of life is a way of using a set of implements and resources then the order through which cultural imagery represents types of order is a distinctive way of being in the world. The notion of imagery is not as a range of pictures or illustrations of pre-existing social practices, but as a language(s) for the formulation of social projects.

The third concept, then, that needs to be amplified, that of cultural change, refers to differences in the way social projects are discursively understood in a particular historical setting (and not just how they are understood but more how it is possible for them to be understood). A recognition that there are differences between social formations and their cultural order does not mean that the process of change from one order to another is an evolutionary progression. For example, that the progression is always from a less developed to a more developed form of life, or that it is governed by a struggle for competitive survival. It is rather that as a social order provides a repertoire of forms for collective consciousness, so the ways of staging or performing that order enact different forms of collective experience. The practice of cultural history involves more than recording continuities or differences in generic styles – there should be an attempt to understand how particular cultural forms can provide distinctive orders of experience.

SOCIAL DRAMAS

Sociological terminology is rich with dramatic allusions (see for example the collection of papers by Brisset and Edgley 1990). There are several ways in which the power of conceptualising social actions as drama or performance has been explored. For example, the conventions that are necessary for social order can be more explicitly seen in the manufacture of dramatic business. This is because the framing, taken to be necessary to mark off a particular piece and type of social interaction, is even more necessary in establishing that what is going on is a piece of staged rather than 'natural' business (the introduction of terms such as framing and keying indicates the significance of the work of Goffman (in particular, 1974) in guiding this approach). Alternatively, the ritualistic aspects of many features of cultural imagery in the articulation of social order has meant that notions of drama can provide a fresh set of resources for the theorisation of power as well as individuality (see for example Geertz' study, 1980, of the staging of power).

16

A focus on the forms and frames of staging should not be taken as purely signifying theatrical or ritual stages. In a number of studies, we have come to appreciate the complexity of verbal art as a mode of performance which involves 'an assumption of accountability to an audience for the way in which communication is carried out, above and beyond its referential content' (Bauman 1977 p. 11). The ethnography of performance then becomes concerned 'to determine the culture-specific constellations of communicative means that serve to key performance in particular communities' (Bauman op. cit. p. 22, italicised in the original), as well as the reflexive constitution of social order and structure in performance. In this approach the notion of performance is taken beyond a dramaturgical metaphor although the idea of a qualitative distinction between performance and other modes of social action is retained.

I believe that we can go further and say that social action in general can only be understood as a performance. What this means is that action is mannered, stylised, aims to be coherent through time and aspires to be able to use the resources for signification at hand. The theatrical terminology of dramatism – role, script, audience, stage, etc. – is metaphorical but it provides for how we articulate the ways in which social action becomes possible. It is of course necessary to retain distinctions between levels and modes of dramatic framing but these are the play of cultural competence. The common root to notions of drama and social is that both involve an imposition of meaning on meaningless sensation. For most of us it is only rarely that the self-fulfilling conventions of common sense knowledge are ruptured so that the artificiality of 'normality' is laid bare. In drama the artificiality is celebrated and intensified, and although feelings of existential terror at the limits of conventional order are only encouraged in a limited range of performance, the transforming power of cultural imagination is at the core of the enterprise.

One way of understanding dramatic force is to see it as a transformation of space: 'The art in the caves of Southwest Europe and the stories of the Aborigines about the landmarks in their range are means of transforming natural spaces into cultural places: ways of making theatres' (Schechner 1976 p. 43). It is in the self-consciousness of drama that the raw materials of personal experience are framed in ways that make them available for communal understanding: 'Just as a farm is a field where edible foods are grown, so a theatre is a place where transformations of time, place and persons (human and non-human) are accomplished' (Schechner op. cit. p. 49). The medium of transformation is a notion of occasion or event in which a distance between action and meaning is emphasised: 'In contrast to the frequently confusing, multi-directional, and uncertain flows of mundane living, the divisible elements of public occasions seem eminently available to the engaged observer' (Handelman 1990 p. 10).

Public events are constituted through a number of features of systematic organisation. Public events or drama turn on the possibility of constructing role(s) as something for which there is both identification of, and to varying degrees identification with, by performers and audience. The display of character and social identity is integral to the dramatic enterprise (cf. Burns 1972). It is possible to make a distinction between social drama and aesthetic drama. Social drama is the more general category and we can see it with Turner (1982 p. 78) as 'the experiential matrix from which the many genres of cultural performance . . . have been generated'. Aesthetic drama, as one such genre, can be characterised through the organising force of a narrative governing the performance, through a commonly agreed sense of a distinction between performers and audience, and through a general recognition that transformations in performance will be limited in important respects. This is not to say that aesthetic dramas can be confined to theatres, if by the latter we mean either commercial performance or a particular structure of interaction between participants.

Drama works through display and partly because display involves an ironic distanced looking or observing of performance, and partly because the taking on of another character is always a dangerous enterprise, the setting for dramatic performance is likely to be a physically and symbolically bounded space. Within this setting, whether it is a church, a pleasure-garden, an inn-courtyard, a purpose-built theatre or a private television receiver, space is transformed and the props of performance are given dramatic significance. Both modes of transformation, of performer and setting, mean that dramatic performance requires playing with forms of social experience. The community which grounds individuality is available for visualisation through dramatisation and this visualisation of communal forms is enacted through forms of public drama (fictions of collective life).

A distinction between social and aesthetic drama is expressed through the significance of several modes of structural organisation in the former. They are issues of degree and type, however, and to that extent they mark points on a continuum. Linking them on this continuum is a category of public drama which draws features from both sides. Which features are dominant depends upon the particular circumstances at hand. For example, the term 'public drama' suggests that it is an occasion taking place in a setting which is not owned or controlled by specific individuals. Participation is therefore voluntary, except that individuals may be caught up in a riot against their will, but it is generally paradoxical to think of an audience seeking admission to a riot. The use of public space does not mean that the occasions are anarchic – firework displays staged by a municipal authority in a public park are freely accessible, but take place in a regulated setting organised through social codes of appropriate modes of participation which might be quite rigorously enforced.

The points above lead to a more general point concerning 'the text' of the drama. Aesthetic dramas are characteristically seen as authored performances, i.e. a specific individual has creative control over the performance (the complexities of this account in media such as film can be put to one side for now). Social dramas are in contrast typically collective and thereby anonymous which does not mean that they are improvised as the form and content may be prescribed by ritual. The notion of ritual, however, is highly prescriptive and may deflect attention from the orderliness of other more incoherent forms of drama:

> The final consideration to emerge from the detailed examinations of provincial crowd activity in this period is perhaps the most significant of all: namely, that analysis of the trends in crowd occurrence and the established forms for describing those crowds produces clear patterns of procedure, location, timing and language.
>
> (Harrison 1988 p. 317)

Although Handelman's typology of different modes of public event is not inconsistent with the distinctions between different forms of spectacle I make in the next part of this chapter, I do not want to follow his lead in concentrating on 'the logics of design' rather than the 'enactment' of public events. It is too easy to treat the historical record of crowd behaviour as self-evidently available and to ignore the extent to which our knowledge of these phenomena is mediated through the perspectives of contemporary reports:

19

Those in power, and those who reported crowd events, wished to be able on occasion to claim thousands of the town's population for *their* cause, and at another time, to be able to damn the masses for their incorrigibility, contrariness and autonomy. . . . This labelling, and the management of this problem object – the crowd loathed and adored – had, however, to operate in constant conflict with the object's own, essentially independent, and formidably coherent, self-definition.

(Harrison op. cit. p. 191)

The lack of explicit authorship should not therefore be taken as an indication of disorder (or celebrated as creative anarchy). There are governing conventions to public drama which provide a variety of textual forms. It should also be remembered that even where there are identifiable authors for public dramas they may wish to suppress their authorship in favour of the anonymity of tradition (Cannadine 1983 discusses the example of those responsible for inventing royal tradition) or the imperatives of history (cf. Hunt 1984 on the new secular festivals of the French Revolution). These examples remind us that public dramas are inextricably embedded in the ideological constitution of social order. They are a form of inscription in which different programmes of collective remembering and systematic forgetting can be enacted (for a particularly focussed discussion of this theme, see Rowe and Schelling 1991 on popular culture in Latin America).

Public drama is therefore collective, predominately traditional and expropriative in the sense that an environment is taken over and adapted to the needs of the drama. Needs which are in essence celebratory: 'Popular culture gives itself to the experience of the sociable and celebratory, its best experience is the festival' (Inglis 1988 p. 76). Is therefore public drama dependent upon a culture, if not of the streets, then of communal interaction? Could it be said, if culture and typically popular culture has in the more general transformations of urbanisation and industrialisation become characteristically privatised, that the very notion of public drama is an historical anachronism in mass culture? I do not believe so because as I said in the previous chapter the relations of dramatisation have necessarily been transformed in a changing ecology of public life. I shall argue through this book that confusions in our language of public life derive from the shifting frameworks of public drama.

The general domain of public drama seems to overlap with a more diffuse sense of the popular. As a category of culture, popular has been used in a variety of ways. There are four uses that are most salient in contemporary cultural discourse. First, to denote general endorsement and approval by common or ordinary people as in 'this type of show is always popular'; secondly, representing a class-based form of life which is resistant to, or in opposition against, dominant ideology – the popular here is defined against other cultural discourses; thirdly, as characteristic of the community or more precisely communal discourses as in populist rhetoric; and finally, as an area of cultural autonomy – practices which are engaged in for their own sake and the immediate rewards they offer to participants. Although these uses may be in certain respects mutually exclusive they coexist simultaneously and all inform the meanings of public life and public drama. An illustration of some consequential ambiguities is provided by the later years of the history of public executions. A dramatic performance designed in part, to articulate a moral lesson to the populace became liable to being overturned by popular action and thereby exemplify a very different text of popular heroism and thus to facilitate a revision of cultures as competing and mutually incomprehensible forms of life.

The multiplicities of public drama are all based in some idea of collective performance which can be described as spectacular show. The essence of spectacle is to provide a way in which to dramatise communal vision through displays which lift themes or values out of the ordinary. A spectacular presentation is an attempt to get the attention of onlookers by forms of display which are sufficiently striking as to be impressive or even awe-inspiring. The crucial point in the form of drama which spectacle provides is that it is images which are privileged through dramatisation in spectacle.

The forms of display are visual enactments of events, actions or roles which are out of the ordinary experience of the audience. It is because they are extraordinary that they can act as a pictorial language of metaphors and analogies for possible, often idealised, rather than actual experience. I think this is the point of connection to the popular often rather derogatory use of describing somebody as making a spectacle of themselves. In this case, the person, either through their actions, their deportment or their dress, etc. has exhibited themselves as transgressing the boundaries of normal expectations. In the constraining world of conventional mores such excess is a source of disapproval, although certain figures, often

21

entertainers, may be licensed to display extravagant even outrageous features by an amused tolerance. And indeed, a style of spectacular excess such as punks and dandies has often served, by flouting decorous conventions, to give a show of dissidence and symbolic revolt.

The spectacular as an invitation to interest and as a characterisation is an opportunity to see something outside of the conventional constraints of everyday experience. It must therefore resemble its subject matter in a way that often runs counter to fantasy and which gives the yet-to-be-imagined concrete form. The spectacular is an opportunity to experience the transcendance of mundane availability, although in the looseness of popular associations we often describe the thrill of such experience as fantastic. But the authenticity of what we are shown does not violate the realisation that the creation of effect is necessarily artificial – our awe is induced by representation transcending reality. Although he is writing of that type of theatre which is a particular mode of spectacle, Neale has a more general relevance when he says that 'it is a mode which seems to involve an oscillating play between not only the exhibition of a visual illusion or effect as such, but also the exhibition of the means – the tricks – used to produce it' (Neale 1979 p. 68).

Spectacle is therefore artifice – it displays cultural invention and yet such has been the power of naturalist aesthetics that running alongside the use of spectacular to mean exciting and impressive is another use in which what is spectacular is specious, meretricious and unnecessarily contrived: 'But it was wonderful only as a spectacle, since it meant nothing' (Bowles 1982 p. 313). Whether it is approved or condemned would seem to stem from the degree to which a commentator takes narrative and/or psychological plausibility as a prime criterion of aesthetic depth or density. In academic as opposed to more popular cultural discourses narrative strength has come to be associated with certain versions of psychological and/or social realism but these in turn stem from specific expectations of theatricality. The strengths of other possibly more stylised forms of representation have been less adequately explored.

Spectacular drama is therefore a mode of performance in which possible experience is visualised in order to impress an audience. The performance may be staged as a celebration, or in order to mobilise the audience for a cause, or to impress upon the audience a moral lesson, or merely to persuade an audience to part with its money in order to either see a daring and complicated stunt or to experience the thrill for themselves (as at a fun-fair). In each and every case the spectacular is literally extra-ordinary – the point is made through the force of performance rather than through rational reasoning. I have described what is displayed as possible experience because although it may be an actual event, through its presentation the experience is fictionalised as representation. For example, the spectacle may recreate a military exploit from the past or it may present a panorama of an urban landscape that is only possible from a unique vantage point such as the top of a cathedral spire, or it may show the moment of conception (spectacular theatricality particularly in the nineteenth century is discussed more fully in the next chapter). The participation of the audience is in a representation of these experiences and, however dramatically effective their presentation, the audience knows that at some point they will be able to step back out of the frame into other more mundane representational scenarios.

The theme of self-conscious dramatisation in spectacle is illustrated by the example of the spectacle of the monarch riding through a city in order to inaugurate a session of the legislature. For the crowds watching, whether on the streets or through television, the procession is actual and real. But what is being paraded is less a particular individual than the institution of monarchy. The possibility inherent in the experience is the capacity of the individual to symbolise an abstract role. The reason for staging the show is to create an aura of majesty which will be shared within a patriotic community. This strand of idealisation, which seems to me to be intrinsic to spectacular shows, leads me to suggest that the imaginative vision in spectacular drama is (loosely) utopian rather than practical (what Manning (1983) sees as a celebration of society) – and this, it seems to me, is the key to the difference between ritual and spectacle. Civic ritual, secular ritual and ritual in a secular society (such as an otherwise unremarkable wedding ceremony) may lack the crucial feature of liminality which underlies the transforming force of ritual, but they only become spectacular when they are staged as performances of ritual (Chaney 1983A; 1987A).

TWO FORMS OF SPECTACULAR SOCIAL ORDER

I have described some aspects of the ways we use concepts of drama and how they trade upon implied forms of social order. In order to take this perspective further so that I can illustrate the dramatic relations of modernity, I shall in this part of the chapter return to the contrast between spectacular society and society of the spectacle. These terms are being used to encapsulate the dramatisation of social order in early modern Britain, i.e. British cultural forms prior to the development of theatrical drama, compared and contrasted with an account of features of spectacular social order in the cultural forms of contemporary British culture.

The basis for my approach here is that drama is self-evidently central to the presentation of collective identity in both eras. More particularly, a concept of spectacle repeatedly recurs as a way of describing aspects of dramatisation, and especially public drama, in these eras. And yet it is crucial for my approach that, although there are certain continuities in the vocabulary of spectacular show, the forms of spectacle are dramatising radically different cultural orders. A social entity (a collectivity) is an abstraction mediated through the innumerable ways it is grounded in personal experience. It is not just that individuals in these contrasting eras would articulate a sense of self in radically different terms, but also that the processes of mediation would be staged in very different terms.

I shall focus upon five features of spectacular drama in the social order of each era. I am only too well aware that an attempt to specify features that are true across the variety of cultural circumstances and ignoring long-term change is necessarily pitched at a high level of abstraction. The accounts are therefore ideal typical: although the differences in meaning of spectacle are important in their own right, in the present context they serve the function of laying a basis for the more detailed exploration of the dramatic relations of a society of spectacle in succeeding chapters. Although there are equal numbers of headings, any two members of each list do not straightforwardly form a pair and within each list their order of presentation is not rank-ordered.

I shall begin by suggesting five headings for significant characteristics of dramatisation in spectacular society. Although presented separately, they are necessarily interdependent.

Ritualised dramatisation

The nature of dramatisation in spectacular society was essentially ritualised, or, more accurately, the business of everyday life was so routinely imbued with formal significance that instead of being something looked in upon, drama was a way of looking out at fundamental truths and values. In general terms the concept of ritual denotes a form to an occasion which is resistant to change. The constituent roles of ritual are independent of any particular performer, and there are governing conventions in relation to individuals' mode of participation such as deportment, which are part of general cultural competence and rarely have to be explicitly articulated. The reason for emphasising the significance of ritualisation in spectacular society is that the charged intensity of ritual experience is formalised in everyday experience. The logic of formalisation was organised around cultural forms in which notions of individuality and personhood were pre-modern. This has meant that a key focus of the development of a discourse of modernism was precisely an exploration of aspects in individuality in ways that still dominate our cultural history (cf Reiss 1982).

Prior to an individualistic ethos, dramatic imagery was personified through masks as icons of identity or through allegorical typifications. The masquerade provides a bridge between a reassurance of recurrence in predictable form, and a *frisson* of uncertainty at glimpsing potential chaos through playing with the mechanics of that form. The overwhelming mutuality of experience meant that all occasions had to be given significance through elaborate ceremonialisation. Tydeman quotes some remarks of Huizinga's to good effect in this context:

> it was not merely the great facts of birth, marriage and death which, by the sacredness of the sacrement, were raised to the rank of mysteries: incidents of less importance, like a journey, a task, a visit, were equally attended by a thousand formalities: benedictions, ceremonies, formulas.
>
> (Tydeman 1978 p. 86)

There is also a wealth of material on the community of magic in Thomas (1973).

It seems, therefore, that in more communal societies the grounds of social order were continually re-emphasised through elaborate codes of interpersonal interaction. These codes provided for a spectacular dramatisation of the relationship and its legitimating norms – a dramatisation in which there does not seem to have been a necessity for distinctions between role, actor and private individual. Bristol (1985) cites Ladurie on carnival in which he uses the phrase 'dual social order' to characterise:

a social world where everything is invested with a sacred character but only intermittently. Every detail of practical reality has a sacred meaning. But that 'moral being' is experienced, not as an idealised spirituality, but in the sheer everydayness and crude practicality of social existence.

(Bristol 1985 p. 53)

The interdependence of formalism and a lack of role-distance (assuming that strong self-consciousness of person presumes or implies role-distance) explains why a strong sense of form was not associated with either 'civilisation', in Elias' (1978) sense, or an elaborate code of manners.

A clear sense of formal obligations and expectations does not mean that the dominant code of honour will not coexist in unresolved tension with other loyalties and values. In later reconstructions of this code of chivalric honour to then serve deliberately ideological ends (at least as well as generating a code to mark caste boundaries – Girouard (1981)), it was assumed that a close identification between the person and the code was a necessity. In not recognising that necessity, medieval nobility was not being cynical (or just 'acting') but was oriented to the symbolic significance of dramatisations which blurred fiction and reality: 'Although chivalric conflict could become a deadly earnest affair, the lists became a natural setting for symbolic games of make-believe, to which allegorical scenic devices, inscriptions, costumes, action, impersonation, and even dialogue contributed' (Tydeman op. cit. p. 87; but neither, as Keen (1984) argues so well, was the performance a fantasy). Chivalric drama ranged considerably more widely than the tournament but in draping undeniably real actions in allegory, mime and spectacle a model of formalisation was articulated.

Indexical dramatisation

Indexical signs are those signs which display a broader meaningful category through their role as symptoms or markers embedded in that particular category. In using the term to characterise public drama in this form of spectacular social order I wish to indicate that the symbolic medium in these forms of dramatic experience is primarily allegorical. The empirical illustration displays an abstract quality or identity – the image or object at hand, in what is possibly all its existential tawdriness, can stand for an idealised entity.

A good example of the process I am thinking of is provided by the dramatic significance of the various forms of procession. Processions within an urban setting usually followed a prescribed route and could be used as a dramatisation of honour or excoriation. The entry of a noble lord to a town, and more particularly that of a monarch when marking a dramatic moment in the reign such as their marriage or birth of an heir, were all occasions for dramatic celebration. The procession indexed the festive community and marked out the progress of its symbolic recapitulation as did more mundane and frequent processions such as the celebrations of guilds' patron saints. Of course the lord generally 'rewarded' citizens' participation by the provision of food and drink and other largesse: more importantly, the political character of the particular agenda of each situation could be highlighted and addressed through the symbolism of the characters and their elaborate forms of address when staging displays at points along the processional route. These displays were extremely spectacular in any conventional sense of the term and drew upon a highly codified dramatic repertoire:

> and everywhere [in Western Europe] in the fifteenth and early sixteenth centuries we encounter the same archways across city streets, assemblages of peasant castles, genealogical trees, tabernacles, mountains, fountains, and gardens and the same groups of allegorical personages.
>
> (Anglo 1969)

In formulating these allegorical addresses and moral dramas the sponsoring bodies, whether urban guilds or municipal authorities, etc. were drawing upon conventions of dramatic presentation in which abstract moral themes were combined with vernacular naturalism – forms of spectacular drama we tend to group under the generic heading of morality plays. The procession has remained a complex dramatic resource but in this form of social order it was particularly effective in condensing complex themes. In relation to Renaissance Florence, Trexler (1980 p. 213) notes: 'The time that merchants and bureaucrats, common workers, and rulers expended in almost endless rounds of processions staggers the imagination. . . . Why did Florentines expend such energy in a form of behaviour that moderns tend to dismiss as mere spectacle?'. His answer to this question is that in such public drama contemporaries believed: 'they witnessed the political process at work' (*ibid*.; see also Pythian-

Adams, 1976; there is also a fascinating account of the changing meanings of processions in a slightly later urban culture in Borsay 1989).

The other form of spectacular procession in which the chief performers indexically displayed their moral character and narrative logic were of course the ritual humiliations and physical degradations through which the outcast literally took on to their body the stigmata of transgression. Foucault's (1977 especially Part 1) account of the changing character and meaning of punishment as a function of modernisation has become very influential, not least in his use of spectacular as a way of characterising the allegorical body of those being punished. The nature of punishment and social control in spectacular social order does not, however, have to be seen exclusively within a Foucauldian framework in order to be significant in understanding public drama. Both the processes of display, in procession and in ritual sites such as the stocks, and in the fineness of calibration between seriousness of offence and form of bodily dismemberment, all suggest that the dramatisation of exclusion was signifying and displaying a form of social order in which the intensity of personal experience was an allegory of the intensity of collective experience.

Inclusive dramatisation

The form of a procession in which the features of the known world are re-framed in order to provide the ground for spectacular display points towards the third feature of dramatisation in spectacular society. I refer to this feature as inclusiveness as I wish to stress the ways in which drama in this form of social order is not limited to a specific sphere but adapts and incorporates mundane experience thereby imbuing it with new levels of meaning. If a defining feature of drama is the re-definition of space, then these cultural forms are remarkably omnivorous in their construction of cultural space. Equally importantly the elements composing a cultural place, as in the physical structure and the integration of light, sound and music in churches, were organised to constitute a form of narrative which dramatised everyday experience and incorporated it in the domain of myth.

This is not to say that there are not ritual sites or sites of strong communal meaning such as church yards, inn court yards, village greens and market squares which are the principal foci for dramatic performance. It is that the boundaries of these sites are only loosely drawn and that within them the hierarchies of social order are at best imperfectly sustained. The dramatisation of order was not contained in tightly framed settings or confined to specified performers. The *charivari* (a mode of social control through quasi-humourous humiliation) was carried forward by a nucleus of performers but the group could absorb or expel individuals haphazardly and the targets of their satire and buffoonery could exercise little control over their roles (cf. Davis 1975 Chapters 4-6; and Burke 1978 Part 2).

A more technical way of describing this process is to refer to a lack of institutional differentiation between cultural forms. The forms of social participation generated by different types of cultural occasion were not distinguished by clearly marked codes peculiar to each institutional setting. There was rather a shifting focus of incorporation that was felt more or less intensely. The spectacle of display traversed the least significant of people and settings and in so doing included them in its transformative power. A good illustration is provided by the lack of clear framing differentiating performers from audience on the medieval stage. Whether it was a cart or part of an open space decorated for the occasion there seems to have been a continuum including both performers and their audience and particularly when several stages were in use more or less simultaneously (Kahrl, 1974). The dramatic action was not limited to one group or to one place exclusively, but rather eddied through all those present, making the community itself a spectacular presentation.

Transgressive dramatisation

A recurrent theme in the features noted so far has been the significance of form and boundary in modes of dramatisation. It is as if in a cultural order lacking a pervasive historical consciousness, and thereby narratives of progression, there develops a complementary complexity of formal structure (again Handelman 1990 in his theory of public events has developed a complementary account). While such an equation is too neat, the type of phenomenon which motivated its inspiration are reinforced by the fourth feature of dramatisation in spectacular society. In highly formalised social orders, tension and conflict are often confronted through violent transformations rather than procedurally governed negotiations. It is a phenomenon that has been noted in contemporary societies in total institutions such as prisons, mental hospitals, boarding schools and military camps. In pre-modern social orders such rituals of inversion are endemic and whether institutionalised or not seem to constitute essential resources for long-term stability and conformity – what Stallybrass and White call (1986 p. 43): 'the logic of the *grotesque* . . . could unsettle "given" social positions and interrogate the rules of inclusion, exclusion and domination which structured the social ensemble'.

Transgressive drama was therefore popular in an oppositional sense and indeed much of the vulgarity which is seen to be characteristic of popular entertainment is a very diluted version of the tradition of transgression (Bristol 1985 more particularly draws out the salience of carnival for the development of theatrical forms). Standing formal order, often literally, on its head is not the only form of transgression – boundaries are by definition imbued with symbolic significance so that their violation, more than simple disorder, affirms an alternative sense of social association. A particularly powerful resource for symbolic violations is the body and the various constraints with which it is hedged about and governed. A cultural licence to wallow in the transgression of these constraints has come to be known by the general heading of carnivalesque following Bakhtin's work (1968) on Rabelais and this term now seems a central characteristic of pre-modern spectacular drama: 'recent thinking has largely confirmed Bakhtin's insistence on the relation between body-image, social context and collective identity' (Stallybrass and White, op. cit. p. 10). Carnival is a zone, of both space and time, within which excess is licensed and the spectacle consists in a parodic transgression of the presuppositions of conventional order.

Tactile dramatisation

Finally, the fifth feature which has been present throughout the discussion so far is the physicality of dramatic experience in this social order. Even within highly formalised. ritualised and complexly symbolic forms of representation dramatic experience was intensely tactile. In part deriving from the lack of clear framing of dramatic imagery and in part from the ways in which drama permeated all aspects of everyday experience, spectacle was a display which was physically present. It could be touched as a physical manifestation of social order – the victim's screams while being broken on the wheel, the devil emerging from the mouth of hell on a guild cart, the monarch's body to be touched or venerated as a source of transcendental power (Starkey 1978), the celebration of crucifixion and resurrection in a church lit, painted and refulgent with incense – which was both a dramatic display and clearly presented to celebrants.

It would therefore have made little sense to draw a distinction between culture and society as one representing or being an alternative to the other. The cultural forms of spectacular drama were so tangibly and intensely inherent in the lived world of everyday experience that they provided a continuous transformation of the materiality of that experience.

The feature of tactility is in this sense paradoxical – it points to both the density of dramatisation and the ways in which the forms of dramatisation need not be governed by realist aesthetics. Naturalistic detail was inevitable and unremarkable but the truth of representation was not displayed through the accumulation of such detail but by being informed and governed by dramatic order itself. In its forms of dramatisation the social pre-empted the meanings of personal experience. In spectacular society, social institutions and their constitutive web of relationships were concretised through dramatic imagery (Hawkes 1973 p. 216): 'a predominately oral culture enacted its own "shape" through a drama which constituted a formal realisation of its own language. In that drama, the unity of language and way of life was both manifested and reinforced by dramatic argument'.

SOCIAL ORDER IN A SOCIETY OF THE SPECTACLE

I have described a number of characteristics of the dramatisation of social order in an era I have called spectacular society. In this part of the chapter I shall set out equally briefly another set of characteristics, this time describing the dramatisation of social order in what I call a 'society of spectacle'. The theme of the form and nature of the arrangements for order will become more prominent in this part of the chapter. The best way I can find for describing the difference between the two parts of the chapter is that form was etched into every aspect of spectacular society. In contrast, in contemporary society of spectacle the formal imagery of dramatisation counterpoints the indeterminacy of personal experience. The characteristics I shall describe all concern the ways in which a public culture (what Horne 1986 calls the 'enchantment' of modern societies) has been created as counterpoint to, rather than the medium of, personal experience. It has become a performance *for* rather than a performance *of.*

Collage characteristic

The first characteristic refers to a widespread conviction that in contemporary culture it has become impossible to sustain any faith in a natural or inevitable authority. It has therefore come to seem that order in any sphere is haphazard – a more-or-less random set of associations that can have the invigorating vitality of a collage. A loss of conviction in the authority of representation has been taken as a defining characteristic of post-modernism, although the term has been used in a variety of ways. The first is as characterising recent developments in cultural representation; the second as a distinctive sensibility; and the third as new forms of economic and political order – perhaps as a synonym for post-industrial. It is not my intention to explore the consistency between these and other uses (helpful accounts of relevant theories and polemical positions have been published in Turner 1990 and Featherstone 1988). The theme that I wish to explore is the common element in its various senses that a commitment to, or a sense of the possibility of aesthetic or normative order has been superseded.

It is of course attractive to apocalyptic theorists of breaks in the periodization of cultural history to exaggerate differences. While it is true that modernity is commonly seen as a world where 'everything solid melts into air' (Berman 1983), such radical relativism was either fought against or celebrated. In a 'modern' world, moral conviction or narrative organisation could still be envisaged. Despite subversive intimations in the most unlikely enterprises (Chaney and Pickering 1986, discuss the subversion of authorship in a documentary project such as Mass Observation in the 1930s), there were many commited to the belief that even if the author is dead, the project of authorship was still a valid enterprise.

The re-writing of authority is therefore a process of gradual and uneven change (and will be a persistent theme in succeeding chapters of this book), and it seems more appropriate to describe the triumph of collage as a characteristic of late- rather than post-modernism. At its most abrasive all forms of representation are equally valid and their combination in any one performance is both a matter of chance and serendipity. The possibility of moral order is therefore superfluous and the social order dramatised in such a society is a sequence of disassociated experiences much as Pateman (1975) some years ago described advertising as 'disassociated impacting'.

Collage as the form of order characteristic of late modernism works in two ways. The first is that contemporary culture has become overwhelmingly a representation through spectacle (see the iconic characteristic below), that is as things to see, and to see through, so that the image has become the paradigmatic means of conceptualisation. The second is that within the most ubiquitous means of pictorial entertainment, images are either haphazardly accumulated or are governed by a form of order that, as an ideology, is in itself merely a more abstract exemplification of the sensibility that experience is an agglomeration of sensations. The essence of this form of order is that the structure of drama is haphazard and attended to haphazardly. For this reason, the industrial character of entertainment in mass society is offset by incorporation into life styles and the negotiation of personal identities.

The flow of television, as Williams (1973) pointed out in one of the earliest discussions of its cultural form, shuffles genres and levels of fiction and reality indiscriminately. The dramatic experience of television is not of a drama but of the privatisation of public drama – the translation of communal language into the ambiguities of interpersonal experience. It is doubtless true that the methods of production and codes of presentation of this dramatic excess are formally very complex, but at so many levels of apprehension the dominant theme is of informality, an egalitarian consumerism which seems to promise new degrees of individuality: 'Spectacle pretends by means of its *élan*, vividness, domestic accessibility (sitting-room television, newspaper, radio) and power so to shape our ways of seeing that we are party to what we can watch' (Inglis 1988 p. 138).

Iconic characteristic

In cultural forms primarily organised through pictorial images, the dominant forms of representation will be iconic, i.e. through signs which in terms of conventional codes will be held to visually resemble their signifieds. In this sense the cultural forms can also be said to be characterised by literalness. The paradigmatic form of representation which purports to offer literal signifiers in this way is photography and in a later chapter I will discuss the nature and significance of this promise. For the present we can note that in a society of spectacle, social order will be more manifestly instrumental. The complexity of late modern society with a high degree of institutional differentiation will seemingly necessitate more explicit and detailed controls, governed by a pragmatic rationality. This is consistent with the personalisation of order noted above.

In a double movement, that will become familiar, the naturalness of cultural imagery will seem to facilitate new forms of participation by the public at large in that there will be fewer barriers between them and themes of drama, but more insidiously the same repertoire of representational resources can be used to provide unprecedented degrees of surveillance. The nature of power therefore becomes problematic in this dramatisation of social order. It is not that there are not complex and extremely detailed regulations governing all aspects of social interaction, but the integration and legitimacy of this regulative complex is naturalised and made to seem inevitable by dramatic transparency. The plenitude of information will paradoxically not make political order seem more amenable to rational discourse but rather induce feelings of powerlessness and impotence and a further retreat into privatisation of experience (Sennett 1976).

An emphasis upon literalness and transparency in representation leads inevitably to broader issues in the nature of realism and the relevance of realist norms to different cultural forms. The issue of realism and the various ways of expressing and displaying realism will come to predominate in mechanically reproduced popular culture (as I have argued more fully before (Chaney 1979 Chapter 3)). I will take up the dramatisation of social resemblance in succeeding chapters. I will merely note for now the more particular character of spectacular realism as exemplified in the multitude of dramatic effects in which the spectator is given an awe-inspiring vision, i.e. given access to the otherwise inaccessible.

Whether it was an urban panorama in the nineteenth century, or an animatronic figure of President Lincoln in Disneyland, or three-dimensional images with enveloping sound in the cinema, or a re-creation of a battle in its original site there are many forms of drama in a society of spectacle which literally enact social phenomena from the real world. However much these performances might blur distinctions between fiction and reality (as in some pornographic movies?), they remain dramatisations which are self-consciously, even exuberantly, aware of their own artificiality. This does not mean that the audience is cheated by the dissembling, rather that they are potentially intrigued by representation that so artfully captures the lineaments of authentic experience. As such these forms of dramatisation are more specific instances of the lure of tourism discussed more fully in later chapters.

Individualised characteristics

I have argued in relation to both the characteristics described so far that the dramatic order of the society of spectacle is to engage spectators in shows that seem designed to intrigue or fascinate their personal attention. This is therefore in contrast with the dramatic order of spectacular society which is embedded in the grounds and routine order of all forms of social experience. In commonsense terms the contrast is clearly indicated in the development of leisure in modernity (Rojek, 1985). In the language of social affiliation and stratification in urban-industrial society one of the meanings of popular that has developed is in conjunction with leisure as a type of activity. To the extent that leisure is a way of spending time, a personal choice, it is thereby a display of autonomy and can claim the mandate of genuine popularity. Leisure exemplifies the form of participation in society of spectacle which is essentially individualised.

The activities in which we participate to constitute our leisure need not be popular in the sense of widely endorsed, it may be ballroom dancing or reading philosophy rather than cinema-going, but they are activities couched in the institutionalised range of cultural forms. The type of occasion is determined not so much by the content or character of specific activities as by the social organisation of occasion in conjunction with the form of involvement of participants (Chaney and Chaney 1979). Thus the type of dramatic occasion may be more or less tightly framed by location, participation and organisation, but a crucial element in their status as performance is the expectations and satisfactions of each individual audience member. Public drama is privatised as personal experience.

The most outstanding example of this process has come to be generically known under the rubric of a 'culture of consumerism'. We need not be detained here by the complexities of periodising this culture (taken up again more fully in Chapter 5); the more significant point for present purposes is that the form and meaning of personal experience has come to be dominated by the display, knowledge of, and command of, material possessions (Campbell 1987). Through the choices made, and the uses to which these choices are put, individuals define a life style that they feel gives them cultural identity: 'Modernity is a post-traditional order, in which the question, "How shall I live?" has to be answered in day-to-day decisions about how to behave, what to wear and what to eat' (Giddens 1991 p. 14). Thus from a repertoire of cultural resources it is possible to articulate a language of individuality (recent attempts to theorise the complexities of the use of culture as life style in opposition to simpler models of consumerism as exploitation have included Fiske 1989 and Willis 1990).

A crucial element in the expression and promulgation of these cultural norms has been the development of mass advertising. Once again the significance of this theme can only be touched on extremely cursorily here, but in the history of advertising it is possible to distinguish four stages. The first is a period when goods were sold primarily through their instrumental utility in terms of practical accomplishments, the second was when goods were promoted more abstractly – more as symbolic entities in their own right, while in the third phase of the middle of this century advertising focussed more on the nature of gratifications to be derived from consumption, developing into a final phase in which advertising tends to concentrate on the style of life constituted through symbolic action with mass-mediated products: 'Who is the person I become in the process of consumption?' (Leiss *et al.* 1986 p. 234). In this latter process the individual is being invited to constitute identity and to engage with symbolic complexity through their personal forms of spectacular display.

Surveillance characteristic

I have already pointed to those aspects of contemporary leisure in which the freedom and autonomy of consumers to organise their own cultural tastes is popularly endorsed. A theme of the fragmentation of public drama into innumerable sub-cultures and mini-cultures will seem flippant when put in its context of the increasing dominance of the market by multi-national news and entertainment corporations. There is in fact a paradoxical interdependence between perceived increases in both personal freedom and the intensity of social order characteristic of the dramatisation of experience in a society of spectacle. I have used 'intensity' rather than 'breadth' because what Giddens (1991 p. 149) calls 'the intensifying of administrative control', is not only all-pervasive but becomes itself the form of interaction. Surveillance by each of others as well as by the multiplicity of administrative authorities has become the ritual space which frames public drama (as Finlay 1987 has argued, treating new communications technology as emancipating within itself without considering the discourses within which it has been embedded is to remain a prisoner of those discourses; see also Thompson 1990).

The starting point of this argument is that it has to be recognised that the repertoires from within which choices are made are in general generated by multi-national cultural bureaucracies whose interests are primarily oriented towards ensuring market conformity and stability. The uses to which choices are put are also governed by extremely detailed and complex systems of regulation – a 'naturalisation' of power that following Foucault has been described as the micro-physics of control. If the 'civilising process' has been largely one of self-differentiation from the community and the acquisition of controls of propriety and sensibility in increasingly detailed terms, then it is unsurprising that in the twentieth century it has been displayed through what purport to be relaxations of codes of control. As Elias (1978) argues, freedom can now be safely sustained within the presuppositions of order.

The intensity of surveillance underlies the process through which cultures, in which great stress is laid on freedom and individuality, such as those of North America, in practice display highly conformist forms of behaviour in areas such as language, dress and attitudes. The transgressive outbursts of licensed disorder in spectacular society are no longer necessary to sustain a collective conformity. In contrast, the moderation of suburban domesticity provides a persistent and unremitting orderliness in which values of self-control, self-preservation and sympathetic attentiveness regulate mundane experience. The dramatisation of order in society of the spectacle dramatises contrasts between public and private spheres – contrasts between spectacles and mundane 'normality' while at the same time adapting spectacular forms to personal use.

The banishment of transgressive outrage from conventional expectations does not of course mean that symbolic deviance cannot be articulated, it is rather that it is transposed to subterranean excess within private settings. Or, more spectacularly, it becomes a paranoia of otherness within public settings. Most commonly here,

37

fears centre around images of rape and pillage in urban centres where an underworld rages out of control and can only be contained by a cordon sanitaire patrolled by an increasingly self-governing army of law enforcement (perhaps underlying a recurrent narrative 'other' of an underclass or culture of poverty resuscitated to haunt accounts of social progress). This dramatisation of transgression is fuelled and reinforced by itself becoming a dramatic spectacle in which we are vicariously absorbed and repulsed by visions of unregulated disorder.

Abstract characteristic

The consequence of the features described so far, and one that becomes a characteristic feature in its own right, is that the social order becomes abstract. In another formulation, the symbolism of culture becomes so pervasive that its symbolic (or signifying) character becomes invisible. Representations of reality in all their partiality and ambiguity become the currency with which reality is negotiated. I recognise that there are strong echoes of some post-modernist formulations in envisaging the autonomy of representation, (see for example, Baudrillard 1983); as I have indicated, I do not want to endorse post-modernism as a package and these echoes are not traces of a 'hidden agenda'. Popular culture in late modernity can, however, be fruitfully characterised as abstract in the sense that the irony of representation is less masked by institutional naturalisation.

The density of semiotic chains does not mean that we, as members of the culture, are enmeshed in a physically given, a tangibly present cultural environment of objects and sensations and lifestyles. It is rather that as signifiers have become deracinated, and thereby capable of infinite recombination and acquiring new connotations in each context, so they are free to act as counters in forms of play which are not experienced as stylised contrast to – but as the stuff of conventional experience. The infinite complexities of the alignments and re-alignments of the stylistic communities of the young are the resource most frequently used by the prophets of semiotic instability; but it seems that, more generally, as the socio-structural grid derived by production-oriented sociologists seems increasingly inadequate to map the contours of forms of collective identity in a society of spectacle, alternative forms of cultural order become more significant (Featherstone 1990 has made a great deal of use of Bourdieu's, 1984 ideas on the sociology of new forms of cultural expertise).

Although I have said that the two sets of features characterising dramatisation in spectacular society and society of the spectacle are not meant to be read as pairs, they are clearly meant to construct a distinct contrast. The contrast between the two sets is conceptualised at the level of the interconnection of features, i.e. at the level of the form of social order. It is the dramatisation of the relationship between individual and community that has been radically transformed, for there are many respects in terms of surface features in which there are family resemblances between spectacular displays in different cultural eras. There are good reasons why in pursuit of a different analytic project one might want to point to persistent continuities in popular cultural forms.

I have been concerned to bring out the ways in which, despite these resemblances, one can detect a transformation in the institutionalisation of social order so that the meanings of both individual and community as well as all other relevant terms have been radically re-written. Concluding this section we can perhaps summarise this transformation by pointing to the ways in which the cultural forms of spectacular society are essentially local while those of a society of spectacle are essentially global. The relations of production through which performances in the first order are staged are specific to the immediate experience of producers and audience. They are governed by the distinctiveness of the habitus they share. In contrast, productive organisations in a society of spectacle are driven by international capital and all varieties of ethnic culture are grist to their mill of international marketing. Differences in systems of economic organisation between late modern societies, although they seem to be diminishing in any case, are less significant than continuities in forms of cultural participation and representation.

SPECTACULAR DRAMA

I hope it will now be clearer why forms of dramatisation are of greater cultural significance than as resources for theatre historians. The organisation of cultural space, relationships between performers and audience, the authority of that which is performed, and the spectacle of performance – all these articulate and confirm social order in other institutionalised domains. We can therefore look to the dialogia of performance as a way of glossing the experience of identity grounded in collectivity.

A transformation in the viability of theatrical spectacle in the transition from early modernity has been used by Barker (1984 p. 10) as a yardstick for the degree of modernity, more particularly as a yardstick for a transition to a newly privatised sense of self: 'In the space of a relatively few years a new set of relations between state and citizen, body and soul, language and meaning, was fashioned'. Relations governing the body are integral to this process as they involved re-fashioning the spectacular relationship between the body and social identity. In modernity, identity became interiorised in a private consciousness, re-located in new institutions of control and exclusion and abstracted into textual discourse (see also the discussion of grotesque imagery in late Tudor and early Jacobean discourse by Rhodes 1980).

In the critical breaks that became modernity the physical theatricality of Jacobean theatre came to seem gross and excessive. In its characteristic physical spectacle of renditions of pain, torture and death are 'images of the body . . . [which point to] . . . the insistence in the spectacle of a corporeality which is quite other than our own' (Barker 1984 p. 22). The emergent naturalism of a privatised consciousness could not accommodate the licence inherent in the common physicality of the social body so that the coarsely physical body (see also the discussion of the same theme by Stallybrass and White 1986), unsurprisingly became the badge of popular as in vulgar cultural forms. Spectacle in this sense came to be seen as the language of pre-modern collectivity and has to some extent survived although a complete transformation in the meaning of spectacle has developed in mass culture.

Modernity can be characterised by being focussed on a sense of the self as both the starting point for any apprehension of the world, and as a persistent and ultimate point of reference, as personal experience, to which accounts must be led. At one level this is problematic as the persons that selves inhabit are not fixed cultural entities: 'What a "person" is understood to be certainly varies across cultures, although there are elements of such a notion that are common to all cultures' (Giddens 1991 p. 53). Although the reflexivity of self-identity constitutes for a person a more-or-less coherent trajectory and place, the performance of individuality in late modern culture is inevitably subject to at least the possibility of ontological insecurity. The idea of role-distance need not be limited to the performance of the roles of bureaucratic organisation, it can be found as a fracture at the core of personhood. Identity from this perspective therefore becomes an abstract point of reference – a repertoire of selves we can see enacted as spectacle in drama and adapt and borrow for our selves.

The spectacular articulation of the self has been presented through a dramaturgy of the body as a medium of signification. The social body transcends and re-works the physical body by acting as a medium of discourse that has underlain the discovery of the body for social theory (for example, Turner 1984). The spectacular quality of the body here is a form of display from which we, as audience or spectators, are crucially distanced. The display, even of our own bodies, is as a theatrical dramatisation, however naturalised. An interesting insight into the argument here is provided by Peters' (1985) history of torture. Crudely summarised, Peters is concerned with the character of torture up until the Enlightenment and its abolition as part of a general shift away from physical punishment (familiar to us from Foucault 1977).

Sadly, the establishment of torture as a routine feature of state policy in the twentieth century must be seen as an element in public life and social order:

> By focusing upon the public character of torture . . . as an incident of some forms of twentieth century public life . . . occurring in other areas under state authority less regulated than legal procedure, less observed, but no less essential to the state's notion of order.
>
> (Peters 1985 p. 7)

Although torture is by and large hidden, it is not invisible. It is a spectre that haunts the vocabulary of public life. The spectacle of torture is not to articulate transgression through the victim's body nor to instrumentally maintain the state's control of knowledge. It is rather to emphasise as forcibly as possible that the social body is subject to a discourse over which the actors have no control:

> The technology of torture in the late twentieth century is in part the result of a new anthropology. . . . It is not primarily the victim's information, but the victim, that torture needs to win – or reduce to powerlessness.
>
> (Peters op. cit. p. 164)

The public drama of the social body is ironically informed by the inherent menace that bodies can be broken by an abstract authority.

How the notion of spectacle can become the language of a completely different order of collectivity, in late urban-industrial society, and thus earlier meanings become inverted, can be made clearer if the tangibility of the social body is treated as part of a broader signification and display of material icons. As bearers of pleasure and identity as well as pain, the latter articulate a language of appearance through which illusion can function as the medium and form of relationship: 'The spectacle is not a collection of images but a social relation among people mediated by images' (Debord 1970 no. 4). The spectacle then is more than a representation of social life; it functions as the practical medium through which order is sustained and the collectivity given an appearance: 'the spectacle is the *affirmation* of appearance and the affirmation of all human, namely social, life as mere appearance' (Debord op. cit. no. 10, *sic*).

The nature of spectacular display in two cultural orders can be further clarified by considering the function of the image, necessarily a vehicle of illusion. The gradual disintegration of the dramatic order of spectacular society was marked by the increasingly virulent condemnation of those who saw images and other forms of display in religious worship as the creation of idols (Aston 1988). Iconoclasm drew on a long history of theological debate about the appropriateness of magnificence in the theatre of the Church (see for example, Duby 1981 Part 3)), but in the sixteenth and seventeenth centuries the movement to transform the nature of worship from an articulation through physical symbolism to an expression through abstract symbolism, primarily of the word, became firmly dominant.

Of course the same movement was inextricably intertwined with associated processes of a shift from communal to individual belief and a transformation in the nature of belief. The relevant point here is that the image was thrown into question because it seemed to embody a physical elision of a radical distinction between this-worldly and other-worldly states of being. The spectacle displayed the metaphor of the body of the Church: 'The ever-increasing number of saints and images of saints bridges all gaps of temporal and spatial existence, revealing the divine in the utmost immediacy' (Phillips 1973 p. 10). The fracturing of this interdependence of imagery, thought and belief was not casual but depended upon radically different conceptions of individual responsibility for moral actions.

A turn away from spectacular society has the consequence then (amongst others) of disembedding imagery. Although in a society of spectacle, images are equally pervasive, and it can be argued that they have supplanted the privileging of writing as the dominant mode of representation, their pre-eminence does not mean a re-capturing of an earlier mode of cultural significance. Images in late modern culture are primarily instrumental, they are radically secular and embody (and I shall argue constitute) conventions of social relationships. As Goffman argues (1976 p. 91) the imagings of what he calls 'commercial realism' (advertising copy) provide: 'something of the same sort of realm as the one a stranger to everyone around him really lives in. The realm is full of meaningful viewings of others but each view is truncated and abstract'. The alignments and for-mulas of interaction rituals not only display structured relationships but will also themselves be used as the subject of displays. Images articulate ontological insecurity and uncertainty – they bring the relativity not the certainty of cultural order into focus.

The limited imagings of commercial realism (as I explore more fully in Chapter 5) are like a kaleidoscopic surface – a flickering spectacular. Realising this the celebrants of simulacra are not striving to express a transcendant sense of collective order – the community their spectacle dramatises is a world of pragmatic play having a history only of dramatic conventions (see for example, Horne 1984 on the representation of history in tourist culture). And even the most rigorous defenders of cultural, and that is social, boundaries – the born-again fundamentalist advocates of censor-ship – are not iconoclasts in the former sense. The censorship lobbies of mass culture (of both right and left) may condemn images as inauthentic but not as idolatrous. In fact they use those images of which they disapprove as a way of smuggling in a broader agenda about the prescription of terms for popular culture. Images are accepted as the dramatisation of popular experience.

I have been trying to elucidate contrasts in uses of image and identity in two uses of spectacular drama as quite different forms of social order. Although there are continuities in theme and style they should not be allowed to mask differences which underlie quite different cultural forms. In early modern spectacular society, the dramatisation of social order works to stage, or to provide a stage for, a language of community. In this sense, spectacular drama enacts an experience of community within its own terms. In contrast, in late modern culture the dramatisation of social order works to stage the 'play' of community. The term play has been used as a deliberate pun, first, to evoke a theatrical performance, and second to evoke a mode of social interaction. Play in the second sense is 'time-out' in which normal constraints are suspended although it may be deadly serious. Community as performance and as game is, however desirable in appearance, a world made available: 'then the world, in cinema, will not only be constituted by the eye, in the sense in which the eye-subject formed the invisible basis of Quattrocento perspective, but the world will be constituted *for the eye*' (Connerton 1989 p. 78, emphasis added; ideas of the social formation of Quattrocento perspective are inevitably indebted to Baxandall 1972).

A performance is always, in addition to being an enactment of a narrative, a ceremony. As I noted at the beginning of this chapter, a dramaturgical vocabulary is sometimes confusing because we seek to reserve terms like performance and ceremony for focussed occasions. To speak of mundane interaction as a performance might be to elide important differences. This is, however, an inherent source of possible confusion in the English language to which we are condemned. There are important differences between different 'levels' of performances, ceremonies and rituals, but there is also a crucial conceptual continuity. This is, that in the self-consciousness of performance we are not just representing social forms:

> The expression of subordination and domination . . . is more than a mere tracing or symbol or ritualistic affirmation of the social hierarchy. These expressions considerably constitute the hierarchy; they are the shadow *and* the substance.
>
> (Goffman 1976 p. 91, *sic*).

The explanation of the constitutive form of ritual (and implicitly in other forms of ceremonialisation) can be detected in Connerton's argument (1989 p. 54) that ritual is not a mythical narrative enacted in another form. In the inscription of collective memory, and other modes of collective identity: 'what the performance of a ritual essentially does do, is to specify the relationship that obtains between the performers of the ritual and what it is that they are performing'. My argument in this chapter has been that this relationship is not uniform, and that we can use crucial differences in relationships between performers and performance to understand the meanings of spectacular drama in two cultural eras.

2

DRAMATISING CHANGE: THEATRICALITY AND SPECTACLE IN NINETEENTH CENTURY BRITAIN

STAGED DRAMAS

In the course of the nineteenth century, Britain became an urban society. During the same period the dominant popular cultural forms were several varieties of theatricality. I shall argue that the ways in which the several forms of drama available as commercial entertainment were staged, framed and performed, worked to display the dramatisation of social order in a process of transition. I want therefore to argue for an interdependence between those changes in social and material conditions through which the majority of people came to see the city as the landscape within which everyday experience was set, and the dramatic imagery with which morals were affirmed, satisfactions fleshed out and modes of identity formulated.

In the course of this argument some of the several ways in which the 'popular' is used, and which have been briefly outlined in the previous chapter, will be played off against one another. One reason why a discussion of changes in forms of theatrical performance leads on to the cultural formation of popular experience, is that the vocabulary of popular culture that has been bequeathed to us is still dense with the compromises that were gradually institutionalised. A second reason is that the 'distance' between theatrical enactment and mundane performance in daily life became a source of moral concern in public discourse. The concern was not so much over the inherent legitimacy of theatrical artifice as over the authenticity of different modes of representation. The 'landscape' of popular experience became a contested terrain for contending understandings and expectations of culture as both a form of life and a fictional or representational repertoire.

A key element in the changing world of English towns as the eighteenth century drew to its close was the gradual disappearance of a traditional spectacular culture:

> The latter was a corpus of beliefs, customs, recreations and festivals, concerned with local rather than national affairs, rooted in magic rather than reason, employing oral and visual rather than literary forms of expression, located in public rather than private space, and intimately tied to the seasonal and Christian calendars.
>
> (Borsay 1984 p. 246)

In its general forms this traditional culture was not restricted to towns, but it provided a base and a framework for a flourishing body of urban ritual and ceremony essentially presented in spectacular forms. The ways in which this body of ceremonial was grounded in urban topography makes it appropriate to speak of the theatricality of pre-industrial urban culture. The notion of theatricality refers to the town acting as a stage for dramas of collective life.

The several types of public ritual and ceremonial can be summarised as providing a structure for a language of community. They worked to dramatise matters important to the community such as the stability of urban administration, celebrations of important visits and events, the terms of social order and the reassuring predictability of seasonal festivals. The integrative force of public ceremonies could also act to contain sources of social conflict through dramatisations of threats:

> So there developed a series of ritual theatres, many located in the town, in which men and women, competing individuals, neighbouring parishes and counties, Whigs and Tories, gentry and popular society, paraded their differences before each other.
>
> (Borsay op. cit. p. 243)

This traditional culture quickly became anachronistic as towns expanded, and in particular because the functional rationale with which it was mutually sustaining became superfluous as different forms of socio-structural alignment were being forged. The modes of disintegration were, first, an increasing polarisation between polite and popular culture most vividly exemplified through social segregation and a restriction of urban space into increasingly

46

privatised zones. Second, there was 'the mutation of traditional into popular culture' (Borsay op. cit. p. 252), with all that this means in terms of commercialisation. Third, there was the development of a national political culture to which communal concerns were adapted and subordinated. While it is important to emphasise that there was not a clear and uniform break between traditional and modern urban culture, popular theatres developed as a response to a cultural vacuum. In the rapidly changing urban worlds of the nineteenth century, spectacular cultural forms shifted into theatres as new forms of staging became necessary in towns in which they had previously been performed and which were now fractured rather than shared.

Although the number of theatres did increase extraordinarily and it can be presumed that it was a response to fill the cultural vacuums of urbanisation and cultural change, it was not just a process of building new theatres. (The exploitation of space as cities expanded meant that not only were traditional 'sites' of entertainment frequently built over, or more tightly disciplined by the new police forces, but that even those traditional 'theatres' of the moral order, churches, were insufficient for new audiences.) More significantly, theatrical performance drew upon different presuppositions of dramatic representation as a metropolitan culture became established. One way of characterising this change is to say that theatrical performance became more self-enclosed and more self-sufficient.

By this I mean that up to, roughly, the first half of the century:

> in a theatre in which the lighting of stage and auditorium was not too dissimilar, and in which the audience was likely to be, shall I say, 'participant', *awareness* of the theatrical experience was constantly being drawn to the attention of audiences.
>
> (Davison 1982A p. 110 *sic*)

Subsequently, awareness has been subordinated to an emphasis upon the suspension of disbelief by the audience as spectators. In these several ways then we can say that drama became more sharply marked off from 'normal' life, although there was at the same time greater emphasis upon accuracy and authenticity within the drama. A consequence of the latter process is that theatrical drama took on a style of hermetic realism – a style which reached its apogee in the commercial cinema and has become the dominant aesthetic in the domestic naturalism of television. A style of realism enclosed within the performance space has come to seem natural so that it is hard to think through the implications of what this style takes for granted about relationships between drama and community. (I do not mean to imply here that all theatre has remained within the naturalist illusions of the picture-frame stage (Orr 1989), but it is not my purpose in this chapter to discuss modernist disruptions of theatrical space.)

Naturalism, as a language of theatrical representation, not only came to dominate the conventions of dramatic performance, but because these conventions were grounded in types of theatrical space, the creation of particular types of theatres has come to seem an inevitable historical progression. The opening-up of collective life to the entrepreneurial activities of new strata of producers of commercial entertainment could also take on this aura. Thus the repeal in 1843 of Walpole's Licensing Act of 1737 which had restricted 'legitimate' drama to a small number of licensed theatres, creating a distinction between Theatres Royal and a penumbra of illegitimate theatres, is often described as an historic step of liberalisation. It is ideologically consistent that the struggle for a 'free' stage can be presented as analogous to and consonant with campaigns to remove legal constraints upon the production and marketing of newspapers. In both cases the freedoms won were to create frameworks within which 'legitimate' popular cultural forms could become institutionalised, and to provide a realm of consensus within which the force of cultural differences was blunted..

Although I have described the relaxation of state controls on two cultural forms as creating new markets, or, more exactly, as bringing these markets into the domain of respectable cultural production, a lessening of state control did not create a more homogeneous audience. Repeal did not mean, therefore, that a distinction between high and popular theatre maintained by a licensing system was subsequently transcended by the emergence of a fully commercial theatre. Rather the opposite, in that repeal of the legislation: 'which had divided drama into legitimate and illegitimate, led, paradoxically, to a far sharper separation of these two forms than had been the case whilst the Act was in force' (Davison 1982B p. ix). The institutionalisation of a particular mode of theatricality, I shall argue, is to be understood as a particularly powerful way of enacting a distinctive being-in-the-world both at the level of individual action and at a collective level. The consequence of repeal was not to destroy popular theatre but to devalue and discredit other forms of dramatisation.

Since 1737 only two theatres in London, those at Drury Lane and

Covent Garden, had held licences entitling them to perform prose dramas of the sort now associated with conventional theatre. There were also of course a number of provincial Theatres Royal. As well as these theatres a number of others held opera-house licences, or limited warrants to present dramas in illegitimate modes which did not infringe the privileges of monopolists. In part, licences concerned the length of season the theatre was entitled to present, and in part were concerned with formal issues of types of permissible drama. In all cases officials of the Lord Chamberlain's office were empowered to adjudicate and therefore acted as effective agents of censorship. Those prosecuted for transgressing their licence, or ignoring its necessity, inevitably pleaded the warrant of public demand and the record of those opposing reform of a ramshackle system is a classic instance of legislative obscurantism in failing to perceive the formation of new publics. What it did mean was that those entrepreneurs seeking to entertain new publics were forced to innovate in theatrical forms: 'The illegitimate forms, melodrama, burletta, farce, pantomime, extravaganza and spectacle emerged as a result of the Licensing Laws' (Cowan 1978 p. 10).

The legal distinction between types of theatre was important in providing a crucible for the development of theatrical forms, and was associated to a limited extent with differences in the social composition of audiences for different theatres. The new forms were not, however, restricted to a particular type of theatrical setting, so that there was not a simple correlation between type of theatre and quality of drama performed. Patent theatres were just as likely to include novelties such as performing dogs and grossly edited versions of Shakespeare. An evening's entertainment at respectable as well as illegitimate theatre would contain a heterogeneous mixture of theatrical forms.

For example, in Leacroft's brief history of the Theatre Royal, Leicester he notes that when in 1836 the management proudly announced the engagement of Charles Kean for five nights: 'on Monday *Hamlet* was performed, followed by The Grand Oriental Spectacle *The Forty Thieves*' (Leacroft 1958 p. 5), a pattern repeated on succeeding nights. Similarly Roy's study of play bills for the Theatre Royal, Hull in 1820 finds that an evening's entertainment took much the same form as in London with a main melodrama followed by a ballet or several comic songs and dances concluding with a farce or pantomime or extravaganza. The popular aspects of these performances were stressed so that:

the stock company was quick to draw attention to those incidents in a play, such as storms, explosions, battles, tournaments, trials, dances and processions of all kinds ... but the effects of which they seem to have been especially proud were the 'new red fire' invented for conflagrations, and the moonlight.

(Roy 1971 p. 28)

The popular character of urban theatre in the early years of the nineteenth century lay in its extravagance of display, the allegorical moralising of melodrama and associated forms, and in a ceremonial-isation which in many ways was a continuation of early modern dramatic ritual now staged in theatrical settings. In the course of nineteenth century urban change the nature of theatrical experience changed radically. The emergent cultural form of theatre, based on new developments, was – through the success of its own innova-tions – supplanted in popular culture by cultural forms such as variety entertainment and the cinema (both in many ways derivatives of the earlier popular urban theatre).

In order to become 'theatre' the audiences of staged drama had to learn new modes of social decorum; the theatre had to become respectable both as an activity and as an occupation; the framing of dramatic experience to be more rigidly marked; and the business of staging and performing had to become professionalised and thereby self-conscious in the sense of reflexively concerned with the nature and function of professional conventions. I will briefly discuss what is meant by each of these necessary changes, and then in suc-ceeding sections of this chapter make some connections between these changes and other aspects of change in public life in an urbanising social order.

BECOMING THE THEATRE

The theatre as it was formed in the nineteenth century was both more tightly framed as a mode of performance, and more tightly disciplined as a social occasion. Each type of control is mutually constitutive of the other and both imply a rejection of the disorder of earlier popular urban theatre. The predominant tone of dismay in contemporary reports of audience behaviour is not limited to the theatre but was part of a more general concern to improve popular culture and lead it towards forms of more 'rational recreation'. In relation to the theatre the need for reform stemmed from a convivial lack of decorum. Nicholl cites a critic's report written in 1827 of *The Pirate's Dream*:

> There was much fighting which would probably have been more effective, but for a real battle in the pit, to which the screams of the women imparted a truth and reality, that quite spoilt the effect of the stage combats.
>
> (Nicholl 1955 p. 8)

There is also Dickens' comment on the opening of *Macbeth* at Sadler's Wells in 1844 which he said was: 'performed amidst the most hideous medley of fights, foul language, catcalls, shrieks, yells, oaths, blasphemy, obscenity, apples, oranges, nuts, biscuits, ginger beer, porter, and pipes' (quoted in Rahill 1967 p. 143). It was not just that the popular audience lacked orderly restraint as that the theatre as social institution licensed the open decadence of the parade and transaction of prostitution.

It is important to focus upon the embedding of performance in local identity when considering the intimacy of the relationship between performers and audience. In a culture where the dividing line between the street and public hall was ambiguous and relatively transparent, it is unsurprising to find that the stuff of sensationalist street literature was quickly translated onto the stage. Thus when an actor in Bristol was convicted of murdering his mother-in-law, within hours his ex-colleagues had offered a dramatic re-enactment of the dastardly deed (Barker 1977). The sensationalism of this topical commentary is exemplified by the licence authors and performers felt they had to change characters, motivations, actions and even consequences. Although it is possible to see these performances as a type of living newspaper there was no attempt at professional or naturalistic objectivity (as there was in the agit-prop theatrical 'newspapers' of the 1930s). Popular theatre was an entrepreneurial hazard in which the end of the show justified any means.

Pillaging was rife both from continental sources and from the work of other playwrights, novelists and any available contemporary source. Attempts at legal redress were common but the relevant laws were so ramshackle that the pillaging continued unchecked (for the significance of the development of a legal framework of copyright for concepts of authorship in literary fiction see Bonham-Carter 1978). Distinctions between playwright, actor, manager and stage designer were not clearly drawn or maintained. The collective character of this cultural form meant that the performance dominated the enterprise such that individual talents were adapted to the show rather than vice versa:

> The actor in the hippodrome, aquatic theatre, and diorama, when he existed at all, became a mass performer, as mechanical as the elaborate special effects that were the central reason for the existence of these theatres. The chief actor became the effects themselves.
>
> (McNamara 1974 p. 22)

What I have called the collective character of production is perhaps better understood as a form of production more akin to that of the workshop of traditional craft guilds. Theatrical entertainment, particularly when it was largely performed by itinerant companies, was dominated by the family as a basis for organisation. Companies were formed around a family, the children grew up in the business, newcomers were 'adopted' into the larger social unit, and there was a high degree of inter-marrying between families in this marginal world of outsiders. A social marginality protected by an argot and limited environment that made it similar to, and sometimes overlapping with, other social circles of the disreputable and possibly dishonest. This ambience changed only gradually and remained particularly true of more popular entertainments (and survived into at least the early years of the commercial cinema).

In the course of the century there was an increasing division of labour with professionalisation. Different tasks became more specialised and there was a greater degree of hiring on merit rather than personal connections. Crucial to the process of professionalisation was a general acquisition of respectability, a process that was greatly stimulated by the founding of the Royal Academy of Dramatic Arts in 1904: 'which perhaps more than any other theatrical institution encouraged middle-class women in large numbers to join the stage and further transformed the social image of the profession' (Baker 1978 p. 107). Conventions of appropriate representation changed to conform with a stratification of dramas by type of audience, and a display of an equation between personality and part became a mark of adequacy in theatrical art as opposed to more explicitly stylised allegories of social types in popular entertainments.

Consistent with changes in the nature of performance and greatly contributing to a disciplining of audience attention and respectful decorum were a series of changes in the physical organisation of theatrical space. Earlier traditions of more privileged members of the audience sharing the performing space had largely been abandoned by the beginning of the century, but now the picture-frame stage became more absolute. Performers were pushed back behind the proscenium arch and the audience became onlookers firmly relegated to a world beyond the stage. It is in this respect that the development of stalls seating is relevant. The area known as the pit had previously been socially mixed. As this area was filled with seats so the great banks of boxes lining a horseshoe stage were pulled back to a vestigial few at the edge of semi-circles of raised seats and many of their former patrons moved down to the new stalls seating. The process of re-organisation was continuous throughout the century and considerably facilitated by many fires which destroyed theatrical auditoria.

The social phenomenology of theatrical experience was further transformed by the innovation of darkening the auditorium during a performance, a development first made possible by gas lighting and then greatly facilitated by the introduction of electricity. Darkened house lights threw greater attention on the stage increasing the status of author and performers, it facilitated the mounting of tricky stage effects, and it encouraged norms of orderly behaviour in that movement and conversation within the auditorium were incompatible with respectful attention:

> The new ideal was to achieve direct communication between the spectator and what was being presented . . . The idea of darkening the auditorium was to enhance this feeling of community between the viewer and the drama by shutting out the social phenomenon of the audience for the duration of the play.
>
> (Schivelbusch 1988 pp. 206–7)

There were analogous changes in the organisation of the evening's entertainment. As dramas became more naturalistic so the suspension of disbelief became more coherent, and the plays became occasions in and of themselves. The tradition of a long evening of mixed entertainment was gradually suspended in favour of a single play. This not only worked to the advantage of authors by increasing their status, as those primarily responsible for the show, but it also meant that plays could start later and become more consistent with bourgeois dinner habits. A later starting time, and a single performance precluding staggered admissions, and more elaborate productions required and justified higher admission prices and so a battle lost at the beginning of the century (when riots broke out at Drury Lane over an attempt to raise prices), was won towards the end.

A change in popular appeal was further stimulated by more comfortable theatres with greater facilities, greater social segregation within the theatre – including separate entrances and exits for different types of seating and thereby different classes of patrons – and more prestigious locations for new theatres. Similarly the introduction of matinee performances assumed that there was a leisured audience who would be willing to patronise something suitably entertaining. In retrospect it seems apposite that a bourgeois, respectable audience was attracted to the innovation pioneered by Gilbert and Sullivan with their light operas, and it became socially acceptable for respectable ladies to attend the theatre unaccompanied by gentlemen escorts.

The processes through which the theatre acquired institutional respectability, or rather became 'the theatre' and thereby contained the possibility of being marked off from popular entertainments, is, as we have noted, inseparably grounded in the articulation of a culture of respectability. It is less commonly remarked that more rigid cultural segregation by social class within a cultural form did not mean the complete abandonment of earlier narrative modes. Indeed in important respects the spectacular dramatisations of urban popular theatre were intensified in the sensation dramas of the latter half of the century. But as the social ambience changed the conventions of theatricality also changed. Popular melodramas did not disappear overnight, continuing to do well in suburban and provincial theatres, but a combination of touring West End companies, changes in clientele, and the development of a film industry had removed these last bastions by early in the twentieth century.

The changes were in terms of theme as much as style:

> The Gothic slowly disappeared; the military and nautical remained. The domestic was stronger than ever and formed the vast majoity of all melodramas in this period . . . dialogue was more natural, plots more skilfully constructed, and the characters more credibly conceived, than in the earlier period.
>
> (Booth 1965 p. 145)

Sensationalism in the respectable theatre did not then involve a complete rejection of melodramatic romanticism but an increased sophistication was increasingly mediated through an atmosphere of social realism. A realism which was based on accuracy of detail rather than narrative credibility of motive or consequence. A social realism that was primarily a concretisation, the antithesis of abstraction – and is therefore more usefully understood in terms of the conventions of naturalism that have dominated the cinema. In general the massive resources of late Victorian stage-craft were deployed:

> to satisfy the public's taste for the pictorial, the richly decorated image, the photographic representation of domestic reality, the visual re-creation of history, and the ostentation of lavish display in an ostentatious age.
>
> (Booth 1979 p. 19)

Essential to all these innovations is the creation of the distinction between a flat scene and a set scene. By the latter I mean an arrangement which consists of independent props filling the stage and around which the action takes place (Southern 1952 Chapter 13). A set scene provides for considerably greater contrivance but in order to gain maximum dramatic effect has to be revealed. This requires in turn a fixed and tightly framed distinction between front and back stages. A re-structuring of theatrical space that was reinforced by increasingly elaborate safety regulations which led to theatres being subdivided into effectively separate compartments. An exhilarating consistency was thus achieved between theories of staging, the needs of adequate access and control, the desirability of social segregation and a phenomenology of theatrical representation that emphasises perspectival distance allied with simultaneous involvement.

The contemporary language conventionally used to describe changes in staging is full of metaphors drawn from perspective and pictorial representation. It was fundamental to the development of respectability as an art form that a single inspiring vision could be seen to authorise the work. The role of authority operated on two levels. The first, as I have noted, relates to privileging the text and its author, while the second concerns the production of the performance. It is central to our understanding of the meaning of spectacular display that actors despite striving for more interpersonally persuasive means of representation were subsumed in a design only available from outside the grounds of the performance, i.e. from the perspective of the audience and imposed by a coordinating vision superior to that of any particular performer. It is in the later years of the century that the roles of first stage manager and then director emerge as authoritative voices invested with the power to interpret the text and assume responsibility for a production.

The idea that the stage. its props and performers, were directed by an external vision, and allied to the development of ever-more elaborate theatrical effects, led to a theme of the stage as a machine. Madame Vestris, first a celebrated actress and later theatrical manager, is usually credited with the innovation of including real pieces of furniture within a stage set and it is appropriate that such an innovation in theatrical realism should have occurred at the same time that Daguerre and Neipce were conducting their successful experiments with photographic reproduction (Appleton 1974 p. 74). As these innovations were developed and built upon, it becomes appropriate to use the analogy of a stage as machine and to recognise the importance of the machinist in late Victorian theatre (Leacroft (1973 Chapters 7–9); Appleton (1974 p. 174) has pointed out of Vestris' 'confections' of the 1850s that: 'These extravaganzas with transformation scenes, elaborate groupings, and opulent decor unmistakably point the way toward the later fantasies of Florenz Ziegfield and Busby Berkeley.'

My account of theatrical developments in the nineteenth century has two purposes. The first is to argue that developments in staging and modes of dramatisation had massive implications for the type of cultural experience theatrical representation was capable of providing. While the second is that these changes were also intimately bound up with and essential for an emergent language of new forms of public drama. Essentially this will be argued in relation to themes in the re-organisation or re-writing of public space. A significant sub-theme of this account is that in relation to some, if not all, cultural forms there is a need to amend Benjamin's canonical thesis that in systems of mass marketing works of art lose their aura. The perceived need to claim a privilege for those cultural forms treated as their area of expertise by intellectual élites and by organisations committed to the propagation of an official culture, in terms of sustaining structures of cultural stratification, has led producers, critics and performers, etc., to need to invent various displays of 'aura' in order to mark their 'art' off from the taint of popular appeal.

This is not to say of course that every form of theatrical entertainment sought respectability through an aura of authorship. I will conclude this part of the chapter by noting some features of the development of the music hall. This was the first cultural form born of popular experience in urban-industrial cities. In the process of commercial development and through becoming a national form of popular entertainment there are clear continuities in the re-structuring of theatrical space. I will argue that in the continuities between this process and the colonisation of the dramatic theatre within the cultural ambit of middle-class culture the nature of theatrical dramatisation changed, but also more importantly that a new series of dramatic metaphors was being forged for communal experience (on contemporary American experience see Snyder 1986).

The singing saloon, which with supper clubs and other informal gatherings is the basis of music hall, falls between the extremes of professional theatre and neighbourly sing-song. Although there was usually a charge for admission to the saloon, partly to be redeemed for food and drink, the publican's real profits lay in encouraging further drinking. The atmosphere was therefore informal, there would be continual movement between tables, and the relationship between performer and audience was dynamic and intimate. In these ways singing saloons were more like penny gaffs and other forms of street entertainment than more elaborate stagings, but they also differed in that the buildings were better furnished, lit and they were licensed.

Their permanency encouraged the emergence of a substantial body of semi-professional entertainers who travelled between saloons. Although the entertainment differed in each locality and retained a regional flavour: 'the songs, dances and tricks were derived from the travelling show and popular theatre, the village green and the street, the drawing room and the church, and the recently-imported nigger-minstrel show' (Bailey 1978 p. 31). The important features of this new cultural form were that it provided a combination of communalism with nascent professionalism; based upon the pub an emergent class pillaged from a variety of sources to provide with pride, ostentation and vitality a celebration of identity that was spectacular in form.

The spectacular character of the entertainment was gradually made more theatrical both through shifting the location from pub to theatre and through the adoption of theatrical conventions, in so doing taking on the form of metropolitan, commercial enter-tainment. The features of a process of transition can be summarised under the headings of: the development of national stars; entrepreneurial investment in lavish settings both in stagings and auditoria; the adoption of formal theatrical conventions particularly governing audience behaviour; and the ways in which national moral panics over the dangers offered by this form of entertainment were accommodated. As these features came to dominate the cultural form, the entertainment provided significantly replicated the conventions of bourgeois theatre, and thereby recuperated a popular form of entertainment within a cultural orthodoxy.

It is not just that Stoll's staging of the Derby, at his newly opened Coliseum in 1904, outdid that great example of Victorian naturalism Frith's painting, but a whole range of music hall characters, such as Vesta Tilley's cross-sex dressing and Albert Chevalier's cross-class impersonation, were far more finely realised than early nineteenth-century characters such as Jolly Jack Tar. Martha Vicinus has suggested that this realism is puzzling unless we accept that music hall in fifty years changed from class culture with class perspectives to a form of mass entertainment characterised by 'the use of stereo-types in which the behaviour of a particular group or class is portrayed, but the emotions are generalised and acceptable to all classes' (Vicinus 1974 p. 266).

It is not so much accuracy as communal significance that provides the implied social world of cultural representation. The norms of pictorial naturalism dissolved the fragmentation of community in metropolitan cities into an idealised normality of conventional truths. It is in this sense that accuracy of detail may be part of an effective neutrality rather than faithful realisation. The humorous or sympathetic or despicable features of those depicted were coins of social exchange that could be used in pictures of social representation independent of the context in which they were generated. My argument then is that the music hall was the first major cultural form to grow out of the experience an urbanising proletariat. It did not, however, constitute a mode of class consciousness preparing for structural transformation but rather a recognition of social difference that in detail and general orientation was consistent with the moralising narratives of spectacular pictor-ialism in other cultural forms (Stedman Jones 1974). A language of social drama that made sense in the context of fully commercial theatres, serviced by national organisations and media of publicity, and catering to anonymous audiences. In such settings entertain-ment was a fabulous alternative to mundane experience, something for the individual to purchase as a source of pleasure rather than the community to celebrate, and drama has become a commodity.

URBAN LANDSCAPE AND POPULAR CULTURE

I have described some features of change in theatrical entertainment in nineteenth-century Britain. I have argued that these changes can be understood as interdependent with other processes of change in forms of social order. The reorganisation of dramatic space in the development of the theatre was inscribed in a more general re-structuring of the cultural landscape – the organisation of space through which social forms are articulated. Both public and drama are modes of inscription: 'besides its single sites, the public exists as a shared social horizon for the members of a society' (Bommes and Wright 1982 p. 260). The notion of cultural landscape is therefore a composite of ways of seeing and the contours of what is recognis-able and seeable (where seeing is itself a metaphor for use). In this part of the chapter I will describe some features of the changing urban landscape.

The idea of landscape, although most commonly pastoral, can easily be adapted to an urban setting particularly when the majority of the population comes to live in cities that dwarf any previous sense of human scale. In the first fifty years of the century the total population roughly doubled and although the rate of increase slowed the population at the end of the century was three-and-a-half times as big as at the beginning. This population was increasingly concentrated in towns. A third of the population were urban residents in 1801; by the year of the Great Exhibition (1851), this had risen to one in two and by the end of the century around 80 per cent were town dwellers. Although what is to count as a town necessarily varies, there is a clear trend of concentration of the populace in larger towns:

> in 1851 30.6% of the population of England and Wales in-habited towns of over 50,000 people and, using the same town boundaries, about 45% in 1901. Using the revised boundaries current in 1901, we find the tendency to agglomerate in towns of over 50,000 people stronger still for then the proportion was 51.1%.
>
> (Waller 1983 pp. 8–9)

The consequences of rapid urbanisation, even metropolitanisation have, rightly, dominated sociological accounts of modernity. I do not intend at this stage to engage with the literature on the nature and significance of changes in community. This will necessarily form an implicit theme throughout the book. All I wish to stress at this point is that urbanisation creates a world of strangers, if only in the ways that Simmel first explored (1971; see also Barth 1980), that interaction with strangers becomes a routine feature of everyday experience. Cities of this size generate a metropolitan imagination – an assumption of mundane anonymity – and in the nineteenth century none more so than London which sprawled from its size in 1800: 'From the Thames a 2-mile journey, either north or south, would bring one to the periphery' (Wohl 1971 p. 15), a journey which had by the end of the century become 18 miles in total.

The other side of anonymity is of course freedom. 'Town air' is 'free air' because the stranger may lack the supports of established social networks but will also escape the crushing weight of habitual obligations. (I do not wish to imply that there are no extensive social networks in urban communities but that they are harder to sustain through generations and, more importantly, are the networks of lifestyles and thus identity in the settings they generate becomes more like a role.) Freedom promises excitement both because the quotidian is thereby possibly less predictable and possibly more amenable to choice and because it is staged against a backdrop of magnificence. The attraction of urban culture is always therefore the promise of possibility, the magnetism is not lessened by however often promises are not kept. And even the presence of magnificence can give a surrogate glamour and significance to the mundane round (Olsen 1986 discusses very well some of the ways that the city as 'a work of art' structures everyday interaction). These features can be detected as core themes in the swirling discourses of urban life in the nineteenth century – the city was more palpably out of control and therefore culture, and more particularly popular culture, came to be seen as a suitable topic for policy (cf. Lees 1985).

The lineaments of social order have to be more clearly asserted when the nature of order itself cannot be taken for granted. This then is the connection within a concept of landscape as it used here between the built environment and forms of popular entertainment. The discourse of the popular as the ways of constituting urban life was and is inscribed in ways of using the environment; contradictions within the discourse bespeak different projects of use.

Even when peddled in the countryside the popular is a piece of the town that is being bought (Burke 1978). In this early modern sense the popular is another name for vernacular or demotic speech. It is what is said unselfconsciously by ordinary people in unmarked settings, and by extension how they dress, how they dance and sing, how they decorate their homes, how they celebrate marked points in the communal calendar and, importantly, how they organise the world of work and the rights and obligations of social contract. Pre-modern, this sense of popular can be presumed to be local but the popular has been increasingly supplied by national distribution agencies. There is therefore an easy elision between the popular as widely endorsed and popular as working class taste or culture. Working people are in some definitions at least a majority of the population so that the popular is a class culture.

This slides more contentiously, however, into more embattled positions. If it is a culture of a class then it must relate to that class consciousness of itself, a criterion is introduced by which something is or can be judged inauthentic – or even validly authentic even if not particularly 'popular' with large numbers of people. There may be cultural forms which are seen as appropriate for popular taste but in their acceptance function as hegemonic modes of incorporation (Bennett 1986). Alternatively, the intractability of working-class culture to norms of respectability may be celebrated by middle-class observers as glorious vulgarity (Nuttall and Carmichael 1977); or be seen to be acting as images of licensed naughtiness for normally respectable voyeurs (cf. Clark's 1985 interpretation of Parisian urban entertainments, particularly Chapter 4). The popular here is explicitly normative, and clearly presupposes socio-structural organisation in class terms.

Possibly the principal novelty of the nineteenth century is that men and women began to use the language of class to describe and explain social order (Stedman Jones 1983; Joyce 1991). Social classes implied both new modes of production to generate distinctive types of social identity and new forms of association, solidarity and conflict within and between social levels. It is not, however, self-evident that either of these types of change preceded the language of class as a dramatic resource which by mid-century had become ubiquitous:

> At almost every turn the English divided up their social and economic life by class; at work, at home, on the trains, in their cemeteries, and even in the ideology that was embedded in a great deal of contemporary literature. The English had come to view social class as normal and proper.
>
> (Walvin 1984 p. 195)

It is precisely because the language of class became so thoroughly entrenched as a popular resource for describing and interpreting social behaviour that it is extremely difficult to use class as an analytic resource to explicate the meanings of cultural performance.

The paradox of this claim is that as perceptions of social difference came to dominate cultural expectations so it seemed more important to contemporaries that class distinctions were not dissipated by heterogeneous mixing in public places. On the one hand there were certain sorts of activities and entertainments which by commanding a particular type of audience marked off cultural fractions within a particular class. On the other side when a cultural form commanded a broader social spectrum the activity had to be so organised that the members of different social strata could participate as segregated from each other as possible. Class and culture therefore interpenetrated each other so thoroughly that the latter was continuously available as a resource to make further fine discriminations within the former. The popular cannot therefore be reserved as the form of proletarian life. Within the increasingly complex battery of social discrimination the popular is generalised as a vaguer referent for any type of taste which does not strive to display its own exclusivity.

This process can be seen to be operating in worlds which are far removed from the bawdy vulgarity of working-class entertainment. In Weber's (1975) study of the development of musical concerts as a cultural form he finds it necessary to distinguish within a middle class audience with a notion of taste publics. The more spectacular virtuosity of, for example, Liszt or Chopin had a romantic appeal to quite different social groups than those who constituted the audience for more classical chamber works. As well as this there are many other themes in this work which are relevant to the present discussion, but in particular one should mention how conventions for appropriate audience behaviour gradually develop, taking the same form as but slightly preceding equivalent conventions in the theatre.

The dramatic force of categories of discrimination and segregation lay in the ways in which they came to symbolise an emergent social order. The lack of physical segregation in the pre-modern city was more than merely puzzling to those seeking to re-shape the urban fabric; it amounted to forms of intrusiveness that could seem polluting or destabilising. British custom from early in the nineteenth century decreed that building design should work so that each bedroom had a single and independent entrance which 'was in contrast to the frequent continental situation in which it was necessary to pass through one bedroom to reach the second, a state of affairs that confirmed the worst English suspicions about continental morals' (Olsen 1986 p. 108). The dangers of heterogeneous mixing with its potential for disorder was also a strong element in the condemnation of the spectacle of public discipline. In contrast, the rationalisation of control and punishment behind the walls of new institutional monoliths of prisons, hospitals, asylums and later schools of the nineteenth century can therefore be seen as integral to the inscription of new forms of order into the public sphere (Markus 1982; Evans 1982).

Another dimension to the changing delineation of public space into increasingly distinct spaces is provided by the discourses of sexuality and death – increasingly segregated from everyday experience and confined to specialised settings and increasingly elaborate euphemisms in public discourse. Even in those works which argue for a revisionist thesis that the repression of sexual desire amongst Victorian women was not as thorough as popular history would suggest (Gay 1984), there is sufficient testimony to the highly formalised character of sexual behaviour in anything other than the most private settings. An illustration of the ordering of death is provided by the number of new cemeteries, at first commercial and later municipal enterprises, founded on what were at first the edges of expanding cities. These cemeteries were to some extent generated by the pressures of increasing urban populations and the toll exacted by inadequate health and sanitary arrangements, but they more importantly mark moves from the casual intermingling of everyday life and artefacts of the dead in eighteenth century church yards to solemnified segregation in rational individualised order. The ubiquitousness of social order and hierarchical segregation was more clearly displayed in the dramatic intensification of respectability after life.

The family home became the physical and symbolic site of boundaries between social worlds so that order could be more explicitly visualised both within the home and between the home and public places. Such has been the success of the norm that a home is the house of a single family that:

> It is difficult imagine today what life was like in the urban houses of pre-industrial Britain. There was a far greater mixture of people and activities: the extended family, friends,

servants, apprentices; private sphere, work, recreation, the care of the sick: all co-existed and overlapped.

(Muthesius 1982 p. 39)

Change was gradual and involved a series of changes in physical layout within the house, in particular the specialisation of room by function and increasingly rigid segregation of the sexes; between the relative significance of the front and the back of the house; and an increasing cultivation of a garden as a private space. A major preoccupation in house design was to clearly demarcate public rooms where members of the outside world could be entertained from more private areas typically under the control of women.

If the home is to be seen as a distinct type of cultural space in which a private world both created by and for women can be enforced and protected from the potential disorder of public life, then its exclusivity can be more radically displayed the more thorough the distinction between home and work:

The romantic imagination indelibly fixed the image of a rose-covered cottage in a garden where Womanhood waited and from which Manhood ventured abroad: to work, to war and to the Empire. So powerful was this dual conception that even the radical fringe subscribed.

(Davidoff and Hall 1987 p. 28)

The gendered equivalences between male and female spheres, public and private spaces and city and suburb have remained powerful cultural frames. Stilgoe introduces his book on the origins of the American suburb by noting that: 'I have encountered for the first time male colleagues and students who dismiss the research subject as a "woman's topic" who see the borderlands as infinitely less important than "the city"' (Stilgoe 1988 p. 16). Studies of popular culture have reproduced these biases leading to a fashionable over-emphasis upon the popular as 'working' class culture.

The flight from the city to the suburb was the main engine of urban growth. The motive force was an intermixture of privatisation, pastoralism and social differentiation (on pastoralism see Stilgoe op. cit. and King 1984). For those who could afford to, moving to the borders of urban space created new cultural enclaves in which drama was set on a stage elsewhere – they could either visit it or purchase a version adapted for suburban scale. The city as theatre had become something for which there was an ever-increasing audience.

Suburbanism did not dissipate the grandiloquence of an urban landscape, indeed the reverse as the centre became increasingly reserved as a theatrical enclave, but rather fractured audiences through the twin strands of class segregation and domestic isolation. House values were increasingly determined by exclusivity, not through upper and middle classes wishing to be distanced from the contaminating presence of lower orders – as servants and trades people they could be contained within exclusive districts – but increasingly fine discriminations were made so that each social fraction could live in a neighbourhood with a distinct and dominant identity. As pretensions to exclusivity became more difficult to sustain so the social orthodoxy of individual streets was more enthusiastically sought. Such exclusivity entailed a high degree of mobility as the class character of districts changed and as individual family circumstances altered.

Suburbanism also required an elaborate vocabulary of physical distinctions to display the appropriate status of each household (cf. Muthesius 1982 especially Chapter 17), a language of class that has persisted as a practical mapping of urban life. Although access to the productive hubs of the city was obviously important, the more that functional elements, such as shops, transport facilities, entertainment sites, were adjacent to domestic residences the more the status of those particular houses was comparatively devalued. The vacuum of what had previously been a shared communal drama was increasingly filled with the sponsored encapsulated dramas of spectacular shows, municipal magnificence and governmental and commercial display.

I have mentioned that exclusivity was more concerned with possible dilution of status through the co-prescence of near-peers, marked differences between low and high status groups within a district could be tolerated and were indeed necessary. Processes of urban migration, inadequate and insufficient housing stock, and poor wages and long hours all meant, however, that there were appalling rookeries, ghettoes and slums blighting nineteenth-century cities within which the working class was concentrated. There were uneven and differentially effective attempts throughout the century to intervene and repair these sores, even if only ambiguously intentioned. For example, when railway lines were laid into city centres, or when sewage pipes or other forms of road improvement were undertaken, it was usually easier to knock through poor districts. These and other forms of rudimentary town planning might be undertaken to break up concentrations of the poor in the interests of social discipline and control, or because such patently unhealthy cesspits were breeding grounds for disease, particularly in the light of dominant miasmic theories of disease transmission, which threatened other class quarters.

More positively, improving transport facilties and rising living standards meant that speculative building for the working class could be lucrative. The ambition to re-locate in suburbs was not therefore confined to the wealthy, and in the processes of re-organisation the social landscape of working class community was recast: 'The forms of working-class districts [changed] in the early and mid-Victorian years from a *cellular* and *promiscuous* to an *open* and *encapsulated* residential style' (Daunton 1983 p. 214). What this meant in practice was:

> change from inward-looking dead ends turning their backs on the public thoroughfares to outward-looking streets; and from a pooling of space between houses to a definite allocation of space to each house. The threshold between the public and private had been redrawn and made much less ambiguous.
>
> (Danton op. cit. p. 215)

The significance of the development of working-class residential districts lies in the way it points us to another aspect of the inter-relationships between class and popular. The culture of the emergent and later mature working class was frequently seen by contemporaries as disorderly and lacking respectability; more seriously it was inappropriate for the disciplined self-control necessary for an industrial and bureaucratised labour force. Other grounds of concern were that it was seen as a fertile breeding ground for class organisation which threatened the bases of social order; and it lacked the crucial institutional frameworks of family and sobriety (Storch 1982). There were therefore a variety of inter-ventionist strategies commonly motivated by the perceived need to instill more appropriate cultural expectations amongst the lower orders.

Crudely we can group these strategies under the two headings of: discipline – attempts to stamp out inappropriate cultural forms; and incorporation – in which the force of class consciousness was dis-sipated through realisation of common interests and acculturation into the favoured cultural forms of more respectable society. To speak of strategies can imply thought-through and planned interventions, which did undoubtedly exist, but more pervasively there were a set of discursive formations within which vocabularies of order and respectability became inscribed in everyday experience.

There are two consequences of this point. The first is that in addition to studies of the role of new police forces in controlling street life, or the suppression of traditional carnivalesque (Donajgrodzki 1977), we need to appreciate the significance of less explicit frameworks such as urban form and cultural conventions in new forms of social control. These interactively meant, for example, that by mid-century observers could marvel at the propriety of visitors to the Great Exhibition as willing adherents to the demands of social discipline and codes of conduct. The second is that it would be misleading to see these discursive formations as simply imposed on a more-or-less recalcitrant popular culture. To the extent that class consciousness became institutionalised it did so within cultural forms that accepted norms of respectability as consistent with or essential to forms of political and religious identity (an example of the sometimes contradictory expectations that could develop is provided by Colls' 1977 study of popular song in mining communities). The popular, then, as it became couched within languages of class became a shifting terrain in that the same phenomena could be seen from a variety of perspectives as part of quite distinct modes of dramatising collective formations.

One of the richest resources with which to illustrate these issues is provided by the development of sport as activity and entertainment in nineteenth-century cities (Mason 1980; Elias and Dunning 1986; Holt 1989). First, because the development of sport in its modern use involved the decay or abolition of traditional forms of play and game, being replaced by more formalised activities governed by agreed national rules and usually involving a national administrative machinery for the organisation and government of the sport. Second, because in popular sports performance was made theatrical in order to be commercialised. Investors had to commit resources to the building of stadia and management of teams and publicity had to be generated in order to stress the spectacular character of the entertainment. Third, the language of class inexorably gave a social character to different sports, or ways of playing within a sport, so that the taste publics of players and spectators came to exemplify class and local identity; institutionalised to the extent that different sports could exist as almost distinct cultural forms. And fourth because despite the appropriation of sports to different class cultural milieux, there could still be articulated themes of disinterested value, reconciliation and social harmony through sport which would provide a dramaturgy of collective, national, identity superseding the divisions of a segregated society.

The salience of a language of class to a phenomenology of urban culture in the nineteenth-century city is then that, through the perspectives of class, inadequacies in traditional discourses of social order were made clearly apparent. There were in a sense new social formations waiting to be given shape and vitality. If the city was no longer a theatre in its dramatic totality more specific stages for new types of social function had to be founded and developed. Principally the legitimacy and dramatic force of the government and discipline of urban society had to be made manifest. In raising these considerations a further use to the notion of the popular becomes relevant. If traditional structures and insignia of authority can only limpingly command their presence in changing circumstances, then their scenario must either be re-written (as happened with the Monarchy, cf. Cannadine 1983), or new modes of political organisation develop. The history of nineteenth century British cities can be written as a narrative of struggle for control over changing instruments of government between competing publics. I am less interested in the politics of accommodation than in the ways in which popular support was presumed, mobilised and displayed. The popular came then to be interdependent with publics and their opinions – the community as imagined entity (Anderson 1983). The artefacts through which imagination was given form and substance, and specific cultural character, are necessarily instances of popular dramatisation.

For obvious reasons these artefacts will cluster in city centres and in terms of national political icons in metropolitan centres. They provide a stage for public drama and in so doing mutually constitute the city centre as spectacular site, and further intensifying the depth of distinction between public and private spheres. Town halls in the nineteenth century, for example, were built: to display local pride; to express the ambition of local influentials; to provide a focus for civic identity for municipalities whose boundaries and character were often amorphous; to provide a centre for social rituals and spectacles of government of newly-powerful urban élites which would rival the traditional pomp of aristocracy and squirearchy; and to give a physical form to a projected community of interests which would blur class divisions and effectively reinforce the 'natural' claim to influence of a middle-class élite.

The frequently medieval or gothic iconography of town halls may seem puzzling as celebrations of political change, but the salience of the past in nineteenth-century urban aesthetics is that it implied a stability in social order. In conjunction with many types of amateur and professional interest, respect for history 'supported the dominant social order by facilitating social assimilation, by screening out problematic aspects of the past, such as economic inequalities, and by fostering the celebration of a common past' (Dellheim 1982 p. 58). The romance of history could be used to create a sense of community and to imbue political power with spectacular dignity and 'to impress laboring people with middle-class values and thus maintain middle-class hegemony' (Dellheim op. cit. p. 175).

We are therefore faced with an intriguing paradox that in important respects the dramatisation of an emergent social order in urbanising Britain was staged through an iconography of the past. The fact that the past visualised was frequently imagined or invented did not lessen its dramatic force (Hobsbawm and Ranger 1983 have edited an excellent collection of essays on 'the invention of tradition', see in particular the essay by Hobsbawm; it should also not be assumed that ceremonials always suppressed dissent and were unproblematically functional for social élites, cf. Hammerton and Cannadine 1981). In the practice of invention the cultural landscape of metropolitan culture, through a variety of resources, was given a dimension through time to complement the spectacular space of the city.

The notion of landscape, then, as a form of spectacular dramatisation should be understood as more than a setting within which identity can be staged, it is the collective identity – in this case Englishness – within which the varieties of cultural taste can be accommodated:

> Élite/mass and avant-garde/commercial were not pairs of oppositional terms but pairs of complementary ones. Each ratified the sphere and responsibilities of the other . . . . the artistic institutions of the national culture simply gathered up and acted as custodians of the best of the national past.
>
> (Dodd 1986 p. 21)

The identity of our imagined communities becomes a claimed 'national character' as well as a national heritage, a set of political and cultural presuppositions that in each case of their use become in so doing a self-fulfilling prophecy (cf. Colls 1986).

The invention or constitution of nationness is a mode of dramatisation which is as much designed for audiences in other national 'theatres' as for the 'internal' audience within the nation. It is consistent with the spectacular character of the dramatisations that it did not have to be phrased through permanent buildings. The frequency of international exhibitions in the second half of the century provided 'ephemeral vistas' through which collective identity could be constructed and displayed:

> At exhibitions . . . 'Olde Englande' came to stand for a range of traditional virtues Englishmen were supposedly ingrained with. Simple, solid, quaint, reliable, unchanging and hardy were the type of adjectives used to describe the English population, more than this they were applied to English culture in general.
>
> (Greenhalgh 1988 p. 122)

These exhibitions drew upon a broad range of popular cultural styles and sources in order to dramatise the pedagogical discourse ostensibly being exhibited, but it is important that it always was a use of popular forms to appeal to mass audiences. In their commercial success: 'the exhibitions heralded the end of vernacular entertainment and the beginning of mass international popular culture' (Greenhalgh op.cit. p. 45). That is the transformation of drama into the imagin-action of dreams (see also Williams 1982).

There is a crucial moment of transition here in the emergence of a mature popular culture transformed by the need to appeal to mass, national and subsequently international, audiences and the, obviously related, increasing domination of entertainment industries by mass distribution networks. The interdependence of popular culture as leisure with a culture of consumerism can be seen to be filling an ideological function of offering mechanisms of social reconciliation that transcend the divisiveness of urban segregation. Both through a phenomenology of personal choice and the anonymity of consumption (any style is accessible providing you have the resources and the wit to purchase it), the manifestness of structural divisions is vitiated: 'It is above all *collectivity* that the popular exists to prevent' (Clark 1985 p. 236). An ideological function that is only made possible and comprehensible, in Clark's account, through the re-structuring of landscape in nineteenth century city development: 'the end of the old patterns of urban neighbourhood and the birth of a city organized round separate unities of work, residence, and distraction' (Clark op. cit. p. 235).

To be sure, this conclusion is reached in relation to Paris only, a city where the re-writing of urban form was so clearly authored within a short period and was so clearly governed by reflexive concerns with what a metropolis should and could be, that it can be argued to be far too coherent for the pragmatic muddle of British urban development. There are, however, and the point of this chapter is to argue for, connections between reformulations of forms of dramatisation and the terrain of urban landscape and the cultural forms of mass entertainment; and one way of focussing their interconnection is through the notion of spectacle: 'as a separate something made to be looked at – an image, a pantomime, a panorama' (Clark op. cit. p. 63).

SPECTACULAR ENTERTAINMENT

Arscott and Pollock (1988 p. 197) have argued that: 'The issue of the city in the nineteenth century was a question of the meanings of new forms of social life.' The point can be taken, as its authors take it, to explain why and how cultural representations of urban life were ambiguous in their appropriateness. Such judgements (by critics and historians as much as contemporaries) are inevitably ideological interventions in what the city should mean or have meant. It can also be read, however, as directing our attention to the interdependence between meaning and form in social experience and emphasising that central to these new forms were precisely the conventions of appropriate expression (the sensibilities) of the city as it was changing. Cultural forms in this sense would not be confined to representing social meaning but would constitute possibilities of social meaning. In the development of metropolitan culture there were opportunities to articulate the outlines of a form of cultural order which could metaphorically be used to ground social and even physical order.

I believe that the city became spectacular in two different but related ways, and that visualisation of urbanism as spectacle became a central resource for negotiating what the meanings of new forms were. The first way in which cities became spectacular was through physical reconstruction particularly of central districts in which new streets, buildings and services such as viaducts and bridges were a public display of wealth and ambition.

The second is that social life in the city became a form of performance in which the performers were increasingly estranged from the drama of which they were part: 'The city, Simmel has shrewdly seen, intellectualized men by demanding more and more consciousness, more alertness and inference, more balance and tolerance for the unexpected, more processing of the immediate environment' (Fisher 1975 p. 386). Although the pressures of interpretation were unremittingly real, through their very intensity they may act to transform reality into euphoric hallucination. In the same way that addicts can become more glittering and alluring when enacting the fantasy of their drugs: 'Commodities derive the same effect from the crowd that surges around and intoxicates them. The concentration of customers which makes the market, which in turn makes the commodity into a commodity, enhances its attractiveness to the average buyer' (Benjamin 1973 p. 56).

A new cultural form appropriate to the metropolitan city which gave an imaginary coherence, and thus a sense of social order, to the diversity and formlessness of urban social experience was the popular newspaper: 'the newspaper is in itself an image of the city, a miniaturized sample of the total life world, not seen in relation but in simple juxtaposition. Column by column, weighted without account of importance, the heroic and trivial repose side by side' (Fisher op. cit. p. 388). The popular newspaper was, in part, a response to changes in urban ecology. As increasing numbers of people spent part of their day either being transported or waiting for transport they sought reading material which was brief, intriguing, sensationalist and varied: 'Newspapers benefited from the experience of city life as spectacle, and they contributed to it. They provided their readers a running account of the marvels and mysteries of urban life' (Schudson 1978 p. 105). The popular newspaper though is more than a dramatic resource in a disordered world, through the jumble of happenings, gossip and sensations it constitutes a form of vicarious participation which is effectively that of an imaginary or abstract crowd.

Complementing the lack of clear order in urban social relations, the intricacy of the urban landscape was integral to the excitement and stimulus of new forms of experience: 'a consciousness of the city as *terra incognita*, a man-made wilderness more daunting than tropical forests, more inscrutable than the Sahara' (Dyos 1973 p. 191). The two strands of the city as a source of wonder and of it as a social environment estranged from the individual are interwoven in the city as tourist attraction. Around the time of the Great Exhibition, publicists, hoteliers, railway companies and others began to cater for visitors to London who needed guide books, maps and all sorts of information about the constantly changing metropolis (Hopke 1986; although there is by now a considerable literature on tourism, MacCannell 1976 is still the best on the social phenomenology of tourism).

It is not surprising that a metaphor of exploration became common: 'The notion of "exploration" which recurs time and time again in the imagery of early urban studies carried with it the sense that nineteenth-century cities, in particular, were "mysterious places" where one section of the community knew very little directly about the rest' (Briggs 1973 p. 87). It was because it could be assumed that the everyday world of different metropolitan communities was different, that in, for example, Dickens' pictures of the London poor: 'He writes like an explorer or anthropologist, clearly assuming that even those who have visited Monmouth Street or Seven Dials will not really have *seen* those places, have understood them for what they are' (Irwin 1979 p. 152; Cowling 1989 is very interesting on the use of anthropological typologies as a pictorial method by later nineteenth-century painters). Being in public was not then restricted to a particular social élite but became characteristic of certain codes of behaviour which displayed a recognition of respectability as social order. In these ways the uncertainties of disordered landscapes could be assuaged.

As an illustration I can point to the social fashion in the second half of the century of eating out, that is lunching or dining in public places. To some extent this was a necessary consequence of city growth – people could not get home as easily, the nature of the working day changed, businessmen were more likely to be involved in journeys necessitating overnight stops, and as city centres became more entertainment centres public dining became fashionable as a form of entertainment. The problem with traditional places of refreshment was their social heterogeneity, they offered little opportunity for social discrimination and privacy and in particular they failed to provide segregated facilities for women. The restaurant, a concept imported from France in isolated instances, became more widespread from the 1860s. The important feature of these new eating places is that not only were they considerably more elaborate and grand than previous types of dining rooms, and in the ritual of formal dining they could match the increasing formalisation of dining in private homes, but they also 'offered a setting in which customers could appear in public while, seated at separate tables, still preserving an immediate territory that was private' (Thorne 1980 p. 243).

The point being made is that the landscape of the urban environment had become so open-ended and mysterious and probably threatening that for any one individual it would be hard to believe that it could be contained within an ordering synoptic perspective. The dramatic conventions that governed the early modern city as theatre can only have seemed increasingly artificial and inappropriate. Nord has described it as ceasing to be a form of theatre which could be observed with detachment: 'The city ceased to be simply a theater, a spectacle, a panorama; and sudden encounters became part of a larger pattern of meaning or the beginning of self-revelation for the observed as well as the observer' (Nord 1988 p. 188; although I quote Nord's point I am actually making a contrast between theatre and spectacular rather than equating the two).

The cultural order, which I believe to have been being formulated, was organised through new conventions of theatricality in which members of the audience were shown representations of increasingly empirically realised scenarios in order to give some assurance to the authority of cultural knowledge. In the concluding section of this chapter I will describe some aspects of the fascination with perceptual representation as a source of entertainment, and its relations with the moral order of melodramatic narrative. In a better sense of the satisfactions of modern culture we should be more able to appreciate the complex presuppositions of our own several senses of identity.

A map gives an abstract, symbolic form to a landscape. Skilled decoders can derive an imaginative sense of what is being represented and in the selection of features to be noticed there is a normative ordering of what is and is not significant. But a map as a vision of social organisation or social order is a narrative that is pragmatic rather than spectacular. An alternative is a panoramic view in which all that can be seen from a particular vantage-point is represented in order to give a synoptic overview. As the intention is to record the variety of social circumstance, as well as the grandeur of buildings or riverscapes, etc., the heterogeneity of possible perspectives can be shown to be subordinate to a narrative vision that is inherently spectacular in its ambition. This type of pictorial synthesis is of course particularly suitable for an urban landscape but need not be confined to a fixed viewpoint but can travel through space, as in a record of a trip down the Mississippi for example, or through time as in recording the phases of a moment- ous battle as in the Bayeux Tapestry. Neither need such panoramas be manually painted but can use technology as it becomes available as in views of the rotation of the Earth as provided by spaceships.

Although the idea of a panorama was not invented in the nineteenth century in that there are a few earlier instances and the first commercially successful panorama, Barker's Panorama in Leicester Square, pre-dated the century by a decade, the era of their greatest popular success was in the culture of changing conventions of theatricality (Altick 1978). A panorama was an immense picture, initially circular although later flat, surveying a view or environment which was housed in a special building to which customers were admitted. In Hornor's Colosseum visitors could see an idealised London free of human and natural distractions. Subsequent improvements on this idea included painting the panorama on an enormous strip which could be unrolled in front of the audience, and the use of special lighting and other effects to simulate the setting. The various forms of pictorial entertainment quickly became very popular and it is not surprising that they were soon adapted as adjuncts to theatrical presentations and indeed came to dominate theatrical style: 'To look at the stage as if it were a picture was by 1850 an automatic response to audiences, and to make performance resemble painting was a habit of managers and technical staff' (Booth 1981 p. 10).

The conventional flat scene hung at the back of the stage in the early years of the century became more complex in two ways. First, the quality and respectability of artists recruited to paint these drops improved to such an extent that the art/entertainment distinction between easel painting and panoramas was lost and artists such as Clarkson Stanfield or de Loutherburg were admitted to the Royal Academy. On the other side, popular academic painting was frequently apocalyptic in theme and style relying heavily on spectacular perspective and juxtapositions of scenic effects (John Martin's cityscapes strike us in retrospect as prefiguring Hollywood spectacle). Secondly, backdrops became more complex in that attempts were made to make their representations more dynamic. There were several ways of achieving this effect, largely through rudimentary renditions of movement and perspectival depth. Complexity was heightened by having two drops, one in front of the other. The first would have parts cut away so that spectators looked through to scenes painted behind.

Another version of spectacular pictorialism was the Diorama originally devised by Daguerre in 1822 before he turned his attention to problems of photographic representation. The audience sat in front of a vast picture elaborately painted on translucent canvas in such a way that when light falling from behind and in front was varied by the use of blinds and shutters the image went through subtle changes and transformations. A romantic ruined chapel, for example, might be suddenly filled with lights and a praying multitude, or an avalanche might overspread an Alpine village. Since the mechanism was too complicated to permit the pictures to be moved there was the innovation of moving the audience instead. They were seated in a circular auditorium which gradually revolved, so smoothly that the audience had not so much the impression that they were moving, as that one picture was slipping away to give room to the next.

The essence of such sensationalist entertainments is the technical ability to generate new illusions and more impressive displays. A key aspect of pictorialism was the persistent experiments with the projection of light throughout the century. Light could be used to illuminate an image in a variety of ways, or to project an image or to project a succession of images so that they gave an illusion of movement. The focus of experimental concern and the basis of one of the most popular forms of entertainment was the magic lantern. First invented in the late seventeenth century, it was not seriously exploited for popular entertainment until the end of the eighteenth and then by a magician called Robertson. The essence of the Phantasmagoria show, which remained popular under several versions of the name for many decades, was that the audience entered into a suitably decorated room and in combination with special effects of smoke and music were scared out of their wits by cunningly projected images of the dead. The entertainments by Robertson and others who developed his techniques were magical in that they played with illusions and transformed reality.

Optical effects and illusions became more complex with the invention of limelight and its development for theatrical use by 1840. Limelight offered a more concentrated beam of light and was very important for all forms of theatrical spectacle. The strength of limelight also meant that the projector did not have to be close to the screen, and while illusionists obviously wished to continue to conceal the source of their effects other entertainers could project images from behind the audience over their heads: 'This helped the magic lantern become the companion of lecturers, an overt presence. Or rather, the magic lantern now embarked on a double life – an overt aide to lecturers, a covert tool for others including magicians and spiritualists' (Barnouw 1981 p. 32; see also Schivelbusch 1988 pp. 213–21). The complexity of the visual effects produced by this sort of machinery should not be underestimated. In the Egyptian Hall in London in the 1870s, for example, complex narratives were presented involving magical effects, a wide range of sensory stimuli and the use of as many as 15 magic lanterns.

The resources of sensational pictorialism complemented and then came to dominate the most characteristic narrative mode of contemporary theatricality. Melodrama is a type of literary structure rather than an historical category but a melodramatic vision – as a distinctive way of picturing social experience, a way which is both spectacular and obsessed with appropriate detail – 'became a natural stylistic mode for the period' (James 1978 p. 87). The characteristic structure of melodrama derives from the formulaic type that 'has as its center the moral fantasy of showing forth the essential "rightness" of the world order' (Cawelti 1976 p. 45). The idea of 'rightness' here is essentially conservative and a confirmation of how different circumstances can be integrated within a simple moral rubric.

The vision of melodrama is not therefore necessarily repetitious, although highly formulaic, rather that novelty – even chaos – can be accommodated by being subsumed to various forms of narrative order. The conservatism is not therefore necessarily political conservatism, indeed much radical literature and drama can be highly melodramatic, but structural in the sense that implicit categories of social distinction, paradigmatically gender (Gledhill 1987), are utilised and displayed in constructing narrative order. However confusing and unpredictable circumstance may appear in the melodramatic vision it is inherently capable of transformation because:

> to the melodramatic imagination, things are necessarily all in the nature of metaphor because things are not simply themselves, but refer to, speak of something else . . . . Melodrama may be a drama which is heightened, hyperbolic because the moral realm it wants to evoke is not immediately visible, and the writer is ever conscious of standing over a void.
>
> (Brooks 1973 p. 209)

The heightened stylisation of conventions of melodrama takes us away from considering the rationality of any particular story and towards a different level of dramatic significance. If the plays are enactments of moral contrasts caught in extreme situations then not only can identification be communicated largely through non-verbal means but the resolution of constituent conflicts has a significance over and above the specific story:

> The good social melodramatist makes us feel that his story is involved with large events of social and historical importance that usually eventuates in some massive public spectacle or event. Our excitement about large events intensifies our feeling about the significance of individual episodes.
>
> (Cawelti 1976 pp. 264–5)

This process of dramatic intensification, of focussing, became an end in itself through tightening the theatrical frame and reformulating conventions of theatricality. It is perfectly consistent with the interdependence of order and episode that sensational theatrical effects were not, with the exception of genres such as pantomime, to deny or supplant 'normality' not an escape from reality but an intensification of reality: "'not only for more entertainment, but, at bottom, for even more reality than real life itself can show", so that audiences did not want nature: "but nature unfettered, exhilarated, in effect transformed"' (Grimsted 1968 p. 234 quoting Melville).

It should be clearer now that innovations in commercial entertainment in the closing years of the century were consistent with norms of threatricality that had become institutionalised. The illusion of movement through the sequential projection of photographic images on to a screen was a natural development of picture-making and also consistent with 'the aesthetic of spectacular romantic realism that dominated the popular arts of the nineteenth century. In the movies that aesthetic has survived' (Eidsvik 1978 p. 112). Film shows were initially part of the cultural form of the music hall because as short novelties they could fit easily a variety bill. Film was, however, more than a cheaper and more reliable form of music hall (Chanan 1980).

The technology of film could be used to re-stage melodramatic narratives with a more arresting use of naturalistic detail and spectacular climax. It was inherently pictorialist and through its form of projection could heighten the illusion and dramatic force of the representation of reality being displayed. Film shows were soon being staged in purpose-built environments that were themselves spectacular celebrations of urban sophistication. The production, distribution and exhibition of films could easily be undertaken by those engaged in the existing commercial organisation of leisure, and through high returns on capital investment quickly develop those relations of production to new heights of complexity. In all these ways film inherited the culture of urbanisation.

The cultural form of cinema was above all else able to combine a breathtaking pictorialism with the logic of melodramatic narrative. The sensations of later melodramas required such complicated instructions in the text of the play that they quite outweigh dialogue and seem to cry out for a camera to act as organising perspective. The essence of melodrama is structure, that is the interweaving of narrative elements to create suspense. Scenes, characters and themes are juxtaposed to create ironic contrasts and to build to the satisfaction of a revelatory climax. Representing on stage these narrative elements required considerable ingenuity in devising what Fell (1974 p. 18) has called 'transitional devices'. These could take the form of using a panoramic backdrop to create the effect of a change in visual focus, or subdividing the stage to show simultaneous but independent action. Film narratives, at least within the dominant conventions of the cinema, have been articulated through the camera being used to replicate the function of transitional devices. The syntax of motion pictures is identical with melodrama's editorial pattern of: 'a progression of pictorial episodes defining a single line of action, or, more frequently, brought about by cross-cutting between two or more parallel lines of action or flashing back to earlier actions' (Vardac 1949 p. 65).

In the 'dream palaces' or 'cathedrals' of the new form (Atwell 1980), the consumer promise of enthralling entertainment for the largest popular audience was made good. The reciprocal obligation we owe to consumerism's promise is popular acquiescence in the social order of mass entertainment. In both the disciplined respect with which mass audiences sat quietly staring at the screen and the ambition to create universal fictions within which the local communal and class cultural concerns are accommodated (however incompatibly), we can see the triumph of cultural order over the increasingly frequently declaimed – whether in hope or despair – incoherence of metropolitan society.

The most satisfying because it is also the most paradoxical triumph of fiction over reality are the ways in which the illusions of representation have come to acquire an unquestioned facticity. In one respect, of course, the ability to capture authentic detail in a photograph makes it a popular exemplification of the pictorial naturalism of Victorian theatricality, but the accuracy of detail tends to blur the salience of conventions of representation. The resemblance an image bears to social reality is still as much an illusion as the resemblance Robertson's phantasmagoria bore to the spirit world at the beginning of the century. However grainy and arresting the conventions that stamp one sequence of images as news or documentary or docu-drama, we should always be reminded to ask: 'How is it possible that we who should know better, no longer think of the images of the magic industry as illusions, but have come to accept them as reality – our window on the world and what it thinks and does?' (Barnouw 1981 p. 107). The most insidious hegemony of conventions of theatricality in metropolitan society is that they have become naturalised to no longer seem theatrical.

3

PHOTOGRAPHIC PICTURES

POPULAR PHOTOGRAPHY

In the previous chapter I introduced an account of some of the ways in which changes in the character of theatrical space were consistent with more general changes in cultural space in an urbanising culture. These changes can be summarised by saying that social life has become more self-consciously staged as something to be looked at. We have become accustomed to seeing as though what we are seeing is framed in a pictorical space, and that pictures are the most natural way of presenting, representing, what we have seen – our experience – to ourselves and to others. If there are substantial grounds for arguing that there are dominant concerns with picturing in a culture of mass entertainment, then the development of popular photography as an everyday means of representation will be an illustrative archive for such an argument. But more importantly, the types of picturing that popular photographers characteristically generate will be particularly significant for a cultural analysis that is concerned with how sociation is 'talked about', represented, in the dramatic forms of metropolitan culture.

These are reasons why the theme of photography is relevant to a more general concern with public drama. I have argued that public drama is the ways in which we stage representations of matters of collective concern. The staging need not be constrained to a framed or marked social space, although it frequently is, and neither need it be articulated through a medium of performance, although it most commonly is. The archaic manners of an English court of law are clearly of major social significance for those concerned and are reflexively devised to dramatise that significance. The staging here is not theatrical but in the dramatic conventions employed clearly very much more is being talked about and displayed than in the, however serious, matters of adjudication at hand (Douglas 1978). Public drama uses the resources of ceremonial and ritual to heighten or re-frame conventions and introduce other aspects of cultural significance (Chaney 1977).

Popular photography, if we think of a set of family snapshots, seems likely to violate these expectations of public drama. It is, for example, characteristically private, in that it is mainly shown only to the intimates who commonly constitute the the subject matter. And yet in the conformism of pose and setting and composition there seem likely to be collective concerns (Hirsch 1981). Although the subject matter is typically considered non-dramatic in that the scenes depicted are usually mundane and unremarkable, there are powerful conventions in forms of representation (Jacobs 1981). It is in the ways of staging the picturing of social forms that we can identify the public or cultural significance of the dramaturgy of popular photography. I shall argue that photography can be understood as a ceremonial form for popular experience.

The relationship between photography and other forms of picturing (and within photography in terms of style) has been obscured in our expectations for different means of representation by discourses through which we have come to divide types of cultures, and their respective audiences, into a hierarchy of taste. It was precisely because the mechanical reproduction of pictorial images, in far greater detail than ever before, became possible in the socio-cultural circumstances in which mass popular audiences were constituting themselves (and of course one of the means of creating such audiences was the invention of photography), that a cultural stratification of types of picturing became one of the resources in social order. It is therefore unsurprising that a distinction between the – auratic – individual and manually produced representation and the – popular – reproducible and formulaic representation should be built into discourses of art and its distinction from commerce (Ivins 1953).

It is against this background that discussions of whether photography can be an art form, what are the dominant conventions of representation, and who should be included in an historiography of significant 'authors', can and have been set. To pursue such a discussion of what can be a form of art is endlessly regressive; I shall therefore discuss the *cultural form* of popular photography. The distinction between an art form and a cultural form is that the former is concerned with the defining characteristics of a form of represent-ation, the latter with the social institution of a type of cultural activity. The reason for developing the concept of cultural form is that the meaning of cultural performance is structured by the ways in which it is made as well as the expectations and pleasures that members of audiences can bring and derive.

The 'story' of any one performance (each instance of the use of a means of representation, in this case a photograph, is a perform-ance) is therefore the institutionalisation of a complex of roles and discourses within which a particular narrative or type of narrative becomes possible or even probable. A commonly made distinction along these terms is between film as a medium of representation and cinema as a cultural institution (cf. Chanan 1980 and Bordwell 1985). The narrative told need not be a story in any conventional sense but a way of talking about a style of life (Chaney 1990A). There is likely to be therefore considerably less concern with the merits and accomplishments of particular 'authors' working in a cultural form and correspondingly greater concern with 'the form of life' promoted or exemplified in a particular type of cultural activity.

Inevitably, any specification of component features of a term such as cultural form will tend to take on the rigidity of a model. Such are the variety of circumstances of cultural production and appreciation that any generalising framework is inevitably only broadly applicable. There are, however, three elements to the general notion of a cultural form and in combination they do provide a comparative framework. The first is the social organi-sation of production. As Rosenblum (1978) has shown, the produc-tion of art photographs involves quite different social formations, organised around function and technology as well as division of labour, than news photographs. Second, the narrative or type of story that is characteristically told or performed conventionally provides the meaning of an occasion; although insufficient for a complete account it is essential. Third, the social occasion of attendance, participation, onlooking or contemplating – whatever and however that occasion is structured, formed and discursively appropriated – will institutionalise a set of activities as a form of life.

There are a variety of aspects to photographic practice which could suggest that there are several cultural forms. The technology of photography can be used in a variety of ways in different organi-sational contexts, for example: accurate copying in a bureaucracy; investigation and enlargement in research agencies; control and surveillance by state agencies for identity records and maintenance of social order; and dramatisation as in illustrations of news stories and displays of consumer goods for advertising purposes. To the extent that these uses are all part of popular photography they are all elements in a cultural form of spectacular picturing.

I have so far referred to popular photography both specifically to designate the activity of photographing things as a leisure activity, and as part of other leisure pursuits by ordinary people who would distinguish their work from the organisational activities above. I will argue more generally here that popular photography refers to the pervasive reliance upon the ubiquity of photographic illustration in organisational practice and indeed in every form of life. Popular photography is therefore heterogeneous because it seeps into other cultural forms and yet provides a distinctive vernacular resource for describing and dramatising that to which attention should be directed. In the process of picturing and being pictured the dramatic structure of popular performance is transformed in ways that are emblematic of late modern culture.

In its most immediate sense popular means here the sorts of photographs taken in everyday social settings – the biographical round with its marked occasions. The popular designates a vernacular for ordering and celebrating the contours of social distinction. The historical record of popular photography is then both a social history of changing mores and a record of technical accomplishment in which photographic devices work to capture reality more simply and more faithfully (Ford 1989 has sought to bring out both aspects). This, however, leads on to a second and more pervasive sense of popular. This is that the domain of leisure, as the sorts of occasions and activities marked as pleasurable and/or significant, is constituted to a greater or lesser extent through the possibility of their being photographed.

Leisure as a generic title for the constellation of lifestyle activities, and contrasted with a notion of work as instrumental obligations, is to be understood as a shorthand way of describing our understanding of choice and style: 'the uses to which we put what is left when subsistence has been met . . . constitute the realm of our private life, the domain of popular culture, and the present battle over the art of living' (Inglis 1988 p. 83). The ambiguous terrain of 'surplus value' colonised by leisure has been increasingly charted over the last hundred years by the constitutive power of photography in defining types of social occasion and activity, and being made to carry the burden of normative meaning. Photography as a form of collective memory is then both a vehicle for and reflexive of the cultural significance of leisure.

The interpenetration of photography with the culture of leisure was jointly dependent upon the technology being exploited and marketed in particular ways. There was, for example, a consistency between the promise for consumers in this new commodity and that offered by other consumer goods: 'understanding mass photography as a practice gains more from looking at the articulation of ther camera with other consumption goods (for example the bicycle in the 1890s, the car in the 1920s, the package holiday in the 1970s) than from starting from the representations it produces'. (Slater 1983 p. 257; the point here is made polemically by Slater as an argument within cultural theory defending materialist accounts from 'excessive' textualism; I am more concerned with forms of life than photographs as texts.)

The mass market, underlying a very profitable industry, is geared towards amateurs who use their equipment – including films and processing as well as cameras – relatively infrequently. To facilitate their use the equipment has been made self-contained so that it achieves certain effects independent of the user's skill or judgement (Allison 1989 and Coe 1989). The legions of 'instamatics' are complemented by a compensating technological fetishism amongst enthusiasts and para-professionals. In this domain, paradoxically for theorists of the manual character of artistic creation, art is not denied by the efficiency of technology but displayed through its mastery.

Consistent with its mass character the photograph as a mode of picturing is indiscriminate. The camera can be pointed at anything or everything and given certain technical constraints it will represent what it is focussed upon. The claim of the representation is that it is faithful to what is to be seen. The conventional character of this, as of any other form of representation, has been frequently commented upon, but deconstructing the rhetoric of the image does not dent its commonsense facticity. The story the photograph tells is of the way reality was on this particular occasion. Photography is instrumental for a variety of institutional practices precisely because of the transparency of the image. The normality of social order is presupposed in everyday imaging and photographs can therefore be inspected as guides to the nature of reality. This may be to see something that is invisible to the unaided human eye, or to observe human conduct abstracted from grounded seeing as in a video monitor, or to categorise types of image in order to construct a 'story' about a relationship between appearance and social truth (Tagg 1988). The photographic narrative is first and foremost telling of the power of the social construction of instrumental knowledge (Neale 1985 Part 1(1)); it celebrates the rationality of modernity.

Frequently, of course, because the camera is able to see, or is licensed to see, or is taken by lucky or intrepid exceptional individuals to see, what is hidden in conventional reality, the photograph can show more than reality – a surreality. The spectacular sight dramatises the occasion of viewing, however casually or superficially we might glance at the photograph, in that what is there is there to be seen by us on this occasion. The seeing is framed by implicit theatrical conventions in which we are, as an audience, located within a particular dramaturgical landscape. The social occasion of photographic picturing is therefore spectatorial – there is an endless and ubiquitous parade of images of ourselves at which we look as at a performance. As well as the incidental pleasures of particular sights, the more general pleasure is seeing and ordering the particular as the general.

PUBLIC MEMORY

A simple approach to schools in cultural studies could group them under three headings. The first are those studies that are primarily motivated by a concern with how culture is made. It is argued that explanations of cultural form and content can all be derived from its means and methods of production. The second approach focuses on the performance, usually considered as a text whether actually or metaphorically. While, third, are those studies that refuse any essential character to cultural phenomena but argue that they exist and have meaning as they are interpreted and used in specific social practices. Although each type of approach has distinct advantages as well as limitations, my project here does not in practice fall neatly under any of these heads. In this chapter I am trying to elucidate the institutionalisation of photographic picturing as a form of dramatisation.

The concept of a social institution refers to a set of habitual behaviours oriented around a particular domain of activity, and which are informed by highly normative values concerning the rights and obligations of different roles within that domain. The significance of a concept of institutionalisation is that characteristic 'habits' are as much cognitive as behavioural. Through systems of classification, logical operations and metaphorical associations, the everyday world is given its natural or taken-for-granted facticity. Cognitive order and social order are mutually interdependent and mutually constitutive of their legitimacy (Douglas 1987). Social institutions do not merely exist, as phenomena to be discovered in theoretical talk, but as important areas of everyday life they constitute the character of the world we inhabit (and thus, regressively, make that character and behaviour and values seem necessary). A cultural form is a mode of institutionalisation, for example the theatre, and also provides or embodies a vernacular for describing, displaying and using some of the characteristics of institutionalisation.

The social institution of photographic picturing is not just concerned with the organisation of photographic 'occasions', those moments when a subject is posed to a greater or lesser extent and the camera pointed, but also with the organisation of picturing as a form of interaction. The occasions of taking photographs are little ceremonies that imbue their subjects with a particular significance (even if the significance lasts only for the duration of the 'shot' and is instantly discarded). The assumption that picturing through photographic resources represents the contours of significance is a more general form of ceremonialisation. Ceremonies and rituals are to be understood in this context as framed spaces within which 'the play' of institutional concerns are more directly enacted, even if the form of performance is through highly symbolised or otherwise condensed utterances.

For example, the ways in which a social identity is ascribed to a new-born baby derive from the institution of family relationships, which are in turn displayed and exemplified through the creation and recognition of social identity. This interdependence is likely to be ceremonialised, and thereby both communicated and celebrated in some *rite de passage* such as baptism. The process of ceremonialising a new network of relationships may also be diffused through a number of ritual forms rather than a single ritual; we can say that ceremonialisation is performed through the taking and showing of photographs rather than a specific rite. That is one of the ways in which the network of affiliation that coalesces in each particular version of identity is dramatised for significant others is through the multiplicities of its photographic image.

The cultural form of popular photography has developed as a form of dramatisation when the resources for affirming collective values and behaviour were changing radically. In a variety of ways the occupational ecology of community, in which social associations were clustered around shared forms of productive activity, has been replaced by forms of symbolic ecology in which the grounds of association more become matters of choice. In circumstances of significant change in collective experience the vernacular of collectivity as something identifiable through time, the discourse of memory, will be at least inflected:

> Public memory is the storage system for the social order. Thinking about it is as close as we can get to reflecting on the conditions of our own thought.
>
> (Douglas 1987 p. 70)

The concept of public memory refers to the dramatic traces, symbolic artefacts, of the institutionalisation of forms of social order; in these traces representations of significant moments, people or ideas will be made available to interpretation and re-interpretation (see for example Sekula's 1983 reading of the photographs in 'The Family of Man' Exhibition).

One type of display of public memory will be through the resource provided by forms of picturing. The pictures need not be literal or restricted to particular sites or forms of exhibition but can be reproduced in innumerably different framings. Although I have noted that ceremonialisation is traditionally expressed through highly condensed representations, it is of course consistent with norms of pictorial naturalism in theatrical dramatisation discussed in the previous chapter that the 'literalism' of the photographic image should be used to 'naturalise' a form of public memory. And that the mass character of infinitely reproducible images encouraged a prosaic, mundane naturalism. I shall argue that the institutionalisation of popular photography has been grounded in questions of the possibility of public memory. The conditions of social order in modernity, and therein authentic experience and communal satisfactions, can begin to be displayed through our reflections on picturing through photography.

An important evocative figure in making these connections is the notion of dislocation in modernity. In terms of personal experience the essence of modernity has usually been located in ambiguity, the lack of a stable and consistent framework for expectations:

> To be modern, I said, is to experience personal and social life as a maelstrom, to find one's world and one self in perpetual

disintegation and renewal, trouble and anguish, ambiguity and contradiction: to be part of a universe in which all that is solid melts into air.

(Berman 1983 p. 345)

A sense of time as something ambiguous, relative, inconsistent, above all indexical in the sense of only being comprehensible in a particular context is fundamental to the discontinuities of modernity. Images of collective experience necessarily become problematical in these uncertainties. An illustration is provided by the difficulties of finding a legitimate iconography for national monuments in democratic society (Oosterbaan Martinius 1986). As well as the difficulty of finding agreement on justifications of their style, the conventional symbolisms of nation, honour and artistic integrity, etc., have all been made at best provisional.

In the re-ordering of institutional categories in modernisation the communal experience of time was changed. The change can be summarised as a move from a patchwork of time grounded in local forms of life to a more external, more impersonal means of exchange like money. The first set of changes introduced a disciplinary apparatus and a new set of responsibilities for recognising the authority of mechanised time (Thompson 1967). In the second set of changes, these paralleling to some extent the development of leisure as a discourse for 'spending' time, the use of time has been individualised through becoming negotiable as a commodity. Individuals acquire greater autonomy in how they structure their consumption of time but no lesser responsibility for investing it 'wisely'. Thus, for example, in Wildenbeest's study (1988) of changing temporal orders on Dutch farms, he found that modern experience was seen as necessitating rejection of traditional constraints and the pursuit of personal advantage. Although, seemingly paradoxically, more modern farmers have not found a 'vertical' ordering of time led to greater freedom than a traditional 'horizontal' ordering.

The logic of mechanisation led to standardisation in the bureaucratic organisation of public time towards the end of the last century. It was not until 1884 that a standard series of time-zones radiating from Greenwich, England, was agreed at an international conference (Howse 1980). The reasons for accepting a common framework for time were spreading communication networks, particularly telegraphic and train timetables, that demanded a degree of standardisation. World standardisation of a public time system facilitated bureaucratic cooperation between military and commercial as well as governmental organisations, and, correspondingly, a bureaucratisation of international communication schedules was dependent upon a formalisation of public time.

The paradox of bureaucratic standardisation in modernisation was that, as I have noted, in the 'cultural' spheres of urban-industrial societies: 'the thrust of the age was to affirm the reality of private time against that of single public time and to define its nature as heterogeneous, fluid and reversible' (Kern 1983 p. 34). Alternatives to the bureaucratisation of uniform time were expressed in the flamboyance and artificiality of urban lifestyles, echoed and echoing in artistic explorations of multiple realities, expressed in philosophical and scientific theorising of relativity, and in theories of different structures of cultural meaning by the founding fathers of modern sociology (Finlay 1990).

The grounds of social identity in modernity are therefore simultaneously personalised and cast within more impersonal, 'theoretical' rather than lived, categories. This can be seen as a shift in the character of the 'epistemic order' of bourgeois society: 'With the present more mechanical in tempo, the past more distant, no longer contained by tradition, and visions of the future more immanent and rational, reality has become a temporal process' (Kern 1983 p. 49). This simultaneous duality in ways of experiencing time, between public standardisation and private heterogeneity, underlies the suggestion that the epistemic break in modernity is the development of institutionalised acceptance of a lack of correspondence between rationality and culture, that is between public organisation and private sensibility. This can be seen to create a divergence in use to which the technology of photographic practice has been mutually adapted and simultaneously accommodated. The incompatibilities of public and private memories have been reconciled in the fragmentary images of an endlessly proliferating technology.

It is the very simplicity of the photographic image which makes it seem inadequate for such protean tasks. In the literalness of representation it seems to be self-sufficient, or at least there is a level of descriptive sense which is accessible to all members of a common culture, but in practice the *subject* of a photograph has to include more than the figures or objects depicted: 'To speak of of the "sense" and "story" of a photograph is to acknowledge that the reality-effect of a photograph is such that it inescapably implicates a world of activity responsible for, and to, the fragments circumscribed by the frame: a world of causes, of "before and after", or "if, then . . . ", a *narrated* world' (Burgin 1982 p. 243 *sic*). The concept of a subject in photography has to include the thing pictured, and the story of which this image is a part (a representative), and an implied seeing subject – the person looking and thereby the social context within which the activity takes place.

It is precisely because photographic technology provides a way of concretising images of the world that it cannot escape being part of how that world is constructed in other forms of discourse. Most simply, photographs need conversation, texts, captions, systems of record and categories of social typology to give them a home and cast a protective or interpretive colouring. The narrativity of popular photography, although dependent on other modes of discourse, reassures both through the facility with which claims can be made upon experience and the guaranteeing of identity as a form of narration: 'Photography's initial tense is the present. It prizes the moment – those serendipitous instants after which Cartier-Bresson capered. But in the act of catching such moments it alters their tense, by consigning them to the safekeeping of eternity' (Conrad 1984 p. 165). The ceremonialisation of photographic picturing works through investing the frequently mundane subject matter with the possibility of historic significance and through entailing a narrated account: 'the set of social interactions that come under the heading of photographing have the quality of a ritual' (Beloff 1985 p. 205).

It is against this background of the ritual character of photographic representation that early uses of photographic technology in the nineteenth century become more comprehensible. In a culture in which the rituals of death began to be luxuriated in as a form of conspicuous consumption, and the physical order for disposing of cadavers became an explicit extension of social order, the celebration of mortality through photography must have seemed natural: 'Social convention, for example, was responsible for the widespread practice of photographing the dead. All photographers included in their publicity material some reference to "Portraits after Death" although very few of these have actually survived' (Braive 1966 p. 82). The conventions of order exemplified here surely speak to commitments to symbolic social bonds. The dead are not rescued from mortality but their relevance to contemporary life is continually affirmed. Some of the same imaginary associations can be seen in the popular sale of *cartes-de-visite* of celebrities by photographers. Those Mayall published of the Queen and her Consort in 1860 helped to legitmate the fashion, and the two aspects of symbolic life – cultural immortality and imaginary communion with symbolic leaders – were intensified by Albert's death the following year when reproductions of his *carte* sold in thousands.

It may be that Victorian luxuriating in the rituals of death has been superseded by a denial of death (Cannadine 1981); and that our expectations for celebrities are different (although the funerary cults for those such as Presley, Monroe and Dean suggest otherwise); but the ritualisation of institutionally significant occasions for small social groups through a photographic record has become more rather than less conventional. We have noted above that the everyday character of family photography means that although it is rarely planned as a distinct activity, except to the extent that it is a 'natural' element in festivals, holidays and other marked occasions, the formulaic character of norms about appropriateness of subject matter, style and composition, etc., is nonetheless significant (Chalfen 1981). (A ritual character that is heightened by the fact the majority of photographers on these occasions is now almost certainly amateur rather than creating a commercial business out of social expectations.)

One example which echoes the morbidity of earlier uses of popular photography comes in an account of a study framework for the 'home mode of communication'. Musello (1980 p. 41) notes the importance of 'traditional' pictures as recurrent themes planned for regular intervals and often using a persistent setting: 'One intriguing example encountered several times was "the last picture". This was seen with groups of older people and groups who were close to an elderly person. They involved posing together at some regular interval in conscious anticipation that one of their number might die soon'. Deliberately casting the memento against the imminence of change is a more explicit and self-conscious form of ceremonialisation, more mundanely a narrative of impermanence is denied by the implicit ritualisation of performance: 'A collection of snapshots may be understood then as an attempt to maintain a particular status quo' (Chalfen op. cit. p. 110). Here more than in any other institutional discourse images of social order acquire a prescriptive authority for everyday experience: 'Family photographers are narrators – "America's story-tellers" as Kodak calls its cameras – who protest against the development of narrative, adhering to the rhythms of recurrence, telling the same tale over and over to a child who loves it because it's known by heart' (Conrad 1984 pp. 166–7).

The more general way, then, of describing the institutionalisation of popular photography is as a way of looking at ourselves; which is not the same as holding a mirror to society. Whatever its inversions or distortions a mirror at best can only teach us to see ourselves as others might see us; a mirror is therefore an *aide-mémoire* for dramatisation rather than a form of dramatisation. What are being dramatised in conventions of looking or picturing are styles of symbolic association. Images of identity, relationship, community, landscape as well as personification are available as theatrical vernacular but independently of theatres. The spectacle of social form can be naturalised as an unassuming technology subordinated to the concerns of other discursive orders. In the next sections of this chapter I will contrast some specific types of looking – at women, at the deviant, and in the more general type of documentary looking – to make some preliminary points on the dramatic conventions of the conditions of our own thought in modernity.

CONVENTIONS OF LOOKING

I argued in the previous section that photographic pictures have provided a medium through which it has been possible to reconcile the rationality of public order with the ceremonialisation of more fragmentary experience. I located the fluidity of the image, the way that it is capable of changing meanings, in its discursive context; the fact that it is always part of some contextualising narrative. The narrative can be described as a directed seeing or as a look and the direction of a look can always be reversed – or rather the relationships of fore- and background can be thrown into question. As in those perceptual puzzles where a shift in focus shows that what was an old lady in repose is also a young girl with head averted, or that two heads in profile is simultaneously a cup in silhouette, so photographic images are ways of looking and being looked at. The technology that pictures aspects of our experience for us can be used to take pictures of us. That is, the camera is an instrument of surveillance and thereby facilitates control.

The order being buttressed in this perspective is a use of power to maintain a social hierarchy of structured inequalities in material and cultural facilities. It is not so much that a ruling group devises a form of order which it then ideologically 'naturalises' in order to disguise its rule, as that collective forms of life which impose massive constraints upon their members, for example racial and sexual identities, are 'seen' to be naturally so. The camera therefore both takes pictures of us which facilitate various forms of bureaucratic control, and also takes pictures of us which when displayed confirm to their audiences the validity of commonsense social knowledge and the naturalness of different forms of life. (Remembering that the audience may also be the subjects of the pictures.)

The argument is, then, that any form of social order is a network of constraints and controls as much as a set of resources. The experience of order as control may be triumphant – it is so 'naturally' right that a practical exemplification confirms an essential harmony; but perhaps more commonly, particularly in metropolitan society, our experience of order is of it as limited and contingent. A set of conventions and expectations which are normal and civilised but which are sometimes more than not met – they seem to be disregarded and rejected by various types of outsiders and rebels. Therefore the very stability of forms of social order has to be a dramatisation. Both through displays of pomp and certainty and through the *frisson* of visualising 'the other side' of disorderly conduct. Animalistic behaviour, paradigmatically sexual displays, may well provoke outrage and demands for censorship and repression (Segal 1970), but in its very forbidden allure our ordered security is confirmed and simultaneously menaced and subverted. Popular photography dramatised the relationship between visualisation and order, touched the intimate interdependence of documentary and voyeurism, and destroyed irrevocably any potential innocence in social observation.

The urban crowd transforms the significance of the stranger. In village society the stranger is sufficiently exceptional and unintelligible to be either an intimation of wonder or the menace of disorder. In metropolitan society the stranger becomes mundane and when in public we acquire, through reciprocal non-recognition, a cloak of anonymity. The social order of anonymity is another way of describing the character of modernity – the fears of isolation as well as relaxations of control. Personal management of local indices of competence and innocuousness become normal social expectations in the anonymous crowd (Goffman 1971). But while these should be sufficient to ward off unsolicited attentions they do not preclude our being the object of others' observations and, vice versa, of our observing others more or less intensively. The detective is, as Benjamin (1973) appreciated in Poe, an exemplar of modernity – through the anonymous gaze the individual is interpreted in social context. The camera as a way of looking is an anonymous gaze both unobtrusive and alert to social detail. It therefore seems appropriate that the first generation of small, mass-market cameras in the 1880s were popularly known as 'Detectives'.

The most pervasive look in a culture of mass entertainment is at an iconography of sexual titillation, an iconography which has largely consisted of images of women – dressed/undressed, singly/ in groups, in direct address/feigning ignorance or indifference to being pictured but always being seen framed by their subordination to a sexual mythology. This is not to say that sexual imagery, and in particular the naked or semi-naked body, was invented or discovered in photographic practice, but that considerably more extensive use of erotic icons has become institutionalised in the dramatic order of a culture of mass entertainment. It is as though female sexuality has come to stand for uncertainties generated in the transitions of modernity. Although the female body is one of the most pervasive icons of consumer culture – as something pleasurable which can be owned and displayed by both men and women – it also signifies a sexuality which is to an increasing extent only ambiguously grounded in the constraints of family and community. A sexuality which offers men the *frisson* of power through control and an object for the rage of impotence.

The naked body is a pictorial and sculptural genre within which conventions vary on forms of naturalism and symbolic import – particularly in relation to the connotations of gender: 'The male nude is typically public: he strides through city squares, guards public buildings, is worshipped in Church. He personifies communal pride or aspiration. The female nude, on the other hand, comes into her own only when art is geared to the tastes and erotic fantasies of private consumers' (Walters 1978 p. 8). The re-writing of public drama in terms of new conventions of collective concerns utilised a consensus of sexual mythology to ground the variety of representational practice: 'It is precisely in the nineteenth century – at a time when older prototypes and motifs were transformed by new needs and motivations – that the social basis of sexual myth stands out in clearest relief from the apparently "personal" erotic imagery of individual artists' (Nochlin 1972 p. 8).

As a 'democratic' medium – i.e. not restricted to particular groups through ascribed features such as status or specific skills – photo-graphy broadened the means of cultural production. And through the ease with which images could be copied, reproduced and printed the market was equivalently massified. Photography can be argued to be the first medium of mass entertainment and as such is the first spectacular form of a dramatised culture. The opportunity for a convenient means of representation was quickly utilised by women and manufacturers of equipment for popular photography oriented their marketing to female customers. These new producers did not, however, in any consistent way use the means to develop new types of sexual imagery, nor did they deflect the relentless growth in images of women as vehicles of sexual fantasy (Ovenden and Mendes 1973; Sullivan 1980).

The spectacle of sexual fantasy is also as I have emphasised a means of control and appropriation – the image is a means of recording, classifying, displaying: 'It's striking that photography and free museums were more or less concurrently born and nurtured but their coincidence is not mysterious' (Maddow 1980 p. 185). For Maddow the coincidence is explained by democratic ideals. I would prefer to argue that those ideals, which I understand to be a commit-ment to popularisation, are a *rhetoric* of participation. The meaning of popular in modernity that is being elucidated is of the *show* (which is *not* the same as illusion) of personal experience. Images of women symbolise desire and the promise of acquisition. The imagery dramatises a symbolic surreality.

The fantasy in images of women does not violate the norms of pictorial naturalism; indeed they are observed with the most extreme scrupulousness the better to create an illusion of accuracy. The invention of stereoscopic slides was popular from the middle of the nineteenth century for their enhancement of affect in all genres but seems to have been particularly effective in pornographic photo-graphy: 'Possessing a compelling illusion of three-dimensionality and preternatural detail, painstakingly tinted, entirely grainless, the visual effect of the hand-colored dageurreotype stereo is the acme of verisimilitude' (Solomon-Godeau 1985 p. 95). Pornographic fantasy is utopian – or Marcus' (1966) 'pornotopian' – in that detail is not governed by narrative coherence and climaxes are endlessly repeated without narrative exhaustion, but the fictive stance has more to do with documentary than, for example, romance: 'pornography resembles the Masters and Johnson sex films, records of animal behaviour, and police forensic photography or medical illustration' (Faust 1980 p. 17). In photography the ability to faithfully explore sexual detail has led to innovations which pre-figure a more general abstract naturalism: 'photography can be credited with the invention of the beaver shot, an image so constructed that its sole purpose is the exposure of the female genitalia' (Solomon-Godeau op. cit. p. 97).

It can be objected that pornography is deviant and exceptional and the early use of photography to reveal, or more accurately to look at, women is more significantly related to Victorian repression than the institutionalisation of photography in spectacular drama. It would be inappropriate to strive too insistently for essential characteristics of spectacular picturing but the impulse in this 'looking' is more fundamentally consistent with picturing as a form of control. There clearly is in images of women a troubled relationship between desire and exposure. There is an 'otherness' in the female body which continually lies beyond the voyeuristic representation. The culture of respectability and the association between feminine and private spheres intensified prurient curiosity of course, but early photographs of women dressing or 'caught' *déshabillé* are echoed in contemporary tabloid sensationalism over a 'celebrity's' inadvertent revelation of a nipple or their panty-line. To look and see what the mighty would rather keep hidden can be subversive but looking and particularly sustained looking is more usually a form of control. The hidden and the mysterious can literally have their shrouding veils ripped away as in Alloula's (1986) reading of French postcards from North African colonies where ethnographic complexity is effaced behind the breasts of young girls and fantasies of oriental licence.

An alternative form of objection would be that the sexual display of consumer culture has taken over the furtive looking of Victorian prurience and substituted a permissive liberalism in which a public nudity is no longer particularly contentious. It is from within this perspective that an apostle of consumer capitalism such as the *Sun* newspaper can celebrate its modernity with photographs of 'Page Three' girls and the 'George and Lynne' strip (Featherstone and Hepworth 1983). In the latter cartoon the resignation to survivalism characteristic of popular strips that Orwell (1961) noted has been replaced with a confident hedonism in which sexuality signifies consumer dreams and vice versa. The principal motif of the equation and very often the physical vehicle of its articulation is still however the body of a woman, meaning that for women in general the scope for personal identity comes to be framed within the terms of that equation. Thus the news report that successful professional women like to be photographed: 'in slinky lingerie *a la Playboy* . . . [discovering this] as the ultimate high, to see yourself looking so feminine' (*The Independent* 10/4/89 p. 13).

The looking therefore, however it is couched in a rhetoric of desire, is a form of control. For one half of the population to be continually made aware that their sense of self is grounded in how they might be looked at or imagined is massively constraining. A form of order is asserted even while its limitations are troublingly apparent. The objectification involved in staring at a picture of a woman's genitals is out of control, desire trembles on the edge of disgust and the otherness is still so tantalisingly present that its display is presented effectively as denunciation. It is this context that makes the massive and pervasive violence which structures gender relationships and in particular male responses to female sexuality at least consistent if not comprehensible. The fear that this violence has increased during the course of modernity and is the dark side of the society of spectacle seems justified. The violence, with the associated rage of racial hatred, is perhaps the abyss at the edge of relativism, the void where unstable order unravels and dramatic frenzy bursts its bounds.

The other limitation of this mode of photographic order takes us back to the inversion of look at the beginning of this section. The very naturalism of the photographic image means that it can capture an undesired and possibly unintended look of challenge and inter-rogation rather than: 'the inviting, compliant expression that signals complicity between the desiring subject and the object of desire' (Solomon-Godeau op. cit. p. 98). It has been argued that the look of resigned complicity in Manet's *Olympia* that initially was so contro-versial and has remained so disturbing (Clark 1985 Chapter 2; see also Hudson 1982 Chapter 7), derives from pornographic photo-graphy (Needham 1973); the degree of derivation is not, however, as important as the revelation of control. The naturalness of order is again shown to be arbitrary.

The argument, then, is that dominant ways of looking are forms of dramatisation. They prescribe the terms of social order although never with complete serenity or without hinting at the limits of the constitutive power of their framing. Popular photography can be said to have conjured spectacular forms of social identity for mundane experience, but as Sekula (1985 p. 6 *sic*) has pointed out:

'We are confronting . . . a system of representation capable of functioning both *honorifically* and *repressively*'. Most clearly in the field of portraiture the camera provides a resource for bestowing dignity on popular life while simultaneously facilitating the creation and operation of bureaucratic apparatuses in legal, medical and intellectual institutions. Such apparatuses are both means of observation: 'serving to introduce the panoptic principle into daily life, photography welded the honorific and repressive functions together' (Sekula op. cit. p. 10), thereby enhancing the knowledge/power of official discourses, as well as normative systems for delineating normality and deviance: 'The development of new regulatory and disciplinary apparatuses was closely linked . . . to the formation of new social and anthropological sciences – criminology, certainly, but also psychiatry, comparative anatomy, germ theory, sanitation, and so on' (Tagg 1988 p. 5).

The photographic record is intimately bound up with the bureaucratisation of collective life ('its mobilisation within the emerging apparatuses of a new and more penetrating form of the state' Tagg op. cit. p. 61), for three reasons. The first is that the mechanical character of processes of representation and reproduction gives an air of impersonality and empiricist objectivity. Second, the form of knowledge of the photograph – the accumulation of bits of information into a portrait – gives the illusion that crucial features can be abstracted and recorded. That identity can be catalogued through defining traces; in the logic of this process information technology has left the relative crudity of the photographic image behind but the bureaucratic rationale has not changed. Third, the brevity and distinctiveness of the photograph makes it an ideal subject for cataloguing, for the construction of frameworks of knowledge which are themselves impersonally available for rational use by those with access to the files, reminding us that: 'The central artifact of this system is not the camera but the filing cabinet' (Sekula 1986 p. 16).

I have so far drawn a contrast between a mode of photographic picturing that acts as a form of celebration and a mode of photographic picturing that acts as a form of control. In both cases the picturing is a type of ceremony that makes two levels of subject visible or potentially visible to those who see the picture. The first is a way of framing the subject of the photograph and secondly a way of exemplifying the discourse or form of knowledge that seeks to celebrate or seeks to control. This second level of discursive knowledge is for some organisational purposes explicit, as when police archives include mug-shots of those who have become instances of bureaucratic record, and is sometimes buried within the self-evident significance of the topic – as in news photographs. Recognising the significance, and frequently the difficulty of identifying, this level of discursive knowledge also serves to point to the shortcomings of a simple distinction between celebration and control.

The history of popular photographic practice has clearly been concerned with the what and why, and less the how, of picture taking; and, less clearly, how the multifaceted dramatic relations of modernity have come to be staged. By the latter phrase I mean the multiplicity of ways that we give ourselves identity both to ourselves and to others. The latter process is, however, a prerequisite for the former because the provision of cheap, reliable and portable means of representation and reproduction has bodied forth a terrain of the average man and of mundane experience both for those who would govern them, and for those who would seek role models, and for those who would discover the terrain. This is then the third sense of looking through cameras – as well as social occasions as communal moments and humans as instances of types and pathologies – we can look as a way of looking at ourselves. As a means of social exploration, as documentary impulse (Lacks 1987).

Most immediately the notion of a documentary camera takes us back to the theme of prosaic or quotidian history that photography could institutionalise. As well as providing a means of displaying families and relationships through time, the camera could be used as a more impersonal memorialist that, as Matthew Brady, the photographic entrepreneur of the American Civil War, described it, was equivalent to 'the eye of history'. Under this rubric early forms of ethnographic photography became explicable as: 'A recognition of the transitory, doomed nature of the lives of peoples existing still in a primitive state . . . They are important photographic subjects because they will speedily recede into the past, indeed they are already to be seen, in the flow of time as fragments of the past' (Thomas 1978 p. 37). The quest to record reality in documentary photography is necessarily voracious, it is motivated by a pervasive curiosity which seeks to explore the present as well as record it for the future: 'From its start, photography implied the capture of the largest possible number of subjects . . . . The subsequent industrialisation of camera technology only carried out a promise inherent in photography from its very beginning: to democratise all experiences by translating them into images' (Sontag 1978 p. 7; see also Buckland 1974).

In practice, of course, the complex of factors and themes that have been used to 'explain' documentary photography draws upon a mixture of cultural and personal concerns. Documentary is used here in the most general sense of recording reality from a collective standpoint. The documentary impulse is characterised by the introduction of some form of self-conscious staging in the representation of reality. Not that reality is modified or interfered with (to do so is to risk becoming propaganda or fiction) but the form of dramatisation is cast in a more impersonal 'voice' – however personally the collective warrant is interpreted (Chaney 1981A). A voice in which science and reform are frequently married to generate a new language of the social such as in: 'the series of "scientific" visual documents of the working class illustrating reformatory texts, government reports or private charitable campaigns' (MacCauley 1987 p. 63).

If we take up again at this point the idea that at one level the meaning of a photograph is dependent upon a form of discursive knowledge, then we can begin to see that in documentary photography there is a 'rhetoric of participation'. I used this phrase earlier in relation to the popularisation of knowledge as a form of legitimacy for the nation-state with a mass electorate. The diffusion of accessible forms of knowledge in modern societies through museums, institutes, publications and educational associations, etc., is both a desire to generate a widespread 'faith in the moral superiority of reason' (Muller 1988) amongst the masses, and a rhetoric of participation that is designed to ensure stable social order. The new media of mass communication and entertainment are obviously basic to the public sphere of mass society and therefore Stange's proposal 'that documentary, a central mode of communication, has assisted the liberal corporate state to manage not only our politics, but also our esthetics and our art' (Stange 1989 p. xv) should be less startling. Photography, as one of if not the first means of mass entertainment for a culture of leisure, provides a clear bridge between knowledge and entertainment that later has become enshrined as the new genre of the photo-magazine – sometimes a separate magazine and sometimes a supplement to a newspaper. In this genre there is a dominant form of narrative based on a concern with the intimacies of ordinary lives.

Photography used for social exposure, even muck-raking, could be powerfully moving as emotional images and frequently upsetting to conservative opinion, but this did not mean that it threatened the legitimacy of the nation-state or subverted social order. In Stange's (1989) history of American documentary photography over sixty years, she distinguishes a series of modulations from photographs as means of middle-class surveillance, through a progressive use of photography in social research to sustain corporate ideology, to New Deal reformist optimism. In the latter phase a dramatic photograph 'could be a vehicle of a seemingly transparent message, whose content could represent for a mass public not specificity but rather ideals and ideality – "symbols of ideal life" that were appropriate for the machine age' (Stange op. cit. pp. 104–5). Documentary therefore makes the premise of spectacular dramatisation explicit – that in representing a world we have in common we can use naturalistic accounts for utopian visions. It should not therefore be surprising that documentary (and documentarists) end up as and in public relations (as for example when the young Communists of Grierson's team in Britain in the 1930s left to join the public relations effort of Shell Oil, discussed in Sussex 1975). The documentary vision is not tied to specific corporate clients but is picturing a public sphere for a dramatisation of social order.

I argued in the previous chapter that the variety of ways of 'exploring' the increasingly alien lands of the metropolitan city combined voyeuristic excitement with moral indignation and intellectual curiosity. The narratives of photographic practice as generated at first by enthusiasts such as Mumby and then in the discourses of news and sensational revelation amplified and institutionalised the theatricality of looking at our society. Looking at our own society is usually done in order to see the remarkable or the significant – to frame the perceptions of those who would look through the representations provided. We would expect therefore to find social reformers seeing a natural correspondence between the impersonal observations of a camera and programmes of collective responsibility or bureaucratic rationality.

In practice, of course, the documentary impulse was frequently cast within iconographic traditions in which social variety and 'local colour' was used to reassure dominant perceptions of inherent consensus and harmony:

The subject-matter of photographic postcards was primarily landscape and historical monuments but also included regional folklore, picturesque types and rural labour . . . . the conservative ideology underlying the majority of ostensibly neutral outdoor scenes of regional festivals, harvests and single figure-types is disguised by the long tradition and thus institutionalisation of such images.

(MacCauley op. cit. p. 66)

A picture of society has come to be constructed through real images which displays an invented landscape; in times of national crisis this honorific world is accentuated in order to assert a distinctive national identity (see, for example, the collection of photographs produced by Doone 1943 to represent Britain both within the country and overseas; a pastoral Britain frozen in Hardy and Elgar).

Another version of honorific ethnography, and one that is particularly salient to the character of popular photography, is that generated through tourist photography. This is clearly a way of storing memories and constructing significant moments in a biographical record but it is also a way of looking at social forms: 'Although the tourist need not be consciously aware of this, the thing he goes to see is society and its works' (MacCannell 1976 p. 55). The tourist and those catering for their interest are necessarily collaborating in a dramatisation of that site, remembering that it need not be a fixed place and that there can be an almost infinite variety of modes of collaboration. Amongst the props that any of the parties concerned might use is photographic imagery for which 'three significant categories are suggested: (1) pictures produced for tourists; (2) pictures produced about tourists and places to visit; and (3) pictures produced by tourists themselves' (Chalfen 1980 p. 26, sic). It is easy and common to criticise the 'inauthenticity' of much of what is represented in the variety of this imagery but this is to miss the more important point. Tourist photography displays the cultural concerns of those who are its audience rather than the world represented. It is a form of documentary in which the criterion of authenticity is inappropriate (although clearly this is contradicted by many tourists' expectations, but in practice their concern with authenticity, paradoxically, talks about a distrust of dramatisation).

More usually the documentary impulse is governed by two considerations that are held to be crucial in sustaining the authenticity of representation. These are that the documentarist should not impose on nor interfere with the 'natural' setting. As has been noted an impersonal style has conventionally been sought to complement a non-interventionist stance. Usually grounded in a bureaucratic discourse as in Annan's pictures of rookeries in Glasgow in the 1860s before they were demolished, the style was radicalised and popularised in varieties of documentary practice such as that sponsored by the New Deal administration in 1930s' America (Daniel *et al*. 1987). In this more self-conscious documentary climate, authorship could be wedded to popular forms most interestingly through a surrealistic estrangement from conventional ways of seeing. In their pictures of British ways of life Brandt and Spender (Spender and Harrisson 1975; Brandt 1983), produce pictures that are disturbing as well as fascinating. The closeness of their observation, despite the melancholy of the fragments and glances they record, is also consistent with the informal photojournalism of someone like Bert Hardy in his work for *Picture Post* (Hopkinson 1975).

It is in this concentrated observation, or commitment to the authenticity of the life observed, that a level of documentary truth as a grasp of social essence is sought. It provides a means for self-conscious intervention, a 'process whereby an "editing of society" can become a personal "poetry" without loss of social grounding' (Trachtenberg 1979 p. 8).

It is because documentary practice of this sort is more likely to be 'authored' it can either be accused of being recuperated into the gallery culture of art, or of being imprisoned within the limitations of populism so that documentarists fail to see how their work can substantiate official discourses (Tagg 1988 Chapters 5 and 6) – the point of such accusations being a concern with how documentary photography can avoid betraying the popular experience it seeks to represent and avoid distortion in the ways it looks at social formations. A more useful alternative, however, would seek to situate the problems of authenticity in documentary photography within more general issues of ethnographic practice or what Clifford and associates have called problems in 'writing culture' (Clifford and Marcus 1986, Clifford 1988; see also Chaney 1979). Documentary photography and photographic pictures in general are ways of writing culture that are also dramatic resources within which particular types of staging as opportunities for reflection become possible. The reason for unpacking the discourses of the popular and some aspects of the formations of public drama in modernity in these chapters, is that culture, as form of life, is enacted within the endlessly refracting mirrors of the ways we see ourselves as a world we recognise. That is, it is not so much a form as a polymorphous show.

The lines of continuity between the self-conscious authorship of documentary photos and popular photography lie in their common anonymity. This is not to say that the identity of those pictured is irrelevant, although for many purposes it usually is, nor that the identity of the 'author' cannot be identified in stylistic features. Obviously we can recognise a particular style and seek it out. What is more important, however, than any supplementary information is that the image mediates between the life-world of those seeing and the life-world of those seen. There is the possibility of a shock of recognition so that as well as knowing what 'they' look like there is the chance of asking 'how might I look if seen by them?'. The particular speaks to a communal imagination and displays continuities of emotion and behaviour within discontinuous social experience. Parasitic upon what can be found the photographer passes on gossip as a way of seeing and framing mundane experience: 'Evans' *actual* subject is time, seen in the beauties of the fallen world . . . . It stares at our customary locales – advertisements, slums, street corners, relatives and passers-by, cemeteries, as though they were of ultimate significance' (Stott 1973 pp. 288–9).

To realise the enormity of the unremarkable, for both documentarist and popular photographer, involves wilful (even if reluctant) estrangement – a willingness to confront necessary ambiguities in any form of representation: 'We tried to present the ordinary in an extraordinary manner. But that's the paradox because the only thing extraordinary about it was that it was so ordinary' (Ben Shahn quoted in Beloff 1985 p. 117). And in this photography is emblematic of modernity – to presuppose the centrality of reflexivity. Style as communal grounds for perception and representation (Ewen 1990), the centrality of images in constituting forms of discourse, and the reflexivity of personal experience: all these are key tropes in photographic seeing and have passed thereby into being key metaphors for the distinctiveness of modernity.

RITUAL AND REFLEXIVITY

I have said that popular photography should be understood as one of that complex of activities that are lumped under the general heading of mass media of entertainment. It is an unconventional member of that set as the industries of mass entertainment usually take the form of national or international distribution agencies which distribute the work of a small number of producers as standardised copies to anonymous audiences. In popular photography the producers utilise standard forms of production equipment which are widely and cheaply available to generate unique images. Given these features and the embedding of this cultural resource in pre-existing social institutions, principally the family so that as I have indicated they become mutually constitutive: 'the activities of making and looking at family photographs have become an integral part of family relationships' (Becker Ohrn 1975 p. 27), could suggest that photography is better understood as a folk form. That is an activity both symbolising and sustaining a form of life generated by its members and significantly functional for institutional stability: 'family history was being transferred, not only through the photographs and collection *per se*, but also through the narratives stimulated by the pictures' (Becker Ohrn op. cit. p. 32).

The making and exhibition of popular photographic images is by and large informal and extremely localised in what is being referred to. What makes this activity a form of mass entertainment is explicable through an analogy with British suburban housing. Despite the individuality of the domestic circumstances within any one house, the form of housing institutionalises certain expectations and ways of being in the world that point to cultural homogeneity in national lifestyles rather than the intense communalism of folk culture. The institutionalisation of popular photography described in preceding sections has been accomplished in ways that similarly facilitate a national mass culture. This is in part because of what we have called the construction of ways of looking in photography, and in part because photography has become so integral to those other discourses of mass society – the industry of leisure, news and public opinion, the culture of consumerism, and the family as an idealised domain of emotional gratification.

A lot of the force of a category of folk form lies in the association of ideas that in folk culture people do what they want to do, through what is meaningful and significant to them. This is in contrast to expectations of mass entertainment that audiences are doing what they are persuaded is socially expected or is a desirable lifestyle or will be a source of gratification and pleasure. (The validity of implied connotations of authenticity is not of immediate concern here, although it has of course been very important in both right- and left-wing critiques of mass culture; Brantlinger 1983.) The terrain of the popular often seems to lie, however vaguely, between this continental opposition.

This is because mass cultural resources can be used through inter-personal readings in ways that inflect, distort, subvert or transform the ostensible meaning of the performance concerned. An example is the adoption of Judy Garland in gay subcultures so that her performances became multiply layered and as a celebrity her persona was complexly ironicised (Dyer 1979 Chapter 3; Fiske 1989 has also provided a spirited, if incoherent, celebration of the autonomy of popular taste). In the same way we can expect to find that ethnographies of photo-graphic use will discover subcultural incorporations of different types of photographic practice. (The creation and dissemination of home erotica, amateurs in ritual poses, is one type of local drama that popularly adapts a mass iconography.)

The insuperable problem for any attempt to provide a definitive account is that meaning, sense, significance are constituted inter-dependently in the process of use by audiences of performances. And the key term here is that of process – there is not a once-and-for-all reading (viewing, attending, etc.) but in all the situations in which it might be re-viewed, recalled, resonate, the meaning of a work is continually being constituted again. More significantly, the reader is an active participant in this process and is therefore to some extent being re-invented in each act of participation. The recognition of plurality of meaning and that even so a work has a cumulative significance beyond our personal interpretation means that through a taking of the stance of the other we can use the position of the work to 'look back' at ourselves. This is a form of self-consciousness in which our understanding of the work can act as a meta-commentary on how we might wish to see ourselves or social circumstances, so that the process of participation may facilitate 'awakening the self momentarily to novel perspectives on those premises of social order in which it is ordinarily embedded' (Handelman 1982 p. 184).

The reflexive character of cultural representation need not be revelatory to this extent but it does embody a duality in consciousness:

> The terms reflexive, reflexivity, and reflexiveness have been used in a variety of disciplines to describe the capacity of language and of thought – of any system of signification – to turn or bend back upon itself, to become an object to itself, and to refer to itself.
>
> (Babcock 1980 p. 2)

Although the significance of reflexivity for social theory has become more generally accepted in the last decade, its paradoxical character is still fundamentally disturbing for theories of human knowledge, the stability of any form of social order and concepts of self and individuality. Both the knowing or apprehending agent and the object known or apprehended are thrown into question if the agency of apprehension is appreciated as dialogical. The latter term, loosely borrowed from Bakhtin, is used to summarise the ways in which each agent and object is in important respects constructed or constituted through their engagement with the other. In the terms of this book, different cultural forms provide opportunities for different types of reflexive participation.

In his conclusion to a set of essays on reflexivity, Rappoport (1980) uses distinctions between a personal journal and communal ritual as instances of modern and traditional genres, respectively. Three important points of contrast are outlined which are based on the difference between the ways in which keeping a journal is a mode of self-construction, whereas ritual forms provide a mode of affirmation for the collective in which a self is embedded (and thereby self-construction). A way of focussing these differences is provided by the notion of participation: writing a journal partici-pates in the self-that-is-writing; performing a ritual is participating in the possibility of participating (accepting a communal warrant). This use of participation is the heart of what I am trying to get at in the dimension of social occasion in the conceptualisation of a cultural form.

The form of dramatisation in ritual is that which is being dramatised: 'what the performance of a ritual essentially does do, is to specify the relationship that obtains between the performers of the ritual and what it is that they are performing' (Connerton 1989 p. 54). It is a relatively small step from appreciating this possibility to seeing that only through participation could one understand repre-sentation, so that one learns meanings through their use: 'Gods, then, are created reflexively by the words attributed to them' (Rappoport op. cit. p. 190). Reflexivity therefore does not only mean the possibility or necessity of ironic consciousness, but also refers to the ways in which, that is the how cultural phenomena contain the resources for, provide instructions for, they are to be understood (used) in the sense of knowing how to go on (Garfinkel 1967).

Popular photography is reflexive, perhaps transparently so, in both senses. It provides a way of seeing how we might be seen by others and it provides a form of dramatisation for the institutional frameworks within which our world is given order, stability and comprehensibility. As has already been noted in this manifest recursiveness, in photography's insistence on the limitations, contingencies, of its picturing – through the salience of cropping, moment, focus and perspective, etc. – photography is emblematic of modernity. And, characteristically, as a mode of social construction the form of participation offered is of a private writing of social forms. In mutually constructing an elaborate spectacle of popular life 'large numbers of persons remain quite individuated, even when together, while they passively absorb dramatic projections which themselves do not necessarily reflect upon any reality known to these spectators' (Handelman 1982 p. 180). Such an account of spectacle is obviously part of a wider discourse of mass entertain- ment, but, accepting its terms for now, it does provide a way in which we can imagine reconciling folk and mass characteristics in photography as a cultural form.

The notion of popular in photographic practice does not then just refer to the sorts of photographs that are taken by amateurs in the settings of everyday life. We have noted in relation to tourist photography that in addition to those taken by tourists there are those supplied as souvenirs or other markers such as postcards. We would also have to include photographs in holiday brochures, tourist guides and other ephemeral literature. In all other forms of leisure activity there is the same mixture of professional and amateur generated images which together intermesh, and are often parasitic in form upon each other, to constitute the vernacular of what is being sought and accomplished in the activity. The point to stress here again is that the authenticity or reality of these images is largely superfluous to their semiotic weight. They are dramatisations of what is possible in guiding the form of identity and style of life.

The perspective of dramatisation is particularly relevant to the vernacular of consumerism: the icons of modernity staged in mass advertising. An advertisement is a public picture, in that it is in the public sphere, designed to be accessible and of interest to an audience who are in general anonymous to each other and to the advertiser. Mass advertising is dependent upon certain technological facilities such as the development of cheap printing, the sophisticated reproduction of images and national media of distribution including poster agencies, mass circulation newspapers and broadcasting networks. More fundamentally it only becomes economically feasible with the existence of standardised packaging of goods, national distribution networks and production lines oriented towards the production of uniform goods across a product range. These and other related characteristics can be summarised as the creation of a national market, and it is in this sense that advertising more than any other cultural form presupposes national integration (i.e. is a mass stage).

The picturing, and it does not particularly matter if it is a single image or a short sequence of images, works through what Goffman (1976) has called a 'scene' as a method of organising understanding. Scenes are fleeting opportunities for viewing which are necessarily truncated and therefore comprehension is dependent upon broad interpretive categories and stylisations. The glimpses provided by the scenes of commercial realism have certain advantages over those of everyday experience in that they are intentionally choreographed to be informative, the perspective from which the audience views is necessarily part of the information to be conveyed, and that which is seen in commercial staging is warrantably seen – there is no suspicion of voyeurism. The public pictures of advertising therefore invite an interpretive engagement: 'The point about an ad is what its composer means us to infer as to what is going on in the make-believe pictures seen, not what had actually been going on in the real doings that were pictured' (Goffman op. cit. p. 83).

The dramatisation is persuasive, therefore, not by the degree to which it corresponds to some pre-photographic reality, but by the degree to which it is consistent with the interpretive frameworks that might be available in popular experience:

> I want to argue now that the job the advertiser has of dramatizing the value of his product is not unlike the job a society has of infusing its social situations with ceremonial and ritual signs facilitating the orientation of participants to one another.
>
> (Goffman op. cit. p. 95)

Ceremony and ritual facilitate mutual orientation through the provision of selves that can be treated for the matters at hand as sufficient (Goffman's notion of the ritual self is clarified in his lecture on the lecture, Goffman 1981A). This does not mean that the use of ritual resources by whatever social entity is always successful; indeed the study of lapses should provide some of the best clues to resources, but that in the focussing and formalisation of interactive concerns dramatic agency can be identified and articulated. How that agency is embodied and given social presence will be relative to different cultural orders, what have been called here forms of dramatisation, and therefore acquire different cultural significance: 'The self . . . is an ideology of everyday life, used to attribute causality and moral responsibility in our society, just as in societies with a denser (e.g. tribal) structure, moral responsibility is not placed within the individual but attributed to spirits or gods' (Collins 1988 p. 50; see also Muller's assertion that: 'The cult of the individual is the abstract core of the modern cultural code', Muller 1988 p. 147).

The dramas of public life are enacted by celebrities claiming some legitimacy for their aura, except for those (un)fortunates who are thrust by random chance into becoming celebrities however briefly; and framed, introduced, commentated upon and mimicked by widening penumbra of parasitic adjuncts who mark out descending scales of dramatic status. In formulating and sustaining public identity the photographic record is a display of the institutionalised self but is simultaneously constituting a popular icon as a model for anonymous audiences. The images of a celebrity display a world in which that identity is possible. To the extent that a radically secular society is inextricably concerned with the dramaturgy of identity, then those who can hint at the bones, the manufacturing process, of identity construction are speaking to substantial concerns:

> The star phenomenon orchestrates the whole set of problems inherent in the commonplace metaphor of life-as-theatre, . . . because what is interesting about them is not the character they have constructed . . . but rather the business of constructing/performing/being (depending on the particular star involved) a 'character'.
>
> (Dyer 1979 p. 24)

Once again the authenticity or validity of that or who is being dramatised is irrelevant to their cultural significance. The highly stylised images of different types of celebrity from domains such as sport, politics and popular music are formal resources for expressing different types of expectation of public life. The plenitude of images common to both public domain and more personal experience is an infinite archive from which allusions and associations can be endlessly spun out. Popular photography is the most pervasive repertoire in institutionalising resemblances between public drama and personal experience.

In conceptualising this sense of repertoire the form of ritual has served as a way of describing the conventions displayed as appropriate in different photographic practices. It also seems likely that certain photographs, singly or in sets, will take on the status of ritual icons for particular audiences (as well as personally highly charged icons for intimate associations (Barthes 1982)). The size, cultural status, coherence and what else is common to that audience will all interrelate in determining the sort of sacred field the ritual icon can focus. There are, for example, very specific claims about both writing history and the aspirations of a specific fraction of the American intelligentsia being made when John Szarkowski, introducing Walker Evans' retrospective exhibition at the Museum of Modern Art in 1971, declared that the photographs had created: 'the accepted myth of our recent past' (quoted in Stott 1973 p. 267).

There are therefore projective claims being made in these as in all other forms of secular ritual (Chaney 1987A). There is no possibility of presupposing a community of belief, so that the use of some images to be emblematic of moments in national history which are acquiring symbolic significance, or the use of others to publicise symbolic figures, or as persuasive encapsulations of desire or fear or other strong emotion are all summoning a community into being. The publication and reiteration of ritual icons aspires to focus attention and emotion as continually re-invented traditions, as a form of collective memory which is reflexive of the future. If in the post-modern world our dominant sensibility is figural rather than discursive (Lash 1988) it is through the theatricality of picturing. It is true that any form of normative distinction between representation and reality has been dissolved by the surreal ellision of the legitimacy of a frame to mark out the stage so that we are all performers while simultaneously being members of the audience. This leaves, however, the popular as all-pervasive – the vernacular within which politics will be formulated.

4

DISCOURSES OF
PUBLIC LIFE

THE PUBLIC SPHERE

In the chapters so far I have argued that in the process of modernisation new relations of dramatisation for collective experience
have been forged. These relations can be characterised by
comparison with features of spectacular drama (if it is remembered that the spectacular is not a fixed form but takes on new
meanings in different cultural forms). The elements in modernisation that have driven out the prior dramaturgy of collective life
have been the constellation of social and economic conditions
that transformed the landscape (life-world) of mundane
experience. I have tried to describe how the production of space
through forms of social action (a landscape) is more than a
distribution of buildings or distinctions between public and
private spaces. It involves the delineation of cultural space:
through the opportunities for performance at a multiplicity of
levels of complexity; through the inscription of audiences for
performance; and through the character of formulas and scripts
for performance. The orderly character to anonymous experience
in the landscape of modernity derives from the conjunction of
both a new set of opportunities for seeing and for being seen.

The most immediately apparent innovation in forms of performance in modernity has been the development of nationwide (and
subsequently international) uniform styles of drama and entertainment. The development of mass audiences has been paralleled by
the gradual establishment of a mass electorate in nation-states. In
both entertainment and political practice a number of notions of the
popular have been developed as a sufficient and necessary mandate
for social order. The ambiguities of the discourse of the popular

113

have constituted an arena within which the implications of democratic forms can begin to be evaluated.

In his provocative history of the invention of 'the people' Morgan (1988 p. 13) begins with the assertion that: 'The popular governments of Britain and the United States rest on fictions as much as the governments of Russia and China'. The essential fiction for Morgan is that 'the people' have some common existence or identity such that they could exercise their sovereignty through their form of government. How and why those fictions have come to seem persuasive, or even necessary for economic development, will only become gradually apparent. (To characterise a concept of social description as fictional is not necessarily to imply that it is untrue or illusory, rather that the grounds of conceptualisation lie in narrative constructions (cf. Chaney 1979 Chapter 4).) If our community is 'imagined' (Anderson 1983), and our language of the popular will a fiction, who is communicating (and how) to whom in the public sphere? I will argue that notions of the popular and the public are not neutral, that is merely descriptive, resources but that they help to form the practical meaning of mass participation.

In the previous chapters the several dimensions of how the popular could be used in accounts of modern culture (and how those dimensions can succeed or overlay each other in almost wilful ignorance it seems), have begun to be sketched in. The political significance of different methods of account has also begun to be apparent. For example, in a perspective that stresses the interdependence of notions of the popular with opposition between classes the politics of conceptualisation are plainly foregrounded. (If politics concerns the differing forms of control over resources, both material and interpretive, and power is the organisation and stabilisation of these forms of control, then cultural forms in which opposition to conventional order is stressed are clearly political.) Equally clearly a version of the popular in which personal choice and the market organisation of popularity are made central would probably be described as apolitical, as for example by those who think it important or possible 'to keep politics out of sport'. The political ideology of this account is articulated through absence – an absence of any concern with how the values which motivate choice are formulated.

There is a more fundamental sense though in which the popular articulates political discourses. The several forms of the popular in themselves demonstrate: 'the ways in which the very recognition of certain cultural forms as "popular" is already bound up in a set of cultural and social discourses' (Shiach 1989 p. 3). In mobilising rhetoric the people are always us, a collective self-consciousness, that is proud of believing in or doing certain things. But the people are also always 'the other' an object of ethnographic curiosity that may be sympathised with, pitied, humoured, admired, entertained or patronised, etc. There is therefore a tension within any use of 'the people'. Not only is the object shifting in character but the person speaking the object is mobilised in relation to contradictory grounds. There is no authorial security although any one 'author' may vehemently ignore this. One consequence of the conceptual contradiction is that political actors in any form of mass politics are necessarily continually searching for a voice through which they can find a way of representing themselves.

The recurrent metaphor of voice and language as a way of 'speaking about' the popular is not exclusively metaphorical. In her study of the politics of language, Smith (1984) is concerned to show why it was necessary and how it was possible to achieve an intellectual vernacular language as a precondition for the democratisation of political discourse. In the eighteenth century: 'Civilization was largely a linguistic concept, establishing a terrain in which vocabulary and syntax distinguished the refined and the civilized from the vulgar and the savage' (Smith op. cit. p. vii). In order to traverse this terrain the new masses had to contest the presuppositions of grammar, the validity of colloquial language had to be established, and in particular the validity of colloquial political discourse had to be asserted.

The language of civilisation, as the embodiment of privilege and unyielding social order, blocked political change at the end of the eighteenth and early nineteenth centuries in France and England. In France revolutionary impetus fractured the constraints of social order and for it to be sustained innovations were required in the rhetoric of expression which in turn provided for new political entities and actors:

> The political culture of revolution was made up of symbolic practices, such as language, imagery, and gestures . . . . In many ways, the symbolic practices – the use of a certain rhetoric, the spread of certain symbols and rituals – called the new political class into existence.
>
> (Hunt 1984 p. 13)

115

What Hunt calls the political culture of revolutionary society was of course not just a concern to devise new words or new rhetorical orders, but an engagement with the need to devise forms of social order independent of the charisma of kingship and the mystifications of religious authority. Although in Britain the revolutionary struggle was not so concentrated or apocalyptic, in practice in both societies the peaks of vernacular and popular emancipation were recuperated, while leaving a new terrain of residual populism. In this new landscape old forms of cultural distinction were transformed and the people were gradually admitted as actors to the political stage.

In a political order in which control over cultural capital is concentrated within an institutionalised élite, 'the voice of the people' will be articulated and, even more complexly, recognised in ways that only ambiguously represent the circumstances within which that voice has been formulated. In each of Shiach's case studies it is apparent that those who would seek to use the popular voice, whether to contain it or to use it as an alternative resource, were not writing in 'isolation from, but always in negotiation with, the texts of the dominant culture' (Shiach op. cit. p. 70). More recently, in the political language of mass democratic culture this negotiation has been elided by recuperating the people in 'the general public', within whose terms difference is, more optimistically (as in 'Coca-Cola' or 'Benetton' advertisements), presented as purely a matter of style rather than otherness. In a televisual culture, particularly one adapting to transnational distribution, any reference to 'the public' is at best a generalising gesture to an audience and their leisure choices.

The interdependence of public with audience suggests that some types of relations of production are more likely to provide occasions for publics than others and that publics are not a cultural universal but historically specific. That is that there will be a complex of circumstances within which publics become a possibility; so that publics are a cultural innovation. In considering the nature of this innovation it quickly becomes apparent that a public is not immediately experienced as a new form of sociality, so much as the ways in which it is occasioned. A public is focussed or collected by a form of communication, some representation with which they engage, and the key innovative aspect of this form of communication is that it is impersonal. Or more precisely that the medium of communication, within which the representation is

116

couched is impersonal or anonymous (cf. Lohisse 1973). A means of communication is impersonal or anonymous when it is not unique, when there is no distinction between the original and copies. A consequence important for our understanding of this type of communication is that it is the social organisation of the process of distribution, not the process of production, which determines those who will have access to the means of communication.

Printing is the first means of communication which possesses these characteristics and it has been forcefully argued (principally by Eisenstein (1969) but see also Febvre and Martin (1976), that printing facilitated transformations in the production and control of knowledge that made possible the modern cultural paradigm (Reiss (1982)), this is that intellectual work is individual, secular and rational. Books are by definition, however, long-term projects. It is with the innovation of printed ephemera that a means of communication was devised that could be used as a forum for political as opposed to intellectual debate (although that distinction in relation to religious conflict is of course hard to sustain). The anonymity of printed ephemera, principally pamphlets and newspapers, refers not to their authorship but to the situation of their reception – their audience. It is printed ephemera that made publics possible, or more precisely that it was in the innovation of newspapers that the possibility of public opinion was constituted (Burns 1977A; Chaney 1981A): 'The newspaper was part of that broad drive for systematic, rational control over the environment which has characterized European civilization since the Renaissance' (Popkin 1989 p. 6).

In its classical use the notion of public society or public sphere implied both a social order of citizenship and a forum for rational discourse encompassing all social institutions – drawing from Habermas, Popkin (op. cit. p. 42) has neatly referred to: 'the concept of "public opinion" as the rational consensus of the private members of society'. Discursive resources became central to citizenship in the eighteenth century because of the opportunity to free communication from the immediacy of interpersonal transmission. In this way the quality of discourse could be separated from the status of speakers. The notion of public discourse entails then an association between impersonality or objectivity and rational discourse, so that for those who would seek to be participants in this discourse 'a "public" consists of persons who habitually acquire their news and orientations from impersonal mass media where they have available to them diverse information and orientations diffused by competing

117

individual entrepreneurs or corporate organizations' (Gouldner 1976 p. 96; some characteristic instances of more contemporary studies of media and public opinion can be found in Part 1 of Curran 1987).

The concept of orientation covers more than rational disinterest also referring to new formulations of cultural space. 'Events' wherever they are recognised to be occurring were being brought within the lived environment of one's society – a simultaneous expansion and contraction of the 'knowable' world solidified at first by railway travel and then by other transport technologies. And these 'events' (as a discourse of actuality, see later in this chapter) are staged in the predictability and formulae of media time thereby generating new forms of synchronicity for public life.

Three points can be argued to have followed from this initial sense of the public. The first is that in its classical form the sphere of public life will be staged in its own physical space as in the coffee houses and theatres of the Enlightenment; as it develops this 'space' will become increasingly abstract by being confined to the means of mass communication and participated in only by privatised individuals (Sennett 1976). Secondly, it seems likely that it will be impossible for ruling élites to contain the proliferation of more specialist publics who may develop radically alternative interpretive frameworks. This may be seen as a space within which emancipatory discourse can develop or as an ever-present danger of a descent into parochialism and irrationality. And finally, developing from Habermas' more pessimistic account that it has become increasingly impossible to sustain the rationality of public discourse as vehicles of public communication have become incorporated in multi-national corporate entertainment bureaucracies (Garnham 1986).

The premise for my approach has been that a study of the ways in which the dramatisation of forms of social and cultural order has changed in the constitution of modernity has to include what Horne has called 'the public culture':

> We now live in a time when there is a demand for what at least appears to be a *shared* "public and visible culture", in which both rulers and ruled can appear to be common, if differentiated participants.
>
> (Horne 1986 p. 54 *sic*)

The demand for a shared culture obviously lies at the heart of any understanding of democratic politics. The development of mass publics means that there can be no arbitrary constraint upon an equality of participation, that is there can be no formal or constitutional discrimination on grounds such as wealth, gender or race. The form of Horne's words ('at least appears' suggests that deficiencies in meeting this ideal, in any one urban-industrial society, can be masked to a greater or lesser extent by the indiscriminate availability (and surrogate sharing) of the media of mass communication. It seems now that 'the politics' of discourses using popular and public can be captured by the metaphor of voice as the mouthpiece through which legitimacy or warrant is claimed. This is to say that we can hear the public that is being constituted through listening to how it is being articulated (or spoken to or addressed) in representation.

Another way of formulating these developments is to say that the promise of the public sphere was adapted to a different mode of collectivity, different forms of dramatisation. There had to develop a language of political community which could command a sufficient legitimacy and authority to encompass the imagination of disparate groups: 'the democratisation of politics . . . [and] the creation of the modern, administrative, citizen-mobilizing and citizen-influencing state both placed the question of the "nation" . . . at the top of the political agenda' (Hobsbawm 1990 p. 83). The recognition of the imperative of nationalism also involved recognising that there could be a 'way of speaking' to and for the public which presupposed and took for granted a social order of communal discourse. A consciousness of the need for dramatic artifice because 'National languages are . . . almost always semi-artificial constructs . . . They are usually attempts to devise a standardized idiom out of a multiplicity of actually spoken idioms, which are thereafter downgraded to dialects' (Hobsbawm op. cit. p. 54). The second point became particularly pressing with the development of national broadcasting networks which could not, at least at first, risk the stratification of publics into popular and élitist that newspapers were then institutionalising.

Mass publics entered the political stage then as actors in a national drama working to a script that offers: 'symbols and rituals or common collective practices' (Hobsbawm op. cit. p. 71), in addition to descriptions and explanations of a new set of disciplinary regimes such as censuses and other administrative records, which could clothe new forms of social affiliation in national garb. The development of mass culture has, even so, been seen as problematic in democratising societies because it can be presumed that

(a) different types of culture embody different modes of communal participation and (b) that intellectuals, as workers in cultural industries, have been faced with distinctive problems in speaking to or for popular audiences. Thus LeMahieu (1988) in trying to think through what might be involved in the development of a common culture in Britain, specifically in the twenty years from 1919 to 1939, treats the dominance of processes of mass communication and the rise of modern commercial culture as interdependent processes and sees the issues as turning around the 'response of the cultivated elites' to these processes. LeMahieu's account of the creation of a 'culture for democracy' is problematic in that he presumes that the effort was successful, and because, emptying democracy of ideology, he can accept that an adequate culture is generated through the incorporation/recuperation of popular cultural forms.

The development of new technologies of mass entertainment undoubtedly focussed concerns about how new mass audiences should be addressed (and heard as speaking), but did not create those concerns. Although a common need to 'educate' the audiences for mass leisure as much as the publics of a mass electorate has often been recognised, it may seem inappropriate to bracket the self-conscious artificiality of dramatised fictions with the taken-for-granted naturalness of national formations. It is the ways in which any repertoire of national identity overrides history while stressing cultural specificity which gives it such self-evident facticity (see Samuel's 1989 account of the images making up any national myth).

The performative language of drama seems inappropriate because it is provisional, processual and, even in ritual, dependent upon the specificity of performance. In contrast the myth of the nation points to conventions of social order which play down any sense of being provisional or conditional while simultaneously celebrating persistent change. It is in this way that the forms of national, and the associated blood brothers of racial and ethnic, identity have clearly become the dominant fictions of our collective experience in modernity. It is within this framework that the abstract crowds of mass politics have become simultaneously the audiences of popular entertainment.

ADDRESSING THE PUBLIC

The generally orderly character to public life in late modernity is based on the incorporation of diverse publics into the audiences and constituencies of mass society. This involves an acceptance within those publics that the ways those audiences and constituencies are addressed, the discourses of public life, provide a system of representation that is an adequate public culture. (It seems that even when the culture proves inadequate and collective violence returns to the streets, as in for example football hooliganism or occasional rioting by the young, what is being staged is not an intimation of an alternative order but a desperate bid for a ritual role – even that of the damned – by those who predominately feel themselves excluded from the performance spaces of consumer culture; contemporary views on football and hooliganism have been ably summarised by Williams 1991.) The development of media of mass communication has been essential for the creation and effectiveness of a public culture, this term to be understood in two ways.

The first is that the notion of public culture is a way of referring to what Thompson calls the mediazation of modern culture: 'By this I mean the general process by which the transmission of symbolic forms becomes increasingly mediated by the technical and institutional apparatuses of the media industries' (Thompson 1990 pp. 3–4); a process: 'which has gone hand-in-hand with the expansion of industrial capitalism and with the formation of the modern nation-state system' (op. cit. p. 164). The second meaning of the idea of public culture is as a form of community sharing common means of entertainment, a cast of public figures and a discourse of citizenship: 'millions of individuals who may never interact with one another, but who share, by virtue of their participation in a mediated culture, a common experience and a collective memory' (Thompson op. cit. p. 163).

The public culture is then composed of the innumerable public dramas that constitute a mediated culture. These dramas will be staged to an ever-increasing degree as events for the media, but in order to become public events they will have to be articulated in ways that are consistent with the ideology of public culture. The concept of voice in public culture is used to refer to the mode of address through which 'the public', as cultural or fictional entity, is made available as practical action to 'a public', as a particular form of social association. In general the practical actions of public life are couched within the ideology of social order which seeks to sustain established hierarchies of inequality. These events are, however, spoken and spoken about and thus addressed to their mass audiences as images of that audience's world. They function to ceremonialize the presuppositions of that world.

It will be helpful if the grounds of public address are initially sought in a formalisation of a way of speaking more than a specific set of topics or an agenda. What is meant by formalisation here is not so much a distinctive vocabulary or a manner of delivery (although as ritual markers they are both likely to be present), as a shift in the footing upon which the address is predicated. Our simplest model of communication is a dyadic face-to-face piece of interaction in which the constituent individuals interchange the roles of speaker and listener. A more complex type of communication (complex to analytically describe not necessarily in terms of what is being communicated) occurs when participants represent a conversation either between themselves or as addressed to an audience so that these overhearers understand the interaction as a dramatic representation. What is crucial about these entertainments is that although the audience is an essential constitutive element in the overall performance, it is conventionally silent during the course of the representation or its interventions are encouraging punctuations rather than the introduction of new material. There are clearly a number of variables operating here, a change in any one of which will have implications for the nature of the performance concerned, but more crucially underlying the interplay of these variables is a pervasive reference to the staged character of any one utterance.

I shall illustrate the relevance of staging to our understanding of public voice through reference to Goffman's (1981B Chapter 5) concept of 'frame space'. Although this chapter is devoted to how radio announcers repair slips in the course of broadcasting, the more general topic is the correction of faults in everyday talk. A frame space derives from the particular relationship the speaker has to the words uttered, such a relationship provides an interpretive framework for understanding those words. Any speaking is necessarily a choice within a set of options and all the varieties of authorship, responsibility, style and direction in speech combine to give a particular identity to an utterance. This identity may be consistent with the frame space that the speaker would normally be expected to be operating with or it may intentionally or unintentionally violate that space: 'To speak acceptably is to stay within the frame space allowed one; to speak unacceptably is to take up an alignment that falls outside this space' (Goffman op. cit. p. 230). There is therefore a normative character to an individual's use of frame space and this normative character can be exploited to deal with the manifold slips and mistakes that litter everyday talk. Part of the informality of such talk is our ability to comment on our own speech production in the midst of doing it, so that awareness of mistakes is displayed through the manner of corrections or apologies.

Neither the speaker nor the listener is likely to be aware of all the slips that are made and of those noticed their significance will be affected by the frame space the speaker occupies. This is a problem for radio announcers in two ways. First, our expectations for the public voice of broadcast speech both make us more sensitive to and concerned about 'faults that we would have to be trained linguistically to hear in ordinary talk [as they] can be glaringly evident to the untrained ear when encountered in broadcast talk' (Goffman op. cit. p. 240). Second, a presumption of an identification between radio announcer and station, and to that extent the sub-ordination of an announcer's identity to their broadcasting role, means that necessary corrections can be expected to be handled through a complicated balancing of self-respect with station discipline. It seems therefore that the frame space for broadcast talk, or more precisely announcer's talk, is more circumscribed as a form of public speech than the informality of everyday talk. For Goffman this formality of address provides an analytic resource for addressing otherwise unremarkable features of everyday talk: 'it is only by looking at such things as delicts in broadcast talk that the liberty we conversationalists have been enjoying becomes obvious' (Goffman op. cit. p. 324). For us this type of example helps to make apparent the stylisation of public settings.

Obviously there are styles of broadcast talk and different stations attempt to develop an identity through distinctive conventions of the normal and the permissible, and in particular a claim to informality is frequently displayed through the ways in which fluffs and mistakes are corrected. Goffman argues though that broadcast talk that is more openly self-referential is judged within the institutional norms of broadcasting to lack public seriousness, and is therefore seen to be only appropriate for low status audiences or everyday, 'domestic' topics. It is certainly true that more serious topics are marked for the audience through ritualised features of gravity and formality, but it is more significant that even the most entertainment-oriented broadcasters feel the necessity to correct mistakes – to display the existence of public as opposed to personal or group norms of conduct and expression.

It is in this context that the self-conscious formality of the early years of public service broadcasting in Britain can better be understood. The British experience has been idiosyncratic in that in a number of fields of public policy a hybrid form of administrative control has been developed. This hybrid, or what Williams (1974, see also Heller 1978) has called an intermediate institution, is a form of organisation which while under the ultimate control of central government retains a considerable degree of autonomy both in day-to-day administration and in terms of policy perspectives and institutional style. This mixture of a degree of significant independence from direct pressures of commercial marketing and from equivalent pressures from departments of state has meant that it is feasible to describe working in such an organisation as a form of public service (Burns 1977B). One can describe this corporate self-image as ideological because it works to mask the conflict of class interests in how forms of popular culture are developed, legitimated and disseminated.

It has become conventional in Britain to characterise the Reithian legacy too glibly: that broadcasters' attitudes were élitist and patronising, and that a broadcasting service was treated as another instance of a colonial mission to civilise savages, in this case the British working class. It has therefore become easy to believe that public service broadcasting is the antithesis of popular or populist culture. (Thompson 1990 more fairly lists the inadequacies of public service broadcasting as susceptibility to state interference, control by a bureaucratic élite, and an inability to adapt to new technologies.) It may be that the institutionalisation of broadcasting in Britain during the monopoly years did take on a very distinctive sense of the public that was being addressed; but this does not mean that other forms of institutionalisation were less public-minded although possibly in one sense less public-spirited (for further discussion see the papers on broadcasting and the public sphere in Collins 1986). More importantly for our present argument this example also makes clear that the notion of voice in public speech is not just a set of conventions concerning degrees and modes of formality, but that the ways in which the public is addressed is constitutive of the public as a space for collective identity. This is not to say that cultural forms determine the possibilities for cultural action but certainly that it becomes more difficult to sustain cultural formations outside dominant discursive frameworks.

An interesting approach to this issue is developed in Frith's

(1983) paper on conceptions of entertainment and popular appeal in BBC policies in the 1930s the 'high years' of Reithian public service broadcasting. The development of a new mode of communication posed new problems in that the audience was no longer a crowd in any sense. Members of the listening public had to learn how to listen and later to watch the new technologies, but producers also had *to learn how to address*, to speak to, this new form of social entity. In a culture of mass entertainment conceptualisations of public anonymity lie at the heart of our experience of collective life. Frith argues that the development of notions of public service broadcasting was not a simple battle between educationalists and commercialists – it was more an attempt to utilise a new form of leisure as a means of communal integration (an attempt that is of course entirely consistent with the nineteenth century ideology of rational recreation), a 'model of how entertainment could work to bind together a community that underlay the BBC's vision of a "common culture" in the 1920s and 1930s' (Frith op. cit. p. 113). The appropriate attitudes and interests were presumed to be those normatively characteristic of the middle-class family: 'Entertainment's contribution to these ideas of democracy, neighbourliness, the community's personality, lay in its organisation of family life' (Frith op. cit. p. 110).

In speaking to the normality of the mass public a pragmatic consensus was presupposed and articulated not just in the discourses of public life, news, current affairs and social conflict, but equally forcefully in the life-world of the cultural horizons of suburban anonymity. The mass public was spoken to in their domestic atomisation, although the latter term should not be taken to imply alienation or anomie. Rather the fragments of a mass audience were drawn into a national community through the security of middle-brow taste as in contemporary films, literature, theatre and music – see for example the representation of working-class culture in the wildly successful Gracie Fields films of the 1930s (Richards 1984; Jones 1987). The immediacy of communion for an anonymous audience was manifested through a personalisation of ordinariness, a dissolution of auratic distance: 'The problem was to fit entertainment as occasion into an intimate routine, . . . The solution lay in the development of a particular sort of *voice* – intimate and authoritative – and a particular sort of *personality* – relaxing and knowable. The radio star was public figure as private friend' (Frith op. cit. p. 115, *sic*). The paradox of public culture is that as membership of households has become more heterogeneous, in terms of the ties that link members, the family has become increasingly idealised as the 'normal' basis for domestic life.

The notion of voice in public drama therefore refers to the discursive presuppositions of collective experience as well as the more immediately available manner of address. The social entities which order and structure personal experience require ways of speaking as themselves, in other words as dramatic resources, in order to constitute the type of entity they can be spoken to be. Another example – I have described the ways of speaking concept through reference to types of formalisation. This can be illustrated by differences in the nature of a letter. A letter to a friend or relative differs in tone and style as well as substantive concerns from one written as a public utterance. A letter written to a newspaper of record is the nearest version we have of a contribution to the public sphere in its ideal typical form. Many of the letters written to the broadsheet press in Britain in the late twentieth century still carry the marks of an obligation to authoritative seriousness. For this purpose a public voice is being used by the author and in so doing a particular form of public discourse is displayed. The letters are open to all to read and the correspondence column is open to all who might wish to contribute, but in practice overlapping circles of interest and influence are focussed by each topic in each newspaper. In this way specific publics are alerted or mobilised within the immeasurable fiction of public opinion. In this context an appeal to personal experience or authority, by for example a High Court Judge, will carry more weight than an analogous appeal from a reader of the *Sun*.

And yet the concept of 'weight' here can be said to embody an acceptance of the conventional view of public opinion as something that really exists which has been so scrupulously avoided so far. The processes of opinion formation – both what it might be and when it might be said to have become so – have only been explored by accounts which work within existing fictions of publics and the people. I cannot remedy this lack and however much one points to the reflexive character of claims to public opinion, there are circumstances in which such claims are clearly self-fulfilling prophecies. The point can only be that in the process of constituting an opinion, as in constituting a fashion, there are clearly gatekeepers, influentials, and privileged points and moments of access. The public so expressed is not and is never expected to be homogeneous or composed of members of equal significance (weight).

The public is therefore a rhetorical figure, both as a mode of address and as a form of social being. The public is a cultural category not just because it is a work of art but more significantly because in its use it trades on shared understandings and interpretations. I have previously pointed to a number of substantial parallels between what I called 'the epistemological stance of popular art and the activities of an ethnographer' (Chaney 1979 p. 10). What I meant by this comparison is that those producing and enjoying popular art are, in ways that they might not immediately acknowledge, exploring, representing and more provocatively constituting their own culture. Popular culture is endlessly reflexive of the form of life within which it is used. Since that publication there has developed a more forceful theorisation of the rhetorical character of ethnography within anthropological theory. Introducing a set of papers on the poetics as well as the politics of ethnography, Clifford writes:

> If 'culture' is not an object to be described, neither is it a unified corpus of symbols and meanings that can be definitively interpreted. Culture is contested, temporal and emergent. Representation and explanation – both by insiders and outsiders – is implicated in this emergence.
>
> (Clifford 1986 p. 19)

Writing (or speaking) a culture is a rhetorical process, it can be done self-consciously in ways that stress the neutrality and authority of authorship or less deliberately in ritual, myth or drama (Brown 1987).

Ethnography is a way of writing a culture (or a form of life within a particular cultural setting). It is usually couched within the authority of scholarship or even science and is driven by a concern to understand, or provide an explanation for, the form of life that is the subject matter. We are then brought back to the nature of representation, the attempt that is to capture some aspects of the flow of human experience in ways that are faithful to the forms of that experience. A representation is, then, more than a likeness or a resemblance in the sense of being a portrait. We can represent, for example working-class life, through plays, novels, films, memoirs and sociological studies and then comparatively discuss their distinctive strengths and weaknesses (as does Laing 1986 for the period 1945–1960), with only a residual sense of facilitating recognition. We represent *reflexively* to make sense of the ways we might form or shape interpretive strategies.

Documentary is a genre of representation that is particularly germane to any consideration of public discourse. In the previous chapter I made some notes on aspects of documentary photography, I am less interested in this section in the iconography of representation and more in the way a documentary formulates its project of representation (I have explored some aspects of the relationships between documentary and public opinion in a paper published in 1981B). The audience is engaged as members of a collective who have some right to feel responsible for or involved with the individuals whose story is being told. It is this presumption of the public relevance of individual circumstance that gives documentary its distinctiveness as a genre (and why very often individual circumstance is treated as allegorical and thereby of normative significance).

In a preface, Corner (1986) treats this sense of public address lying at the heart of the documentary endeavour as the sociological dimension of documentaries, a dimension which clearly supports the idea of documentary as a form of mass communication. More practically, the technology of mass communication is presupposed in documentary, as: 'it is the technological capacity to record the visual and/or aural elements of a particular piece of the world which provides the primary *evidential* quality sought by documentary accounts' (Corner op. cit. p. viii *sic*). The term 'documentary' was only formed in the 1920s as a response to new means of apprehension and new forms of perception (Stott 1973; Chaney 1981A) (there are of course precursor instances which can be detected before the term was developed, cf. Paget 1990). Documentary is therefore an instance of one of the discourses of public life bridging the domains of entertainment and politics with a discourse of citizenship.

It is important to note that there is not 'a' documentary project, and indeed the history of documentaries is the history of recurrent attempts to reformulate the meaning of the term. What, however, has been a persistent and necessary feature of these documentaries has been a concern with the public that is more or less explicitly being addressed. We should expect that this self-consciousness would be more apparent in a documentary movement than a particular film or performance, and in the work of the early British documentary movement in the 1930s, Mass Observation, we find the metaphor of an instrument of mass communication being used as a way of both characterising their work and as a way of locating the public as subject and as audience: 'Through Mass Observation you can already listen-in to the movements of popular habit and opinion. The receiving set is there, and every month makes it more effective' (Madge and Harrisson 1939 quoted in Chaney and Pickering 1986). The documentary movement was therefore a means of apprehending (listening-in to) the public and the means by which the public could know itself – it could act, as they said, as 'the voice of the people' (amongst the several accounts of the early years of the Mass Observation movement see Pickering and Chaney 1986).

Although there are many dimensions to this project that could be explored, the most immediately relevant is a recognition (however confused and uncertain it was in Mass Observation writing) that different dimensions of public culture were being brought into being, I more generally use the term being constituted, through the process of representation – or as in the terms of this chapter 'form of address'. Amongst those responsible for initiating the idea of Mass Observation, it is clear from contemporary articles that they believed that the seemingly simple project of observing everyday life can transform the literary activity of the observer from that of privileged individualism to that of co-author. In an avant-garde attempt to rupture the recuperative power of public culture they argued that if a documentary or ethnography is to engage with new social entities, then the 'reality' of collective experience will be found to lie in the random juxtapositions, the collage, of everyday happenings as much as in the hierarchies of official representations:

> The proper arrangement of cultural symbols and artifacts is constantly placed in doubt . . . . The ethnographic attitude must continually pose these sorts of questions, composing and decomposing culture's 'natural' hierarchies and relationships.
> (Clifford 1988 p. 132)

In ways that anticipate post-modern themes in the deconstruction of representation, contemporary movements in France and Britain, in the former case in a manner that is more self-consciously intellectually aware in its use of socio-anthropological and surrealist sources, both raised issues concerning the dramatisation of public experience. Those involved in the Mass Observation movement in

Britain and with the College de Sociologie in Paris (Hollier 1988) both offered the possibility that the ideology of social order is more effectively subverted by querying the sufficiency of representation than intermittent outbursts of spectacular rage. They also both chose the concept of ritual as a vantage-point from which the relations of dramatisation could be unpicked. The promise of their initiative both for our understanding of fiction and drama as well as for our sense of social order is only gradually being realised.

THE DISCOURSE OF ACTUALITY

A concern with the representation of public life necessarily draws attention to the generation, organisation and publication of those happenings in public life that are generally covered by the composite category of news. Contemporary news is not equivalent to public discourse which would cover many types of publication and genre. It is rather more accurate to say that news is a category of, or form of, or genre of, public discourse. We would therefore expect to find certain generic features to this type of writing (and of course speaking), features that are more usually referred to as 'news values' (cf. Tuchman 1978, and see also Darnton 1975 and Schudson 1982).

The concept of genre in this context is immediately controversial because it implies predictability, recurrent features and orderly characteristics. The romantic adventure of journalism usually implies an exploratory quest to discover the way the world is – and to bring the random, the unexpected and the dramatic into the domestic ambit of private experience. Above all, a commitment to accident is a theme of journalistic practice whereas the sociological perspective offers a study 'of the generation of news [which] aims to find and make plausible an order behind this sense of accident (and to understand as ideology journalists' failure to recognize such an order)' (Schudson 1989 p. 264). I do not intend to characterise the genre at this stage. I am less immediately interested in what sort of thing news is than in the news as a way of speaking to publics and how we might understand the significance of this form of address for social order.

One reason for the multitude of news studies has been a widely shared feeling that news as a common resource acts as a mode of legitimation, in fact the central legitimating resource: 'Clearly the apparatus of cultural manufacture and distribution is such as to provide explanations, symbols and rhetoric which make the social order appear both inevitable and just' (Golding 1981 p. 63). The interesting element in Golding's argument (and he is being used as example of a very general tendency in the field), is that broadcast news or any form of news is a core element in the explanations, symbols and rhetoric which justify social order. One aspect of why this approach is so widespread is that it is driven by a functional necessity. If you begin as Golding does with the assertion that 'The contradictory coexistence of gross inequalities and the apparent acceptance of them by the large majority of those worst affected [in industrial societies] continues to be *the key problem* for modern sociology' (*ibid.*, emphasis added), then this problem clearly generates a need for an explanation of acceptance.

It is also worth noting that Golding's formulation presupposes that there is a functional interest, by those advantaged by gross inequalities, in securing the acceptance of those disadvantaged; so that there is a determining (and thereby explanatory) force driving the mechanisms of the cultural apparatus: 'from a systemic point of view, the features of non-reflexive consciousness appear as logical expression of what the vested interests of the social order require' (Dahlgren 1981 p. 111). This apparatus would only be successful if it is popular. Therefore the popular as it entails and displays acceptance, or acquiescence, in a rhetoric of justification, by definition becomes in this perspective a language of exploitation – the popular becomes a synopsis of 'the key problem' for modern sociology.

The majority of news studies have obviously been accounts of various forms of news as displayed through readings or analyses of characteristic content, sometimes held to derive from the ownership of news organisations. Although this research has displayed dominant themes and limitations in the versions of normality available through news discourse, there should not be a naive expectation of objectivity – a professional mythology (Schiller 1981). The sociological problem with the development of news as a form of public discourse is not that news is not an objective resource for the rational imperatives of the public sphere. It is rather that there are significant implications for public culture in themes of social description. For example, in their study of the reporting of riots in Britain in 1981 Hansen and Murdock (1985) attempt to locate specific themes, such as the presumed gullibility of crowds (as in other 'marginal' groups) within a much broader historical canvas of patronising discourse. This discourse not only informed political and judicial utterances and actions but more specifically dominated paper voices through 'a series of mutually reinforcing oppositions which serve to depoliticize events, deny their social causes, and to reconstruct them as an unprecedented outbreak of criminal violence' (Hansen and Murdock op. cit. p. 236).

As an alternative to accounts of the news which have been focussed as it were 'from above', there has developed a considerable body of work which has studied the production of news from below. In these studies the organisation of agencies within which news is collected in order to be published, and the nature of bureaucratic constraints which both constrain individual creativity and ensure a predictable character to the news that is published and broadcast (e.g. Fishman 1980) is emphasised. Although this work has provided an essential corrective to claims of the media as public watchdog, it should not be thought to be surprising or sociologically problematic that news as public discourse is conventionally cast within the symbolic forms of institutional imagery and stereotypes. The orthodoxies of popular fiction are rarely subverted or contradicted by news accounts and indeed organisations such as the police or hospital staff may find it necessary to cast news accounts of their work in the dramatic categories of media discourse. Ericson *et al.* (1989 p. 379) discussing how news sources negotiate for control over issues and presentation point out that 'The bad-news formula – with its related core ingredients of dramatization, sensationalism, personalization, and focus on the unexpected – must be accepted as the limitation of news discourse', and within those limits the formula can be exploited to organisational advantage.

If the focus of studies of news production is kept within the boundaries of what we can call the sociology of organisations, these studies could be seen as another instance of sociologists discovering that what people think they are doing offers only a very limited account of what they are actually doing. If, however, the focus is shifted to consequences of production procedures for the way the world is talked about, that is the consequences of news-making for news content. It becomes in effect a study in the sociology of knowledge. The change of focus is possible because news does not just tell us about its subject matter – it tells us through its own display how that subject matter is reliably known: 'News provides knowledge about who are the authorized knowers, where they are in the knowledge hierarchy, and what claims they make to knowledge' (Ericson *et al.* op. cit. p. 395). Thus there is a triple process of news telling what is known (for example about the dangers from terrorism), who are the authorised knowers (in this case *inter alia* representatives of state agencies), and the social framework within which their authority is legitimated (here the setting of a political agenda), with the consequence that 'news . . . incorporates important social dramas pertaining to community and democracy, order and change . . . News acknowledges order as it is preferred by members of the knowledge élites, and creates the class of political spectators' (Ericson *et al.* op. cit. p. 398).

The common theme which pulls together many of the strands in sociological studies of news is that a reality or a version of reality is being constructed in news accounts which is not governed by a need to correspond with real reality. The governing principles governing news realities are held to be variously ideology, professional norms or bureaucratic imperatives or some combination of them all. Although reality is frequently used as a reference to the subjects of news reports (e.g. Tuchman 1978), in practice it is normality that is the real subject matter. Whether it is crowds or local government or crime waves that are being constructed (in the sense of being put together through symbolic resources), the reiterative frame of reference is the predictability of accounting procedures: 'Reporters clean up and repair flawed bureaucratic proceedings in their news stories. Their model of cleanliness, orderliness, and normalcy is a bureaucratic one' (Fishman 1980 p. 135).

The concept of construction then implies a frame of normality – the two are interdependent as they are used in relation to news discourse, they underpin our sense that news is a distinct genre of public culture. In order to bring the characteristics of the genre out more clearly the concept of constructing normality can be subdivided into three component elements of: knowing; knowers; and events. This framework presupposes that news is a form of report which can be substantiated, the report deals with places and actors that can be given some gloss of familiarity. A new revolutionary leader can be given an identity in terms that share a reader's frame of reference, and a difference in patterns of religious affiliation can be located within a familiar category of fundamentalism. Of course there will be recurrent conflicts in which members will attempt to contest or re-write the terms of their institutionalisation. But in order to do so they will have to draw upon other dimensions of institutionalised knowing. Key elements in how occurrences are to be known are strategic semantic markers as for example in relation to political violence (Taylor 1986).

The process of knowing in relation to news is then the provision of a set of terms and a narrative structure within which an event or set of events becomes reportable. This is not say that there is only one knowing frame for any particular event, news is contentious because it is inherent in the genre that any report is provisional. If the language of knowing is highly formulaic in that actors, roles, actions and motives are all articulated in a vocabulary that transcends the idiosyncrasies of particular experience, then sophisticated performers can violate category expectations, reverse their roles and ironicise their image (Klapp 1964). Of course these shifts in dramatic casting will often be involuntary and stem from events beyond actors' control but there are other re-scriptings which are deliberate and knowing as in rock stars playing with gender and sexuality. We can then take over Cohen and Taylor's use of scripts as 'the battleground and launching pad for identities' and particularly their notion of master scripts as cultural resources which structure and organise particular events (Cohen and Taylor 1976). The script is another version of the genre which organises what the event will have turned out to be an instance of.

Knowing is done by those who have some privileged access to the events in question – the knowers. Naively we might expect that the participants will be authorities but they might for various reasons be unable to furnish a report, the criminal is only exceptionally available as an authority on crime. In practice, participants are hierarchically organised in terms of status and authority so that certain positions can structure the knowing and the reports of others even those more personally involved in the event. For example, in a fire in an underground railway station the warranted authorities will be representatives of fire services and other emergency services. Other experts such as agents of the railway company and authorities on fires will contribute to the report and this weight of expertise will frame the more emotional contributions of those rescued and the relatives of those still to be rescued.

The grammar of reporting whether it is in print, sound broadcasting or a film report will articulate these differences in status and provide for different modes of presentation and interrogation. Orchestrating a variety of voices in reporting will be the author or reporter who may themselves be framed by a presenter who, in broadcast news, synthesises further levels of input, expertise and authority. In print journalism in keeping with norms of objectivity and sustaining a distinction between fact and value, the reporter has traditionally sought a dispassionate voice. In broadcasting this neutrality has become a middle ground of normality in which the presenters usurp the popular voice to articulate the commonsense of accidents, scandals and disasters (Kumar 1975 distinguishes three levels of presentation in the BBC in relation to different types of legitimating authority; the character of this form of celebrity will be returned to in the next section).

It might seem that the constitutive significance of different forms of knowing in conjunction with differences in the authority of knowers is such that public events are merely vehicles for different strategies of news telling. In that the events have actually happened to some degree they are not completely subject to the narrative domain of their telling, but more significantly a world of public events marks a transformation in the characteristic manner of the being in the world of reader/listener. Events are occurrences given significance through an interpretive frame, principally a biographical narrative which can be told in a multitude of ways to a multitude of audiences (see for example Bruner's 1987 study of biographical narratives). In the discourse of actuality in public culture a new (compared to the local knowledge of pre-media culture) form of collective memory is being expressed: 'the content of an individual's conceptions of the history and the future of his or her collectivity comes to depend on the processes by which public events get constructed as resources for discourse in public matters' (Molotch and Lester 1974 p. 103; see also Lester 1980).

The generation of public events involves a shift in temporal axis from a narrative frame through time to one organised through the simultaneity of events:

> What is the essential literary convention of the newspaper? . . .
> Why are these events so juxtaposed? What connects them to each other? . . . The date at the top of the newspaper, the single most important emblem on it, provides the essential connection – the steady onward clocking of homogeneous, empty time.
>
> (Anderson 1983 p. 37)

The logic of symbolic time, the cultural time of publications and programmes, is that not just the meaning of the events but the participation of their audience is transformed. The event is framed by a dramatic order which seems natural and inevitable but is simultaneously arbitrary and impervious to idiosyncratic use: 'The privatized reception of media events is typically *fragmentary*, in the sense that receptive activities typically take place in locales which are segregated and dispersed in time and space' (Thompson 1990 p. 243). There is therefore, as Anderson argues, a deep analogy between the imagination of actuality in news and the imagination of community in national identity.

The basis of the dramatic order in news is that the events in a newspaper are collected by their publication together but not only do they lack a narrative logic, also the manner in which they are read (used) is likely to be incoherent and arbitrary. Newspaper editors will attempt to repair these issues as Harold Evans in a training manual has recognised:

> The problem [of newspaper design] is to communicate within the same physical context not one message but a series of disconnected messages of infinitely varying significance, and to do this with speed, ease and economy in a recognisably consistent style.
>
> (quoted in Rushmer 1990 p. 45)

'The problem' is not, however, a fault of poor design but inherent in the public sphere. As publics are reflexively constituted in forms of communication which relativise authorial coherence, so the 'voice' of that communication becomes less that of specific authors or editors and becomes more that of the mode of communication in itself; or more precisely the phenomenological stance of the implied reader of that mode of communication.

There is, of course, a class of media events which function as festive occasions – they are given a licence to interrupt, and thereby heighten, the discourse of actuality: 'Postponing their programs to make room for the occasion, the networks interrupt social life, depriving it of the rhythms conferred by non-stop broadcasting in its function as collective clock' (Dayan and Katz 1988 p. 162). Although ideological in that they are couched in a rhetoric of consensus, media events are frequently ambiguous because the happenings reported acquire their meanings in the processes of dramatisation. Media events therefore invite an hermeneutic engagement by their audience: 'The interruption it [a media event] represents triggers social reflexivity' (Dayan and Katz op. cit. p. 182). In part this happens because a media event is very rarely enclosed within a single cultural form but is rather being continually echoed and developed in inter-textuality with other media (the notion of intertextuality has been developed by Bennett and Woollacott 1987 in relation to the stardom of a cultural myth such as James Bond).

There are two features of the practice of news retailing, the discourse of actuality, as a form of knowledge which help to identify the voice of the public in contemporary mass communication. The first is the significance of arbitrary associations in public discourse and the second the consequences of structural amnesia. They can both be explicated through equivalences between the narrative performance of mythical tales and a narrative of news, and contrasts between them both and the authored narratives of literary fiction.

The first reason for an analogy between myth and news is in their lack of structural coherence. The narratives of myths and news are equivalently 'anonymous' in that the tellers are voices for, or in a fundamental sense the puppets of, mysterious concerns shrouded 'back stage' (although we should recognise of course that some would claim a deep structural logic underlying a corpus of myths). The commitment to objectivity in news is a belief that the author, even if s/he is identified, is speaking on behalf of a more authoritative command. In contrast to the authored perspective of a novel (at least in its classic form), narratives of myth and news bring together unlikely conjunctions of occasion, character and consequence. An arbitrary bricolage of significance and association is characteristic of post-modern narratives, but this is not as recent an innovation as has been claimed. Rather it becomes a characteristic feature of the dramatistic staging and articulation of public opinion and public discourse in a culture of mass politics.

The second feature of news I want to describe I call the consequences of structural amnesia. By this I mean that a focus upon simultaneity and novelty induces a radical indifference to the past. This is not to say that the past is not a valuable, indeed, frequently overwhelming resource for nostalgia, but a sentimental dramatisation of the past is not an historical perspective. Nostalgia is alien to history as cumulative unfolding, to accounts which focus upon institutional structures rather than personality and allegorical idealisation. Nostalgia is alien to historical perspectives taken as the foundation for any account of social structure and ideology: 'broadcast news is . . . inherently incapable of providing a portrayal of social change or of displaying the operation of power in and between societies' (Golding 1981 p. 80). Structural amnesia means that the past exists as a series of spectacular tableaux and allegorical figures, so that, for example, Hitler loses an historical specificity and becomes a generalised reference for all subsequent charismatic leaders of totalitarian states. The sheer flow of actuality that continuous live television coverage provides has usurped the traditional role of print journalism, but precisely because it is mediating public events into private homes it is peculiarly susceptible to government control, and its news is inherently anodyne (Fisk *The Independent* 8/1/92 p. 13).

I do not think it is stretching terms too far to point to a parallel between societies without history, as in pre-modern village societies, and mass politics. In village society gossip 'is composed of this daily recounting combined with lifelong mutual familiarities. By this means a village informally constructs a continuous communal history of itself: a history in which everybody portrays, in which everybody is portrayed, and in which the act of portrayal never stops' (Connerton 1989 p. 17). In the social formations of mass politics and entertainment news may be seen to be serving the function of gossip as the voice of collective memory in which everybody may be famous for at least fifteen minutes.

I began this section by quoting Michael Schudson's contrast between a journalistic commitment to chance and a sociological search for order. I believe that we can see now that the two aspirations are not incompatible, indeed that they coexist. The character of news as narrative genre is marked by incongruous association and allegorical dramatisation, and yet the performance of this genre gives coherence through the forms of its telling. More precisely, the public, as the imagined social context within which these narratives are presumed to make sense acts as a form of ritual. By which I mean that the ways in which the public can be addressed act as a ritual frame, so that the news can be seen as a mode of ceremonialisation:

> to consider the newspaper as a vehicle for symbolic forms in which large parts are occasionally pre-empted for ritual performances or as itself a symbolic form which occasionally takes itself seriously as the 'Voice of the People' or 'The Voice of Britain'.
>
> (Elliott 1980 p. 171)

The idea that news functions as a form of order directs our attention to the ways in which the practice of news may provide a voice of normality while articulating change. The illusory contrast between journalistic chance and ideological order is echoed in a further contradiction between Connerton's theme of how collective entities such as societies remember themselves and 'the very principle of modernity itself [which] denies the idea of life as a structure of celebrated recurrence' (Connerton 1989 p. 64). In the public dramas of mass politics there is an inherent tension between narrative disintegration and a rhetoric for identity. There is therefore a good reason for expecting there to be circumstances in which tension can be seen to be being avoided or displaced by being shifted to grounds of possible reconciliation in ritual recurrence and mythic characterisation. We need studies of what I have called 'the distinctive language through which collective ceremonies are constructed and reported, the language of imagination in media accounts' (Chaney 1987A p. 122).

The orderly characteristics to news stories detected in sociological accounts are, then, more than stylistic features generated by professional socialisation and training procedures. They are also more than generic features of distinct story types such as murder, royal romance or international diplomacy. The order in news is a way of detecting and describing certain dramatic conventions. The reason for calling them dramatic rather than fictive or rhetorical is that they provide for the organisation of the lived environment of the audience. They govern the space or the stage within which the cast of public life can act and gives their actions a plausibility and dramatic verisimilitude. It is in this sense that dramatic conventions in news telling operate as in effect a 'vocabulary of motives' (to use Gerth and Mills' phrase (1956 Chapter 5)). This applies as much to professional or full-time actors such as politicians as to occasional and unintended performers such as those individuals caught up in tragedy, disaster or the inconvenience of interruptions to air flights. The conventions of news more seriously mark off a symbolic space as a zone distinct in character from the local or private worlds of the audience.

The democratic structures of mass politics, in order to sustain the fiction of the mandate of the people for government policies, require three interdependent opportunities. They are: the untrammelled access to information of the populace as the basis for public discourse; the possibility of the presentation of competing perspectives in public discourse as the basis for the mobilisation of public opinion; and mechanisms for the institutionalisation of publics within political structures. It is not my purpose to attempt to assess the extent to which any of these can be said to exist in any democracy, although it seems that any claim to meet these criteria in any instance must be heavily qualified. We as members of the public have an untrammelled right to access to the public sphere but our access is as members of the audience looking on looking at versions of ourselves. The range and flow of information may be far greater than anything previously imagined so that the dramatis personae of public life are more intimately accessible to our personal judgement and identification. But this has not meant that our participation in public life has correspondingly increased, rather that we have become as vicarious spectators more engagingly caught up in the verisimilitude of the spectacle.

PUBLIC FIGURES

The theme of identification introduced at the end of the previous section prompts a concern with the forms of identification in different discourses of public and popular. The argument here is that the values, lifestyles (mores) and pleasures which constitute the culture of a group will be concretised and made specific and, perhaps most importantly, given dramatic force through personification. By this I mean that an individual performer can provide a means of affiliation or identification through their dramatic identity so that members of the audience can feel themselves caught up with or at least recognise themselves within that culture. It could be argued that this process is a universal feature of dramatisation, although there will be differences in whether the performer is playing an allegorical or more individualised role. While this is true, there are distinctive features to a culture of modernity which have generated significant emphases upon identification of, and with, a continually changing galaxy of public figures.

Some of the reasons for this claim of the significance of personification are inherent in the public drama of modernity and will be grounded in the architecture of this book. By this I mean that public drama is both a conceptual device for describing the dynamics of social order and a metaphor for the transformation of space inscribed through social structure. The book has an architecture in that guiding us through the transformation of space the theme of each chapter is a different dimension of performance. As these are related one to the other so some of the interrelationships of order and structure should be displayed. In the dimensions of performance discussed so far recurrent themes have been the re-writing of the means of marking space and time so that they have become increasingly abstract, arbitrary and symbolic.

My premise is that in a world that is simultaneously meaningless, lacking conventional forms of regulation and coherence, and meaningful, in that the ascription of cultural meaning is more clearly seen in modernity to be a human enterprise, the paradox can more easily be reconciled through dramatisation. In what Williams (1975) has called 'a dramatised society', the relationships between drama and social action are acted out by performers who are resolutely naturalistic even if the framing narrative is fantastic or ritualised.

In terms of public discourse the voice through which publics are addressed is diffused through an intimacy of association with a multitude of performers. As audiences for media of mass communication are by definition anonymous to each other and to those who address them, they have been studied as markets, 'as objects of knowledges' – a phrase used by Morris (1988 p. 200) in relation to the positioning of women in the discourses of marketing and social knowledge. (Morris also recognises that any attempt to 'evade' the authorised knowledge of constitutive discourse will need: 'to produce a mode of [alternative] address', *ibid.*) In bridging the spaces between their own discourse and the heterogeneity of popular experience the public voices of mass communication speak to and attempt to surround and contain those who are privatised and are users rather than makers of the public domain. (These terms should not be read as implying that these relationships are the same or immutable in all cultural forms; as Morris also points out in the production of meaning we need to study how 'classical theories of modernism fall short of women's modernity'; Morris op. cit. p. 202); in Radway's 1987 study of the involvement of women readers in romance literature there is a spirited rejection of the view of audience as cultural dopes.)

The traditional modes of public address at, for example, a public meeting or state ceremonial or theatrical excess have been recognised to be subverted and made obsolete by the intimacy of media of presentation, paradigmatically television, which transcend conventions of dramatic staging and provide ever more intrusive engagement. The practice of politics has been transformed as more adept performers have realised that it is inappropriate to address the audience as collectivity but that each member can be spoken to individually (a discovery made virtually synonymously by Baldwin in Britain and Roosevelt in the USA). The dramatic metaphor of front stage and back stages becomes superfluous in forms of dramatisation where dramatic conventions are infinitely ironicised as resources for a play of style. In consumer culture the dominance of materialism can be subverted by being turned into what Chambers (1986 p. 7) has called the: 'secret language of style', most characteristically in youth cultures where all artefacts are symbolic resources signifying arbitrarily. It is unsurprising in this context that those who have been committed to structural transformation through mass action (conventionally understood, it should be noted, as an almost exclusively masculine form of action), have been most reluctant to accept these changes in the appropriateness of different modes of political address. Because the political publics of mass politics have become an abstract crowd, the dramatisations of address in mass communication are suspected of presupposing a consensus of normality.

The other implication of all-pervasive means of reporting the activities of public figures, which effectively dissolve functional distinctions between front and back stages, is that a new discourse of collusion develops. The paradox is that rather than an excess of public surveillance leading to new norms of public sobriety, the ubiquity of representation is used to sustain dramatic identities. No news source is able to take upon themselves the responsibility of a sustained assault to show that the president of a country is a fool, or a liar or a satyr, or whatever. There is therefore a ghetto of collusion in which the enormity of a gulf between the front stage of identity of public figures and the intimacies of back stage are known to professionals, but are judged too disruptive of audience expectations for the discourses of public life. There is in this silence an echo of the paradoxical consequence of continuous live television coverage noted in the previous section. Again, rather than broadening the terms of public debate, all-news channels have proved particularly susceptible to news management and of failing to question the orthodoxies of state power.

It may seem absurd to point to a collusion in sanctity when so much of popular journalism consists of scandals in which the sexual peccadilloes of the rich and the famous are exposed. The justification of my argument is that those thus humbled are rarely the powerful but members of that crowd of mountebanks and charlatans who constitute the gossip of celebrity life. (When through force of circumstance the powerful are forced into exposure as liars and crooks the shock to political order is such that rituals of re-integration have to be devised – see Alexander's 1988 discussion of 'Watergate'.) The second point is that there is an ambiguous line between heroism and villainy for these figures. Their alcohol problems, their homosexuality, their association with known criminals, will all be known for a long time. These 'failings' will be colluded in for so long until for reasons that may be particular to each case there is a shift in casting and a pack is let loose in favour of the previously secret.

Public figures are as Klapp (1964) has recognised symbolic leaders, their identity constructed out of dramatic resources. Their public status is not given in a once-for-all way by an organisational context but is rather provisional, dependent upon means of presentation, liable to be ruptured or to be re-framed in ways they might or might not be able to control. Identity for public figures is therefore more clearly a performance, an enterprise whose authenticity is at least open to being questioned. There is no reason to distinguish between public figures in terms of some being more 'authentic' than others. There may be differences in style between domains, as between politicians, royalty, sports people and entertainers, but they share a common stage.

The self-conscious creativity of public identity leads to curious problems of framing for more self-conscious performers who might seek to sustain a distinction between performance in different settings and selfhood, such as certain theatrical performers. There is, however, an inevitable elision between role and self, particularly for performers in dramas of everyday experience such as televisual soap operas, with the self becoming subsumed in the role. In this respect it is reasonable to suggest that the low status usually accorded to film stars as actors stems from a feeling that their identity is subordinate to and swamped in a stereotype role. Therefore the publicity industry which is an inevitable part of stardom, and which is the basis of their news value as public figures, makes them marketing strategies rather than creative artists.

The idea of stardom leads to a further type of status as public figure. I have already made reference to announcers as mediators between public and discourse, but announcers are members of a broader category which includes a host of ways of being a personality or celebrity. As examples we can point to those introducing talk shows, being a pundit on something(s), having an idiosyncratic expertise or an idiosyncratic manner in presenting a more common skill, or more generally having once been identified the fact of identity is sufficient to generate further occasions for identity. In Lowenthal's study (1961 Chapter 4) of changes in the characteristics of those portrayed to a mass audience as heroes of public life, he notes that: 'we called the heroes of the past "idols of production": we feel entitled to call the present-day magazine heroes "idols of consumption"' (p.115). Lowenthal writing in the 1940s, and basing his account on an analysis of the content of biographies in popular magazines, is principally concerned to condemn the values of what he calls passive consumption rather than '"the talents for creating, organizing, and directing"' (p.123). We do not have to share his commitment to entrepreneurial productivity to recognise a distinct mode of identity.

The supplementary industries of being interviewed, pictured, described, explained are not a bridge between audience and public figures, they are the ways in which personalities are constituted and sustained. The effectiveness of identity construction here is that any and all of us feel able and are willing to pass judgements on the motives of public characters. Thus a new Russian leader or a Pope can be 'trusted' or derided in millions of domestic sitting-rooms. The personalisation of politics seeps out from national leaders and their constituency to a global audience. More complexly, there seems to be a process of sympathetic identification either for or against either vamping popular singers or sports stars who violate norms of fair play.

There is an ambiguous relationship between this class of celebrities and the more traditional sociological category of charisma. The ideal type of charismatic leadership taken from classical theorists is of an individual who, either by possession of some divine attributes or through a willingness to act violently, is able to focus resentments and offer the promise of a new order through the redemptive grace of the force of their personal vision. A stress upon transformation is not irrelevant to democratic political orders, but seems unnecessarily restricted, even in relation to political leadership, and does not really address charismatic status in other institutionalised areas such as religion, sport and entertainment. In all these areas it seems more appropriate to suggest that the nature of the appeal of contemporary celebrity status is to forms of re-communalisation – ways in which individuals can feel themselves to be a member of a collectivity with recognisable norms, order and existential validity: 'The stars, in representing community ideals associated with what it means to be a person in America, are experienced as *individualized social types*

– a mode of being that reconciles personal identity with social identity, and individualism with conformity' (Reeves 1988 p. 150, *sic*).

Sports stars, television personalities, politicians and even terrorists, etc., constitute a galaxy of public figures who share many of the features of traditional spectacular theatricality. That is, they are highly stylised, rather conservative once identity has been formulated, and are in essence figures of display rather than introspection. Although stardom is a marketing strategy for mass entertainment industries, this does not explain the appeal of particular celebrities, and in particular the ambiguous appeal of anti-heroes – 'bad girls' such as Jean Harlow and Margaret Thatcher. It seems too simple or tautological to say that the constructed character of stars' identities works solely as a fantastic escape from reality. We could rather say that it is the wealth of tangible detail we know about the lives of celebrities, it is the consistency with which their personal relationships are caught up in the web of public identity, all of this gives them an existential reality which is perhaps more substantial than everyday experience. It is the essential paradox of fantasy entertainment, as it is of consumer culture in general, that the utopian dream is not articulated through other-worldly experience but is very firmly grounded in recognisable features of ordinary life. Each celebrity's work at the real/unreal transforming divide is distinctive and it is therefore hard to generalise from individual examples. What seems generally true is that style is the key to identity and style works through a compelling mixture of tangible detail and persuasive rhetoric.

In discussing public identity two dimensions have been identified – authenticity and fantasy. The pairing is intriguing because they are not opposites and yet in this context they make a revealing contrast. In looking for celebrities whose identities can be trusted as authentic the audience can be said to be looking for people whose use of a public stage can be seen to stem from motives, ideals and attitudes which are essentially ordinary. Politicians usually strive to sustain a common touch and like to be seen to be able to speak to the vulgar and undertake vulgar actions. One of the best studies of this appeal is provided by Merton's study of Kate Smith's war-bond drive, itself one of the first studies of mass persuasion (collected in 1949). Merton argues that Smith's extraordinary success was possible because 'For many, she has become the symbol of a moral leader who "demonstrates" by her own behaviour that there need be no discrepancy between appearance and reality in the sphere of human relationships' (Merton op. cit. p. 145).

To unquestioningly accept that celebrities are popular as figures who exist out-of-this-world is to take one form of publicity too literally. As Dyer (1979 pp. 48–50), amongst others, has pointed out the ideology of popular success usually attempts to reconcile the uniqueness of the star with an emphasis that their ascent to greatness involved a mixture of luck and hard work and that the celebrity maintains a popular perspective. In Lowenthal's study (1961 p. 127) of 'mass idols' he emphasised that the biographies of these heroes demonstrates that: 'Success has become an accidental and irrational event . . . The outstanding has become the proved specimen of the average'.

The tenor of these notes on public figures is that in being identifiable, so that they are noticed when they are seen in settings other than the stage upon which they achieved public status, does not mean that they become role models. There may, of course, be a variety of forms of incidental learning from dramatic displays but that is inherent in analogous experience being represented in public discourse. Identification of celebrities is an identification *of* a world that is shared in common rather than an identification *with* a celebrity as someone upon whom identity can be modelled. The world of public discourse is therefore glamorous, frequently outrageous, literally extraordinary but it is simultaneously domesticated and made accessible through the attractions and resonances of the shifting populace who carry and articulate a variety of styles of being in public. In this sense, then, the celebrities of the public stage provide a series of reference points through which a multitude of publics can reflexively identify themselves. It could be said that celebrities provide a voice through which they both address their constituencies and through which the constituencies can speak themselves (and this can obviously happen both through positive and negative identifications).

Public figures therefore provide a vocabulary of style and manner, a lexicon of character traits as in the differences between Presidents Nixon and Bush, and implied lifestyles as in what Jimi Hendrix and Arthur Scargill have in common. And spelling that out, what they have in common is an implied form of life within which an attitude or a stance can resonate as a mute but known content to forms of relationships. It becomes clearer in this account that the public figure is a vehicle for mannerisms, style, value and it is entirely irrelevant whether the qualities with which they are identified are 'really' true of them. Re-writing a character as is sometimes attempted by a celebrity may be sympathetically articulated but it is not thereby a more authentic performance, rather a performance that carries different connotations of authenticity that seem to command some degree of affiliation with a public. Not only is it irrelevant whether a public figure's identity is 'true' of them it also follows that it is not necessary for them to be a real person – they can be a cartoon figure, an elaborately stylised dramatic role, a computer simulation or even a (possible) figment of the imagination as in the case of the Loch Ness Monster.

What I have called a vocabulary of qualities is not the more general concept of public discourse but it is in part the means through which that discourse is spoken. Public figures literally but not exclusively provide the voice through which publics are addressed and accounted. The galaxy of public figures is therefore analogous to the news (as well as largely constituting the stuff of the news of course), in that anchoring the excess of human actions is the normality within which they can be framed. The public as a world (or stage) shared in common is other than the bulk of personal experience (for the general run of audience members), but can be accommodated within the routines of private spheres by grounding otherness in dramatic conventions whose terms both include and exclude the audience of spectators. They are included by the intimacy of identification and excluded by the artifice of representation, by the symbolic character of the public sphere.

5

MARKETING CULTURE

THE ABSTRACT CROWD

The theme of this book is that the fictions of collective identity are inextricably intertwined with the institutionalisation of social order in modernity. In the course of the book I have tried to indicate how some aspects of changes in dramatisation illuminate modernity. Of course the term, dramatisation, is metaphorical but the lineaments of drama – the conventions, staging, perspective (imaging), address, attending and above all reflexivity of re-framing – can be pointed to in characteristics of forms of popular entertainment. I can summarise the thesis by saying that changes in forms of representation (the modes of dramatisation) will allow for the characteristic ways of being in the world that we recognise and describe as collective. It is in these characteristic forms of representation that we delineate and articulate the differences that we celebrate or deplore as modernity.

I have argued that social order is mundane complicity in the reciprocity of perspectives of everyday experience. Social order is also and unremittingly a language of control. It is a network (a capillary) of disciplinary arrangements through which order is exerted and imposed on the recalcitrant circumstances of misfortune and disadvantage. We should therefore expect to be able to read in changing forms of public drama, shifts in forms of control and constraint, although any one cultural form may be expressed and experienced as opportunity rather than constraint. In this chapter I will discuss the opportunities for and constraints on audiences that the development of mass cultural forms has staged. It is in the marketing of representations that we can gain another perspective on the constitution of social order.

The starting point for this approach will be a return to the theme of disciplining the abstract crowd that was briefly mentioned in the previous chapter. The point here is that the audiences of mass entertainment, despite being privatised in their form of attendance (and therefore presumably exempt from at least most of the contagious poisons of the crowd mind), might still be suspected of escaping the constraints of orderly participation. In the largely unsupervised viewing or listening of the mass audience there is a risk, to social order, of a chaos of meaning and possibly therefore chaotic behaviour. This is why I argue that censorship is not an accidental feature of mass entertainment. Censorship is inherent in the distrust generated by the abstract crowds of mass entertainment and will only become superfluous if the relations of dramatisation are radically altered. It is in this context that new forms of discipline for audiences of mass entertainment can be seen to have been institutionalised through new cultural forms.

The scope of the discussion need not be limited to forms of entertainment or dramatic (staged) representation. The development of self-discipline in an audience is not unrelated to the development of 'autonomous individual self-controls . . . such as "rational thought" or the "moral conscience"' (Elias 1978 p. 257), which Elias sees as informing the elaborate moral codes of the civilising process. Although Elias is writing about the drama of interpersonal conduct his model can be fruitfully applied in accounts of entertainment in mass society (see Elias and Dunning 1986). It is fundamental to Elias' approach that he should warn against treating concepts of individual and society as static, separate entities. In contrast he argues that if the social order of civilisation is an innovation it is not at the level of society acting on individuals but rather an interdependent process displayed in figurations such as social dances: 'The same dance figurations can certainly be danced by different people; but without a plurality of reciprocally oriented and dependent individuals, there is not dance' (Elias 1978 p. 262).

During the nineteenth century in every area of life new disciplinary arrangements began to be accepted as necessary and appropriate for the unruly popular crowds of urban entertainments. As an introduction I have in Chapter 2 used changes in the physical and social form of the theatre, as both an important illustration, and as a metaphor, for the character of changing norms of order. The theatre literally dramatises the practice of representation and as such forcibly encapsulates a relationship between social actors and frames of performance. Theatrical changes in the course of the nineteenth century can be summarised as: (a) a shift of focus away from performances which were paralleled on stage and in the auditorium; and (b) to a subservience of the latter to an increasingly engrossing spectacular representation as staged performance. While there is no doubt that popular entertainment became in certain respects more respectable, the nature, speed and form of the changes is not consistent in all forms of entertainment or leisure.

Shields has argued that within the transformations of leisure and popular entertainment it was possible that: 'a *site of the carnival-esque* was formed and maintained as a setting or infrastructure which not only supported but encouraged the carnivalization of social relations' (Shields 1990 p. 40, *sic*). In this paper he argues that the beach at Brighton could act as a liminal zone, an interstitial space, to license the relaxation of conventional norms of propriety (see also the later version, Shields 1991 and other chapters). The notion of carnivalisation describes therefore actions imbued with the transgressive, transformatory power of medieval carnival. The persistent suggestion of impropriety that clings to the seaside for him explains why 'Victorian essayists so hotly condemned working-class behaviour on the beach, where lewd "fun" became a threat to not only the social order but also the moral order which has been taken to be synonymous with "civilization"' (Shields op. cit. p. 52).

Shields traces a schematic history of Brighton from its discovery (invention?) as a Regency resort through various modes of scandal to recent moral panics focussing on disorderly behaviour amongst the young. In part this possibility of disorderly violation derives for Shields precisely from the ways in which the beach could act as a site for the physical crowd. Rather than being a source of dehumanisation and anonymity the crowded beach licensed various forms of transgression however mild they might be. Although I feel that Shields' account romanticises one version of 'the seaside' and that his use of the notion of the carnival is misleading, he does, valuably, emphasise the argument that all forms of entertainment are bound up with codes of social and moral order. It is therefore possible to take holidays as a subject of and, more controversially, as a display of disciplinary control.

Tourism, as a particular form of 'going away' and being outside the conventional order, obviously has a specific history and raises many issues about the organisation of pleasure to which I shall return. The central point to be made at this stage in the discussion is that the touristic excursion should never be seen as a carnival; or even as a disturbing transgression of conventional constraints. There are many forms of excess associated with tourist sites and entertainments but these are persistently governed by highly formalised codes of appreciation. Rather than tourism being a transformation of the carnival into some more modern epistemology of transgression (see Stallybrass and White 1986 for an exploration of carnival as a form of knowledge), tourism acts as a powerful illustration of the disciplinary codes governing the abstract crowds of mass entertainment.

In order to illustrate the idea that a change from being a crowd to being an audience can act as a form of social control I shall discuss the development of audiences in several forms of entertainment. The thesis is that learning to think of oneself as a customer, that is as an individual purchasor of entertainment rendered as an object, carries with it a shift in the cultural space engendered by the activity. The cultural space of a form of action is the network of relationships and their physical placement in social space. A piece of dramatic business transforms a physical space, through the ways in which it re-frames that space as a site for playful actions; but it also transforms the cultural space of relationships so that actions and interactions are to be understood as playful. In this sense then, the actors change their footing, they are literally performers in a different sort of activity and thereby take on a different identity for the duration of play or of the performance.

All I wish to do is to explore the implications of treating commodities as invitations to drama, and of treating drama as a commodity, and thereby transforming the interactions of performers and customers. An example of the process I mean is provided in the actions of the British state in relation to the popular press in the nineteenth century. In the first three decades the feared power of newspapers to mobilise crowds to insurrectionary activity was countered by repressive taxation. A Stamp Duty levied on each newspaper was intended to restrict the readership to those who could be trusted to respect established authority (on the popular press in the nineteenth century, see Hollis 1970 and Lee 1980). In practice a policy of explicit discipline and control through the financial powers of the state was not only ineffective, in that it created martyrs of those imprisoned for producing and distributing unstamped newspapers, it also intensified a language of collective identification amongst those excluded from the reading public. The system of discipline therefore worked to intensify a sense of class as an identity for the crowd and made interclass conflict more rather than less likely.

The perceived inadequacies of the policy led to the Stamp Duty gradually being repealed. This laid the basis for the development of a popular press oriented towards an anonymous readership attracted by an increasingly sensationalist journalism. Both the expenses of sensationalism and an acceptance of the interdependence of news and commodities (discussed in the following section), further led to a press dependent upon being able to act as a marketing vehicle for advertising campaigns. Newspapers may be able to offer a critical interrogation of 'the news' they report, but this is necessarily embedded in the gossip of public culture.

The disciplinary code implicit in the historical constitution of an audience is analogous to that shown in the respectful attention granted to the cinema screen by the shrouded audience in the auditorium. Although the abstract crowd of the cinema audience is physically co-present they are abstract as a collectivity in their personal appropriation of the performance. The cultural space is pre-given and dramatic interaction for participants is governed by norms of respectful disattention characteristic of those who habitually live in a community of strangers.

The popular newspaper is not of course as engrossing as a film show and it is rarely read collectively so that the crowd occasioned by the performance is more clearly abstract. The address of the newspaper is, however (as I have been arguing in the previous chapter), more clearly situated within the presuppositions of drama as normality. It is consistent with this approach to see television as closer to the newspaper as a cultural form than the cinema. Despite the similarity of moving images on a screen the cinema, even in multiplex venues, offers the attractions of theatrical entertainment, while television is essentially a form of pictorial magazine – itself a form initially devised for an audience of female readers. The imaginations of community on these media derive from a recognition of the idiosyncrasies of personal experience allied to the commonality of dramatic identification. In essence, my argument is that the disciplinary code of the abstract crowd is effective through the impossibility of exempting oneself from that crowd. It is the ubiquity of dramatisation that envelops the possibility of transgression.

(Another way of phrasing this point is to say that it is the conventional impossibility of changing or leaving the frame space of the dramatisation of normality that ensures society becomes a spectacle for itself. This was of course one of the most provocative insights of the Surrealist movement and it underlay the ambition to excavate the foundations of normality in search of fantasy; a project that, as I noted in the previous chapter, generated forms of utopian sociology in London and Paris. In succeeding parts of this chapter I shall return to the significance of intimations of utopia in spectacular marketing.)

Sennett's argument (1976), that in the abrogation of public life we are abandoning a concern with civility, is relevant here. For him, it is almost as if in the ubiquity of dramatisation we have lost the formalisations of theatrical discourse. In part, this is expressed through increasing distrust of public figures so that as 'the audience lost faith in itself to judge them; it became a spectator rather than a witness' (Sennett op. cit. p. 261). While on the other hand, an inability to play – to become an actor deprived of his art in Sennett's phrase – that can also be called a reluctance to self-consciously explore the artificiality of representation, throws all action over to be judged in a court of authenticity. The consequence is a narcissistic regression to an obsessive concern with the legitimacy of self-actions. The audience as spectators is disciplined (or effectively constrained) through the lack of boundaries on spectacular stagings: 'The mass media infinitely heighten the knowledge people have of what transpires in the society, and they infinitely inhibit the capacity of people to convert that knowledge into political action' (Sennett op. cit. p. 283).

A further example of the fashioning of an audience within a new vocabulary of mass participation is provided by the development of opinion polling or audience research as measures of collective taste. If the predominant model of collective behaviour is that of a market in which each individual customer makes their choice, and it is only in the accumulation of choices that values are created, then cultural choices should be able to be adapted to fit the same model. If each member of the audience is an individual expression of taste, then, within the terms of the model, it makes sense to accumulate the judgements of each and every actor to arrive at gross characterisations of collective views – and thereby values. This as a model of the democratic process clearly provides an opportunity of participation for every member of society; but it also entails a structure of decision-making that treats choices between dramatic options as equivalent to choices between cigarettes, perfumes or cars.

This is the path that was reluctantly followed within the BBC in the late 1930s with the development of an audience research department to poll audience views (Chaney 1987B). It is unsurprising that the new department was created under the tutelage of advertising executives because the model of dramatic affect drawn upon in such polling is essentially that of mass advertising. The war in 1939 established the need for the new techniques of charting audience taste as it seemed overwhelmingly necessary to establish popular support for the war effort. As polling has become more sophisticated so it has represented the audience more faithfully while simultaneously facilitating the fragmentation of cultural space.

Representation in advertising works to dramatise a subject (whether it is a product, an idea or an identity), and create a relevance, however fleeting, between the subject and the anonymous members of an audience. The conventional complaint about advertising is that its promises are illusory but this is to mistake the character of the drama being performed. In the process of dramatisation the consumer is not offered a vicarious space in the performance but a promise of association and of relevance. Advertising is therefore populist, it must seek to appeal to its audience, but it is also didactic in that it provides instructions for 'viewing' the subject. Michael Schudson has wittily described the idealisations of advertising as capitalist realism to point to an analogy with the socialist realism of countries with a different model of citizenship (Schudson 1984 Chapter 7).

The narrative frame of advertising presupposes a set of values and conditions of normality in order to be able to tell its stories so elliptically (this is perhaps why advertising has tempted commentators into treating instances as myths; see for example Leymore 1975). Above all, advertising assumes that it is addressing its audience as individuals. (Collective appeals, as a variant of advertising, such as forms of political symbolism like the CND logo provide a pictorial slogan. They may seem to articulate what the community of affiliates has in common, but in practice they are another form of promising the possibility of individual appropriation.) Advertising, in its individualised and yet indiscriminate address, articulates and presupposes the disciplinary codes (that is the social order) of the abstract crowd.

MASS COMMUNICATION AND MASS CONSUMERISM

The development of processes of mass communication has involved messages or representations being formulated in ways that make them available for marketing. It has frequently been argued that the massness of mass communication does not lie in the standardisation or industrialisation of cultural production. It is rather that there is a mass character to networks of distribution. The basis of a system of mass distribution is that there is no necessary distinction between an original and copies, and therefore all versions can be seen to be of equal cultural value. It is because each instance will also be of equivalent economic value that those involved in recruiting an audience can be sure that they are marketing standardised goods. This is the basis of the view that the cultural significance of innovations in mass communication technology is analogous to, and formally parallels, innovations in marketing consumer goods.

In order to take my account of the disciplinary codes of the abstract crowd further, I shall develop the idea of parallels between performances of mass entertainment; the leisure of mass tourism; and the commodities of consumer culture. Although the development of printing is, correctly, usually pointed to as the first instance of a form of mass communication, there is clearly a difference between the manuscript of a text and a published version. These differences are, however, mainly relevant to the attributions of economic value to different modes of inscription or representation. The more objects are unique or in short supply they can acquire a distinctive value based upon a number of considerations such as features of the author or circumstances of the process of production. There is a shift to a different way of negotiating value or meaning when we consider products which are composed purely as signifying systems – lacking any basis as an authored or personally made they can be endlessly duplicated.

Amongst multiple produced commodities the market value of any one instance will depend upon a number of circumstances of which the perceived prestige of acquisition or appropriation to the customer or audience member will be one. But this prestige will derive from what we can call the cultural status of object or representation as negotiated resource rather than anything 'inherent' in the entity in itself. Thus if we consider an individual's choice of a motor car, once s/he has decided upon the manufacturer and model any particular instance of this category will only be differentiated from others by contingent circumstances. Of course if the car sought is no longer being produced then it may acquire some of the qualities of an antique and thus be subject to a different set of considerations. Or, as a further variation, value may be added by the fact that the car was once owned by a famous personality but in this case uniqueness is being coincidentally pasted onto a standardised product.

It is not necessary for me to embark upon a technical discussion of the factors involved in the creation of economic values in cultural forms. These are obviously relevant to the resourcing of production and distribution organisations but the central interest here is with the creation of different modes of significance for audiences, and with relationships between significance and signification. The implication of products being marketed as anonymous (in terms of authorship) performances is that a conventional distinction between use-value and exchange-value becomes irrelevant. It is obviously true as Haug insistently notes that: 'There is quite a difference between asking what use a thing is and whether it is saleable' (Haug 1986 p. 97), but the difference does not mean that one scale of evaluation is better or more authentic than another. The fact that use-value is prior to, in some evolutionary or geological sense, exchange-value does not mean that it is more authentic, merely that the framing of layers of meaning of commodity or performance is less complex when we concentrate upon instrumental function.

It may or may not be true that creating a market in the latter sense of promoting saleability is necessarily accomplished through illusions (such as those offered by advertising), but it is not a cause for dismay that 'Ultimately the aestheticization of commodities means that they tend to dissolve into enjoyable experiences, or into the *appearance* of those experiences, detached from the commodity itself' (Haug op. cit. p. 72, emphasis added). It is through the dramatisation of experience rather than the validity of representation (however that might be gauged) that mundane resources for evaluating experience are assembled. That is, that we create values for social action through our 'languages' of representation: 'consumer culture through advertising, the media, and techniques of display of goods, is able to destabilize the original notion of use or meaning of goods and attach to them new images and signs which can summon up a whole range of associated feelings and desires' (Featherstone 1990 p. 114).

To say this does not deny that resources for creating the appearance of enjoyment will in socially inegalitarian societies be more available to members of élites. Those who lack this power will, therefore, find themselves in various ways imprisoned within appearances over which they have only limited control. Although, it should also be recognised that while working within the illusions of appearance, there are a number of studies which explore the ways in which subordinate groups, particularly amongst the young, are able to play (in every sense) with the complexity of appearance and representation (cf. for example Willis 1991).

My argument can be summarised by saying that processes of mass communication are characterised by standardised forms of distribution through which commodities are made available to anonymous audiences. The commodities which are marketed are distinctive in that they are forms of entertainment, this used in its very broadest sense, and thus particularly concerned with the creation of the appearance of enjoyable experience. The goods or products of mass communication industries are therefore almost entirely governed by the criteria of exchange value. As with a meal in a restaurant its use in terms of providing fuel for sustenance is there but is a very minor consideration. The functions and gratifications served by mass entertainment are driven by the illusions or ideals of norms of identity (both personal and collective). We can see that both the means of representing economic value and the commodities sought after or acquired are equivalently arbitrary resources for signification. They are meaningful through the uses they facilitate and the ways they are used.

If capitalism can be described as the organisation of economic relationships in which the dominant scale of values is to treat all possessions and relationships in terms of their worth as capital, then consumerism is a late development of capitalist economies in which the circulation of commodities is stimulated by inculcating values in society in which the acquisition of consumer goods is accepted as a primary criterion of status and a language for social identity (see for example Ewen 1976). A consumer culture is therefore one in which the values of consumerism, that is a desire for new acquisitions which can never be exhausted, become dominant indeed overwhelming (Campbell 1987). Featherstone (1990) distinguishes between three common views of consumer culture: first, as deriving from developments in capitalist commodity production; secondly, as developments in imagery of status; and thirdly as a set of emotional pleasures in an enhancement of sensuality.

Consumer values consequentially are first, hedonistic (enjoyable experience is sought and commodities are assumed to provide at least the appearance of enjoyment), secondly this-worldly (secular) and thirdly have a necessary stress upon innovation. Traditional patterns for the use of objects cannot remain dominant and choices become governed by the peer evaluations of fashion. These are of course the paradigmatic characteristics of modernity (see for example the account of theorists of modernity, in particular of Simmel, in Frisby 1988). Particularly when allied with the development of mass advertising as the engine of consumerism (see S. and E. Ewen 1982). And yet there are a number of studies, such as McKendrick's account of the consumer revolution of eighteenth century England (McKendrick *et al.* 1982), and Mukerji's study (1983) of the growth of consumerism in early-modern culture, which suggest that to assume the modern-ness of consumer values is misleading.

The grounds of this confusion lie in the meaning of terms and are similar to the more familiar problematic of the nature of popular culture. There is a perennial choice between stressing continuities in forms of social action across periods and cultures, or arguing that formal similarities mask differences in meaning and significance. In particular, in this case whether the 'audiences' for popular entertainment and fashionable consumer goods in early modern and late modern cultures understand their participation in their respective activities as sufficiently similar as to be equivalent. My thesis in relation to this point and throughout the book is that the differences are more important than the similarities. It was not just that there was a lack of technical resources to service a mass market in pre-modern culture, but that more importantly there was an absence of the dramatic form of a mass market.

In Mukerji's study of the development of modern materialism she is concerned to subvert the orthodoxies of social change by arguing that 'The hedonistic culture of mass consumption was probably as crucial in shaping early patterns of capitalist development in Europe as the asceticism usually associated with this era' (Mukerji 1983 p. 2). The instruments or means of hedonistic display in early modern materialism were principally symbolic commodities, goods such as pictorial prints valued at least as much for their expressive as practical qualities: 'Pictorial prints . . . were the first form of mass-produced images for popular markets. As such, they were an early form of mass culture that helped to cultivate consumerism in the lower echelons of society' (Mukerji op. cit. p. 38). In pioneering new markets for the distribution of symbolic commodities, another name for cultural goods, print makers also engaged with other characteristics that have become familiar to us in marketing culture: the stratification of audiences by levels of taste and the use of formulas as narrative resources.

There are two lessons I wish to take from Mukerji's study. First, to assume a simple line of historical development from ascetic capitalism to decadent consumerism is inappropriate. And, secondly, that in formulating modernity the cultural significance of changing forms of representation is at least as important as technological innovations. New forms of representation, implicated in new dramaturgies of social action, concerned relationships between community and the individual and the grounds of those relationships. The goods and commodities through which new forms of relationship and a new dramaturgy of action were staged were most often a combination of aesthetic form and practical resource – clearly illustrated in Mukerji's study (op. cit. Chapter 3) of the publication of maps.

The fact that this new genre, maps, in the cultural form of publication depended on contemporary developments in the technology of printing is not of course coincidental. To return to the theme of this part of the chapter, printing as the first form of mass communication became functionally viable because it could service (and at the same time help to create) a market for consumer goods. Another way to describe this market is as the creation of mass forms of popular culture. As Mukerji points out, maps are both a way of formulating social space and a means of controlling space for new forms of political administration (see Brody 1986 for a more recent account of the use of mapping as a resource for cultural inscription and political control).

I have referred several times to the expressive values or rewards of consumer goods as resources for signifying changing forms of identity. By this I mean there are opportunities for displaying taste, expressing social affiliations and articulating values and attitudes. Lying behind these notions of style as the presentation of self is of course a more fundamental re-writing of notions of the person and the self as moral actor: that identity is neither necessarily fixed nor homogeneous (for a discussion of the social organisation of the self and the development of selfhood in modernity see the essays in Carrithers *et al.* 1985). Individuality as a dramatic resource is not only a defining characteristic of the emergence of theatricality in early modern culture (the terrors and pains of the embodied self are explored in Barker 1984), but becomes a root metaphor for the collective fictions of modernity.

The interdependence of processes of mass communication with the development of a mass market for consumer goods was only hinted at in early modern Europe. To describe some of the several modes of printing, for example of maps, prints and calicoes, as forms of mass culture is provocative rather than strictly descriptive. Even in eighteenth century England when the 'birth of a consumer society' can be detected (McKendrick *et al.* 1982), the social world of leisure, fashion and consumerism was only imperfectly articulated. The values of conspicuous consumption, allied to new forms of entertainment as leisure, were being institutionalised amongst emergent urban populations other than the aristocratic élite in ways which were essential for subsequent developments in a national culture. Marketing was, however, still predominantly interpersonal rather than impersonal and standardised (an alternative approach stressing the interdependence of modern consumer values with the cultural innovations of romanticism is developed in Campbell 1987).

In practice the consumer values of eighteenth century England are inseparable from contemporary developments in publishing. These, on the one hand, led to enormous increases in stature of newspapers and new political publics, and, on the other hand, to the emergence of a personalised, secular and naturalistic form of prose representation in which there is a recurrent emphasis on novelty (see Hunter 1988). The commodities displaying new life-styles were significant resources in constituting and staging new structures of social relationships such as the increasing salience of a distinction between public and private spheres. (Even though the Evangelical subjects of Davidoff and Hall's book (1987) on suburbanisation might not seem good examples of a consumer culture, they are clearly in so many ways dependent on national cultural forms.)

The full flowering of a consumer culture during the last hundred years has obviously depended upon the possibility of truly mass markets. It was both the combination of the existence of a fast, reliable and standardised transport network and industrialised production and distribution systems that made a mass national market possible (Fraser 1981). In the last third of the nineteenth century department stores as symbolic homes for new consumer relationships and physical palaces for the hedonism of popular luxury were the vanguard of cultural innovations (Miller 1981; Chaney 1983A; and Bowlby 1985). In the department stores new forms of leisure were dramatised, a new anonymity of being in public was pioneered, and indeed the process of marketing style became a spectacular show. The appearance of enjoyable experience now overwhelmed other modes of signification; to the extent that processes of shopping in metropolitan centres or being enthused by metropolitan values was to seem to inhabit 'dream worlds' (Williams 1982). These were also the worlds of the birth of audiences for mass entertainment.

The values of consumer culture point therefore to new forms of dramatisation for public space in two ways. First, because, in the positive accentuation of illusion and the fantasy qualities of popular hedonism, individuals are encouraged to dramatise mundane experience (in part of course by the increasingly widespread use of drugs as transformations of reality). The kaleidoscopic landscapes of city centres 'summon up half-forgotten dreams, as the curiosity and memory of the stroller is fed by the ever-changing landscape in which objects appear divorced from their context and subject to mysterious connections which are read on the surface of things' (Featherstone 1990 p. 23). And secondly, more literally, because there are enormous extensions in the range and scope of forms of dramatic entertainment.

A consequence both ways of dramatisation generate is that the status of consumer values as languages of order is at best ambivalent. A realm of illusion allied to a meticulous concern with fashion can be seen to encourage extravagance, self-indulgence and the pursuit of immediate gratification. (These are all values which are frequently catered to and yet deplored in popular entertainments; one example from many is the extravagance of cinema architecture – the extraordinary exuberance of a building form that made a spectacular frame for and of popular taste; see for example Atwell 1980).

Systems of social values in which self-indulgence is strongly emphasised or which encourage a willingness amongst audiences to be dazzled by the illusions and fantasies of tawdry spectacles can be seen as provoking the danger of a chaos of meaning. At the beginning of the previous part I noted that processes of mass entertainment were faced less with dangers of disorderly behaviour amongst the physical crowd than a chaos of meaning amongst the abstract crowd. It is therefore unsurprising that those who seek to articulate a moral agenda for social order should so often regret that the values of hedonism are neither rational, nor respectable nor responsible.

This is not the appropriate place to begin a detailed exploration of the functions of censorship in mass entertainment, except to note that across the political spectrum the dangers of disorderly culture, whether of topics or of consumption, are seen to lie in the dangers of transgressive personal excess. This has been inflected in one way by those moral entrepreneurs who, dismayed by the social stratification of popular culture in urban-industrial society, have sought a re-integration at the level of culture which will transcend the irreconcilable perspectives of a fragmented and unequal society – a re-integration that is usually posed in the forms of traditional values. Quite contesting inflections have been generated by those who, seeking to end exploitation through structural transformation, have seen the illusions of popular hedonism as false consciousness or exploitative fantasies.

Both critical perspectives apply more generally in theories of popular culture as well as to the innovations in consumer marketing in the last century. The reason for this is that, as I have said, censorship is not an aberrant distortion of the market but inherent in the development of anonymous abstract crowds. The fears of consequences or effects are fantastically enhanced when the frames marking drama and normality become blurred. The paradox of mass culture is that dominant values of relativism and liberalism are continually challenged or counterpointed by intransigent cultural minorities who, in asserting their identity and resisting discrimination, seek to control the agenda of collective representation and to forbid images seen as damaging or dangerous. There is consequently a balkanisation of cultural identity between mutually antagonistic groups underlining the paradoxical feeling that in a common mass culture there is no shared culture.

LEISURE AND THE THEATRE OF SHOPPING

In my account of changes in the cultural organisation of dramatic space, changes I have described in terms of the transitions from crowds to audiences and have summarised in the previous sections as the management of the abstract crowd, I believe I have also been drawing in some of the contours of a leisure culture. There are of course many attempts to mark out leisure as a social phenomenon, not least because there have been historic changes in the pursuit of leisure as a way of accounting for or describing the quality of life during processes of modernisation (see Clarke and Crichter 1985 for an account that seeks to situate issues of leisure within an historical context).

One reason for leisure becoming more significant is that it clearly has become central to any description of everyday experience in urban-industrial society (Gershuny and Jones 1987). And equally clearly it can be used by actors as a way of investing their personal experience with distinctive meanings, so that the manner of their leisure is in important ways an expression of personal identity. The repertoire of leisure activities common in any one community will provide a shared framework so that personal practice can be both an affirmation of typicality allied with individuality. Leisure, as I have argued in a previous discussion (Chaney 1979 pp. 91–102), is a private activity, a private means of using collective resources. The notion of leisure is therefore intrinsically descriptive in contrast to a concept of play which I have described as an analytic concept. By this I mean that play refers to a structure of relationships – a form of performance that can be imagined as a different mode of dramatisation.

My argument is, then, that leisure is a characteristic of modernity. It is not so much that leisure is a particular form of public drama, rather that the activity of leisure can be defined as the mobilisation of audiences for popular culture. There are some accounts in which leisure and popular are counterposed, the latter is seen to enact or articulate a transgressive stance while the former is collaborative consumption (that is leisure collaborates in systems of oppression; Fiske 1989). It is only possible to make this argument with a prescriptive, and I believe misleading, notion of the popular (cf. Chaney 1990B). Neither are the two terms synonymous unless the popular is merely used to describe the peaks of consumption.

The popular, as I have been trying to argue throughout this book, involves a variety of forms of dramatisation of collective identity. Leisure is the ways in which the popular is marketed. It is therefore an industry like advertising which deals with the appearance of experience. The concept of the popular refers to forms of collective interpretation such as collective remembering while the concept of leisure refers to what is common to a number of marketing organisations. Leisure is therefore those forms of the commercial organisation of the production and distribution of popular culture, through which audiences are generated for spectacular shows: 'The circularity here helps to bring out that the essence of audience concern is their involvement in consuming/spectating themselves' (Chaney 1979 pp. 97–8). In this approach while leisure and popular cultures may be overlapping, and indeed enacted through the same performances and activities, the distinctiveness of leisure lies in the marketing of culture. A choice of leisure activities therefore parallels being a member of an audience for entertainment or a customer for consumer choices.

A commercially significant element in the leisure industry, has been the development of holidays as a standard feature of consumer society lifestyles. As tourists we are above all else performers in our own dramas on stages the industry has provided. Although the clearly constructed landscapes of theme parks and pleasure grounds are exceptional, in practice all tourist locales can be seen to involve degrees of staging. There is in them all a management and clear articulation of cultural identity oriented towards what Urry (1990) has called 'the tourist gaze'.

To say this does not imply that tourism is an unchanging practice, we should rather see the history of tourism, or better the development of popular holidays, as encapsulating the theme of transition from crowd to audience. I do not think it is necessary to review that history here (cf. Urry op. cit. Chapter 2; see also Urry (1988)), but it is clear that traditional themes of battles between respectable reformers and popular hedonism made the 'holiday' an ambiguous area in terms of moral order. Even in those disciplined spaces of holiday camps with their regimentations of fun, there was a persistent and well-founded popular lore of licensed relaxation of sexual mores. And it was of course central to the holiday experience that resorts should combine the brash excess of the fairground with more utopian, other-worldly architectures and entertainments (Thompson 1983).

Some types of tourist may go in search of a licensed space for transgression, or for a 'natural' authenticity. But whatever the shape in which s/he chooses to detect that which they seek, in the production of a more-or-less persuasive dramatic space the tourist is as implicated a performer as any of those managing the stage on his/her behalf. I take this to be one of the central themes of MacCannell's book (1976), with the further implication that the suspension of disbelief is not generated by qualities of an 'attraction' but of the ways in which we could say it is 'visited with'. Another way of putting this point is that there is only a matter of style in differences between explicitly designed-for tourist resorts and mundane sites that tourists happen to visit for whatever reason, such as say the sewers of Paris: it is in the practice of gazing that tourism is staged. A tourist is a distinctive type of stranger, collaborating in the spectacle that is being performed.

The dramatic representations of tourism are therefore staged for a potential audience. The managers (if I can so refer to the myriad forms of service industry constituting an attraction) of tourist sites draw on narrative formulae much as the producers of other media of mass entertainment such as film and television. They cannot, however, fully control how they will be seen and appropriated. As the production essentially rests in the processes of visiting by the audience, that audience becomes in effect an abstract crowd as in other more privatised forms of popular entertainment. This may seem paradoxical as in moving what have been called 'the golden hordes' (Turner and Ash 1975) along their pilgrimages of pleasure they will (in general) seem far from abstract. The abstraction lies in the personal criteria through which they each come to formulate and evaluate 'attractions' and 'a good time'. The principles of appreciation are the ways we learn to adapt to, and consistently conform to, the codes of activities and places.

I claimed in the first part of this chapter that tourism is misunderstood if seen as a disturbing transgression, that it acts rather as a network of disciplined conformity. How can this theme be reconciled with a history of hedonistic licence which has persisted through a shift of locale to more exotic resorts? Even though holidaymakers have traditionally used their holiday as an occasion for licensed debauchery and excess, and a holiday is in general still an occasion of extravagance and usually conspicuous consumption, the practice of holidaying has become a display of citizenship. Even when grossly exploitative as in tours of the bars and brothels of Thailand, or merely vicarious as on the naked beaches of the Aegean and Adriatic, the tourist is expected to conform to a script of orderly consumption. The script may be conjured from personal dreams but the dreams themselves: 'are not autonomous; they involve working over advertising and other media-generated sets of signs, many of which relate very clearly to complex processes of social emulation' (Urry 1990 p. 13). The illusions of pleasure (or the appearance of experience) are as pervasive here as in other forms of consumer choice.

It is also relevant that the collective character of popular entertainment in holidaying is changing with other patterns of commodity acquisition to more individual patterns of consumption. Despite the possibly greater investment of personal significance by audience members there is, however, nothing in a more volatile or more fragmented market to suggest that individual behaviours are likely to be either more innovative or more disorderly. Indeed the cynical 'post-tourists' (see also Urry 1988) who have transcended mass entertainment may well have no illusions about the authenticity of their entertainments but in this they are consistent with mundane 'normality'. To the extent that post-modern tourists have abandoned a search for cultural meaning, they have also accepted the limitations of artificiality to any form of social action when there has been a radical dramatisation of everyday life.

The strip of actions involved in negotiating with another to secure ownership of an object or access to a service or participation in a performance, might traditionally have been seen as being purely governed and driven by functional considerations. It is, however, the starting point of sociological interest that such practical activities can provide the basis for other types of enquiry. (Although I am pointing to continuities in all forms of 'audience-ing', I will for the sake of brevity concentrate on consumer choice for next few paragraphs.) These will include a concern with structures of relationships, the positioning of self in relation to a collective and the conception and involvement of different audiences in the performance concerned (Chaney and Chaney 1979). Thus the settings, whether they are markets, fairs, stores, theatres and resorts constructed for the routine performance of such transactions can without strain be seen as stages for the dramatisation of ritual concerns.

As the stages of performance (the dramatic frame) change, so the expectations and opportunities brought by customers or audience change. Similarly, the objects of transaction too take on different meanings. For example, it is useful to establish the differences between an object such as a pair of shoes made by a craftsman for a particular customer; a pair of shoes made to standardised patterns and sold nationwide under the brand name of a manufacturer; and a pair of shoes that is not only an instance of particular genre, such as training shoes, but is made by a particular manufacturer and has a number of fashionable design features. The object in the latter case is a member of different system of significations. Only minimally grounded in instrumental purpose, the objects of transactions in a complex system of marketing are free to take on other roles.

In advertising, which is the cultural form of representation for consumer goods, it is necessary to appreciate that the product is a transitional signifier. Rather than there being something signified, an object which is being displayed or referred to as itself, the product or service is indicating a process or a form of life that is *being*

166

brought into being. What this means is that in the cynicism of post-tourists and other modes of commentary, there is a necessity for a discursive milieu in which what is signified is endlessly malleable. The play of sophistication is that it can and will be treated ironically.

The shifts in the level of meanings I am trying to describe has been developed in a different way by Leiss and his colleagues (1986) in their study of changing appeals within mass advertising. They distinguish three paralleling quadripartite distinctions in the history of advertising. The first is in the ways that advertising agencies have sought to create a distinctive area of expertise; thus they sought to sell through, successively, a product-oriented approach, followed by symbols of products, then personalization and most recently through a claimed grasp of market segmentation. Paralleling this history they distinguish four basic formats which have been used to advertise products. The earliest was through product information, next through creating an image for the product, then through personalizing the product through customer identification and finally a format implying a lifestyle. Through participation the member of the audience becomes an actor.

Finally, in 'the theatre of consumption' they distinguish four successive cultural frames for goods. These concern the relationships between goods and their consumers; they are summarised as idolatry, iconology, narcissism and totemism. They are four forms of metaphorical worship in which we go from false gods to aesthetics to self-veneration and finally to the constitution of clans as principles of social order:

> During the present totemistic phase the identifying features of the three preceding periods are recalled and synthesized . . . . Consumption is meant to be a public spectacle, a public enterprise. Product-related images fulfill their totemic potential in becoming emblems for social collectivities, principally by means of their associations with life-styles.
>
> (Leiss *et al.* op. cit. p. 295)

It is impossible to say that one of these theologies is more authentic than any other.

The several forms of the appearance of pleasure, or given a sacrilegious intimation of the sacred, within the representations of advertising point to a crucial difference within late modern culture. Within élite society, particular goods and their manufacturers can be used to display the wealth, taste and general competence of their purchasers (see the traditional critique of the decadence of élite fashions by Veblen 1925, and a celebration of the play of choice by Wolfe 1977). The cult objects of popular fashion are necessarily less exclusive but the networks (system sounds too precise and specifiable) within which they signify are more complexly interwoven (Hebdige 1979; Chambers 1986). Fashion always works to create boundaries between those who can use its language and those who cannot (Lurie 1982). The ironic sophistication of popular consumerism is to recognise and celebrate that there may well be a multiplicity of languages being spoken simultaneously (an idea also explored in Featherstone 1990, particularly Chapter 6).

If style is the language of cultural projects then it has to be bracketed with design as the medium of distinctive signifiers of goods (on the self-conscious borrowings of artistic and consumer innovations; see Martin 1981). The notion of design as a distinctive area of study, and therefore something with an historical specificity, has been appropriated in at least three quite different ways. The first approaches design as an adjunct of the history of art (and indeed teaching art in Britain has been continually caught up in the competing claims of 'fine art' versus the 'trade' skills of design, see for example Pearson 1982). In this approach the aesthetic qualities of good design are studied much as architectural history might seek to chart the continually changing reconciliation of form and function. In a second approach, design is abstracted from substantive function and purpose, and now celebrated as a reservoir of cultural iconography. It may be the cult status of an object such as Levi's 501s or the use through slashing of such an object, but in either case the object itself is an arbitrary signifier of the heterogeneity and vitality of popular taste (Heide and Gilman 1979).

The third approach to the history of design begins from the realisation that design is constituted in processes of mass marketing:

> While pottery was a craft industry . . . the form of a pot was most likely decided by the man who was to make it. However, when the manufacture of pots was broken down into processes carried out by different workers, an additional stage was required, the preparation of instructions for the various workmen to follow: in fact, a design stage.
>
> (Forty 1986 p. 34)

What Forty's point about the transformation of a craft industry makes clear is that design, as a self-conscious process (that is as a deliberate choice of style), is a function of the mechanisation of production (Schivelbusch 1988 has made the same point).

Two further closely-related points follow from this insight. The first is that self-consciousness of style parallels (and replaces?) the loss of aesthetic aura as a consequence of the mechanisation of production. The second is that the design stage is analogous to the use of genres or formulas in mass entertainment. Both are serving the needs of mass distribution by giving an integrative point of reference for differentiated forms of creative activity. This also applies in the discipline of anonymous audiences: the design of a product, working in much the same way as the role of the star in an entertainment show, serves to signify the aesthetics of shared values.

Amongst the first to realise and to theorise the role of design as a constitutive frame for how audiences can read and understand objects was William Morris (although of course this terminology would have been foreign to him). Thus he used design as the basis of a critique of the organisation of production, and, secondly, as an argument that a design should be able to be read as a relationship between a specific use and the form of life within which that use was employed. In this sense design is never socially neutral but always articulates emancipation or exploitation. I will return to the politics of design in the final part of the chapter. At this stage I note only how the sociological critique opened up by Morris allows for a more provocative reading of mundane design than whether it is based on illusion or not. For example, it is instructive to read how the social relations and values of cleanliness, domesticity and femininity (and their implied equivalence) are embodied in the forms of products. The processes of the construction of gender are made to seem 'natural' and become invisible in self-evident 'objects of desire' (this is based on Forty's (1986) account, Chapters 7–9; see also some of the essays in Fox and Jackson Lears 1983).

The particular example of the marketing of electricity illustrates a number of themes that recur throughout this chapter. In the first half of the century in the UK it was feared that it would be difficult to sell electricity as a mass source of domestic power because of its expense. The design of appliances was seen therefore as being particularly important in promoting the attractiveness of electricity: 'Propaganda about electricity made much of its being a uniquely "modern" fuel, and descriptions of electricity promised unheard-of benefits' (Forty op. cit. p. 190) – in particular through the provision of cheap energy providing an unparalleled democratisation of leisure. In important ways, then, the objects that were designed to use electricity had to symbolise through their design the modernity of new lifestyles – they had to become part of popular culture.

Another view of electricity, its forms of production rather than consumption, was equally symbolically important. As electricity began to permeate the fabric of modern urban life, not just in domestic settings but also in powering public facilities, it became apparent that the organisation of the production of electric power was an important path breaker for new forms of corporate monopoly capitalism: 'The concentration and centralisation of energy in high-capacity power stations corresponded to the concentration of economic power in the big banks' (Schivelbusch 1988 p. 74; see also Sandgruber 1990 p. 50: '[electricity] paved the way for comprehensive instruments of supervision and manipulation'). In this promise of modernity, in which a combination of the rationality of corporate organisation could be allied with a utopian vision of beneficent social engineering, electricity neatly straddled the 'opposition' of capitalism and socialism, thus providing a model for the emergent industries of mass entertainment.

I have in this section been concerned with the parallels between marketing and culture, or more precisely the parallels between the marketing of consumer goods and forms of mass entertainment. For the audiences for both types of product the transaction involved in acquisition, attendance or participation is a stepping stone in the activity of practical aesthetics. By this I mean that in the choosing, evaluating and savouring of objects and activities as well-formed enterprises over and above those objects' and activities' instrumental function, we are engaged in a practical activity. An activity in which we indicate, however obliquely, how we wish ourselves and immediate settings to be seen: 'aesthetics simply *is* the form of most people's theorizing; it is the discipline of popular culture' (Inglis 1988 p. 17 *sic*; in relation to landscape see in particular Part 3 of his book).

UTOPIAN INTIMATIONS

While I have stressed the gradual emergence of modernity through the creation of markets, audiences and publics, the institutionalisation of new forms of shopping also inscribes new norms of subjectivity:

Around the turn of the century a fundamental cultural transformation occurred within the educated strata of Western
capitalist nations . . . a new set of values sanctioning periodic
leisure, compulsive spending, apolitical passivity, and an apparently permissive (but subtly coercive) morality of individual fulfillment.

(Jackson Lears 1983 p. 3)

The search for an authentic lifestyle is inherent in a quest for
meaning which is itself a utopian project. In this part of the chapter
I will try to show why and how the marketing of culture has
engaged with the unlikely promise of utopia.

While one sees the creation of department stores as marking a
crucial point in the development of mass marketing, it would be a
mistake to assume that mass markets were solely dependent upon
this innovation. The stores did provide a manifest symbol of new
possibilities, and to that extent they focussed new attitudes and
re-wrote the topography of the city. But the stores were themselves
dependent upon the development of mass advertising, a cheap, fast
and effective transport network, and new skills of accountancy,
packaging and stock control amongst others. The goods of mass
marketing embody a changed cultural significance from the
purchases made in local markets. They had to be manufactured,
branded, packaged, patented, advertised and retailed in different
ways as Strasser (1989) makes clear. But perhaps most importantly
they are semiotic markers of different relationships between manufacturers and consumers. In ways that directly parallel all other
forms of mass entertainment, since the turn of the century these
relationships: 'have flourished at the boundaries of public and
private life, . . . where the products of corporate decision-making
are transformed into intimate objects that people use daily' (Strasser
op. cit. p. 28).

In Chapter 2, I noted how the theatrical frame of the new department stores at the end of the nineteenth century is consistent with
the design and grandiloquence of contemporary spectacular. We
can take this parallel between being a customer and being a
member of an audience further: 'The illuminated window as stage,
the street as theatre and the passers-by as audience – this is the
scene of big-city night life' (Schivelbusch 1988 p. 148). There was
both a physical crowd thronging the aisles of the new stores and an
abstract crowd who were oriented towards the stores' merchandise

as a narrative of modernity. The latter is more significant in that the demands and compulsions of affiliation are more pervasive than in the former. The freedoms of consumer culture were and are grounded in a disciplined order as Schivelbusch has captured with a distinction between two forms of light, one is: 'advertising light – commercialised festive illumination – in contrast to street light, the lighting of a policed order. Commercial light is to police light what bourgeois society is to the state' (Schivelbusch op. cit. p. 142).

There is a further dimension yet to the theatricality of mass consumerism, however. In an innovation characteristic of mass entertainment the architecture of the new stores, as with railway stations and other monumental forms, was used to clothe functional refinement in an eclecticism of stylish drapery. The rational organisation of resources to achieve specifiable ends could then be re-staged as the transcendance of practical concerns into an idealised social imagery. In addition to 'dressing' particular buildings as characters in a spectacle of magnificence, the broader urban landscape was more consciously shaped to display a social realm that transcends mundane considerations. In this way public space is made didactic and a series of exhortations. Few architects and urban planners may aspire to the megalomaniac visions of Nazi urban and political regeneration (although it is important to remember that the well-springs of ultra-nationalist values lay in populist traditions, illuminatingly described in Taylor 1974, see also Lane 1986), but I shall argue that such utopian intimations in the landscape of late modern culture are the language of imagination of mass culture.

It is the interconnections between the changing social forms of the metropolitan city and new forms of commerce and entertainment that lead me to believe that the idea of consumer culture is underestimated if it is restricted to audiences for new products. Consumerism entails re-writing social and physical space; it creates new forms of cultural space for performance. The forms and boundaries of the conventional life-world are inscribed in a variety of ways in expectations and understandings. The world around us can be thought of as both a physical terrain and as ways of organising and interpreting its physical components (recent contributions to re-thinking the spatial as cultural environment are to be found in Shields 1991 and Short 1991).

One way of interpreting this theme can be taken from an idea by Girouard (1990) in his book on English towns. He comments on the continuity of his interests by drawing a parallel between a country house and a town (op. cit. p. 5). Of both, it is reasonable and fruitful to ask, what is the way of life which produced it?; and what are the services and functions which sustain it? A significant difference may be that while many country houses can display an authorial vision, few towns, and only those aspiring to utopianism, can claim to be authored. Towns therefore are authorless narratives told in forms of fact and fiction. In one sense because the metropolitan city cannot be contained within a single narrative and any progress is as a documentary exploration, and secondly, more literally, because a town is indexically inscribed through its documentary records such as newspapers, archives, visual records, etc. Both in relation to a nostalgic communalism and in response to the other of urban menace, the city in entertainment becomes a terrain of narratives – an increasingly imaginary zone.

This new stage for performance (terrain) can frequently, if loosely, be described as utopian in its idealisations. An initial form this frequently takes is nostalgic. Idealising a vanished community, social history is reconstructed as entertainment in museums and theme parks, such as that at Beamish in the North East of England: 'Local heritage is the focus of the visit to Beamish, . . . Beamish is a commemoration of a mythical past; objects never intended to commemorate anything are transformed into monuments of mythical meaning' (Shanks and Tilley 1987 p. 83). More usually, the idealisations of consumerism offer a bridge between the securities of the present to the promises of modernity. We come back to Strasser's point about marketing bridging the domains of personal experience with multi-national manufacture, although it seems that bridging may not be the most helpful metaphor. The process I am trying to capture is the ways in which the promise and the grandeur of modernity could be staged within the petty intimacies of suburban lifestyles.

In Marchand's study (1985) of American advertising in the decades between the two world wars, he argues strongly that the composite picture of social concerns in advertisements is not an accurate guide to reality. But, more interestingly, advertisements can be read as a guide to how mass society was shown to be adaptable to personal relationships. Advertising at that time provided a means of affiliation that simplified the enormity of corporate marketing. Obviously, advertisements as the cultural form of consumer culture, simplify by distilling a dramatic narrative into a tableau that can be quickly apprehended (Goffman 1976; see also Winship 1981 for an illustration of the invisibility of a cultural repertoire in dramatising the use of goods). But the notion of simplification here goes beyond this to refer to the relationships between any element in that culture and the grand mythologies which motivate the cultural order governing social actors and their cultural resources.

My argument in this chapter is that the metaphor of marketing in consumer culture provides a set of grand myths for (or we can say provides a means of dramatisation of the complexity of) modernity. In their various forms the myths can be summarised as attaching great importance to the possibility, through spectacular forms, of personal appropriation of moments of cultural significance. Further, that this promise, of personal appropriation, is inseparable from the forms of representation we have used in a struggle to articulate a sense of modernity. And yet the promise of change, recurrent change, and the re-writing of social order inherent in individual-isation that is offered in modernity because they disturb conventional order are likely to be seen as threatening in many ways. The simplification I seek to describe should be understood as the means of accommodations and adaptations to these threats.

Given the lack of a clear object to be dramatised (i.e. modernity) it is unsurprising that the simplifications I am concerned with have, as I have indicated, usually been couched in the dramatic form of spectacular show. Thus the imaginary, the illusory and the artificial have celebrated and mocked the rhetoric of cultural change. I have consistently argued in relation to the stars, shows, tourism, adverts and of entertainment that, as spectacular entertainment, there is nothing behind the facade. Without endorsing his technological determinism it might be helpful to revive Marshall McLuhan's once influential slogan that the medium is the message (given its most thoughtful presentation in 1964). In the spectacular excess of pre-sentation all customers can feel of equal status as patrons. The wonder of modernity is made accessible and comprehensible through utopian forms.

I hope to be able to clarify the ways in which an intimation of utopia has acted as a simplification of the simultaneous promise and threat of modernity through some brief notes on modernism. McLuhan's slogan is interestingly consistent with the formalist dimensions of modernism. I have referred to the perceived threats of modernity, threatening because they seem to stand as prescrip-tive expectations to embrace an uncertain social world. The very lack of solidity in the social forms of modernity (stirringly celebrated in the now famous set of essays by Berman 1983), has been theorised in the representational innovations of modernism (Bradbury and McFarlane 1976; see also Kern 1983 and Finlay 1990). Modernism clearly was (is?), whatever else it might be said to be, in its various forms a series of attempts to engage with the implications of modernity (Clark's 1985 essays on painting by Manet and his followers are one attempt to trace representations of the myths of modernity). The formal innovations of modernism are usually presented as what were felt to be necessary responses to the times, that is as an avant-garde necessity to renew its innovations.

Although it is clearly inappropriate to create a firm distinction between the naturalism of popular culture on the one hand and the formal abstractions of modernist high culture on the other (an incompatibility that has been tendentiously played up in the Philistine populism of Left and Right). If the codes of modernism have come to stand as a symbolic language for the demands of modernity, then to the extent that these demands are seen as threatening, so modernism will become alien and antagonistic to popular experience. In all the varieties of modernist innovation, one recurrent concern is with the appropriateness of the relationship between the formal resources for signifying and that which is to be signified. This becomes particularly problematic when the signified one is dealing with is the built environments for new forms of communication and entertainment. (In a typical collection of illustrations of modern British building styles in the first 40 years of this century all the examples concern communication, including transport, and entertainment; Forsyth 1982). In these respects the iconography of modernism is giving form to the future as what will be known. Modernist forms, and in particular modernist architecture and planning, are therefore constitutive of visions of collectivity and community. There is, if you like, a predisposition to social engineering.

An intimate connection between a theory of an idealised built environment and a utopian community (or idealised system of social arrangements) is not an innovation of modernism (see for example the history of utopian forms traced in Rosenau 1959). Theorists of utopia have traditionally postulated a physical space outside the conventionally known world in which a completely new form of social organisation can be inscribed (Kumar 1991; Levitas 1990). And those who have in practice sought to exempt themselves from the constraints of the imperfections of normal society (or who have sought to protect others as in Owen's or Cadbury's communities) have usually created new designs for living in their physical environments (Hayden 1976; Davey 1980; Peterson 1987). The innovation in modernity to this long and interesting history is that utopian theorists of modernism, whether as characteristically English as Ebenezer Howard or as characteristically French as Le Corbusier, have had a distinctive influence on the social policies in different national contexts which have informed what Ravetz (1986) has called 'the government of space'.

It would be a simplistic generalisation to pretend to know whether the modernism of urban planning and architecture has been as consistently unpopular as has been presented in populist tracts (even creating an unlikely social campaigner from a leading member of the British Royal family). At the time of writing it is clear, however, that there is a very widespread loss of confidence in programmes of social engineering. This has meant that innovations in communication and entertainment, where they have continued to engage with and in some sense display the promise of modernity, have usually done so in very bowdlerised accents of modernism. It has also legitimated an enormous variety of modes of communal nostalgia which in addition to being a very simplified form of collective remembering also seem at times to constitute a flight from modernity. The utopianism of consumer landscape frequently has the paradoxical character of a personalisation of community.

Interesting examples of the dilution of modernism are provided by the development of out-of-town shopping centres or shopping malls which are the most current form of the utopian promise of consumer plentifulness (cf. Kowinski 1982). I have published a study of the largest British instance of the form (Chaney 1990A) and will take some points from that account. In many respects the MetroCentre in Gateshead is a utopian zone from which the menaces and threats of urban disorder have been removed. In the regularity and coherence of its built forms and its little nods towards rural idioms, such as the scattering of trees and plants, it would gladden the heart of any theorist of the need for planned communities. It is also dependent upon a road network and a massive building programme of suburbanisation both of whose forms directly derive from entrenched tenets of urban planning. The MetroCentre as a cultural form where commerce becomes leisure is therefore one instance of the routinisation of modernity, and characteristically the trappings of modernism are very skimpily applied.

Here, very clearly at one of the points where international manufacturing is accommodated to the personal intimacies of mass customers, the monumentality of public architecture is dissipated into suburban forms indistinguishable from other aspects of the mundane vernacular.

Another example of the recuperation of modernity by more traditionalist simplifications is provided by the rise of religious broadcasting in the United States – what Hoover (1988) has called the 'electronic church' (this account is largely based on his book). Closely associated with the rise of evangelical fundamentalism over the past three decades the electronic church functions as a version of an imaginary community with particular appeal to those who feel themselves estranged in mass society. Transcending the conventional doctrinal disputes of established denominations, and celebrating an eclecticism of sentimentalised and frequently charismatic faith, religious broadcasting is able to operate as a para-church. It is therefore an example of the sort of de-institutionalisation that has been hailed as a mark of post-modern social forms. And yet the post-modernity of de-institutionalisation is articulated through a rigorous traditionalism affirming values and beliefs otherwise seen as threatened by modernity. The paradox may inhibit the spread of evangelical fundamentalism but it has revived and reshaped conservative politics.

The paradox of using very advanced technology to affirm traditional values, is not peculiar to the electronic church. The paradox of a privatised participation in communal forms it seems is the utopian dream of a culture of marketing. The explosion in communicative resources in modernity has generally worked to privatise and personalise audience control of communication facilities (including transport). And yet, simultaneously, the anomie inherent in this fragmentation of public space has been counterpointed by an idealisation of community, although it is a community articulated in subjective experience.

A theorisation of the utopian promise of marketing culture has appropriately been furnished by an architectural critique of social engineering. There has in recent years in most media, but particularly in architecture, been an avant-gardist rejection of modernist aesthetics in favour of the eclecticism of post-modernism (cf. Jencks 1984 for example). In one of the early manifestoes of the movement by Venturi and Scott Brown (1972) the centrality of spectacular imagery to consumer appeals, discussed earlier in this section, is celebrated. They argue that what we should learn from Las Vegas is that the high modernist architectural aesthetic of form enclosing space does not exhaust the order of cultural space. The alternative they detect in consumer culture is to recognise that communication can pre-empt aesthetics. The architecture of casinos, garages, motels and shopping malls, etc., is essentially that of functional sheds. The architectural interest for post-modernists is that on these sheds has been draped a spectacular imagery which symbolically reorders space (of course inheriting and echoing the innovations in mass marketing in department stores at the turn of the century). Stylistic hypereclecticism can and does cannibalise any and every source for this symbolic repertoire.

The Strip in Las Vegas is therefore very modern as a set of new buildings which have colonised the desert. It has been built on a place without a history, at least architectural history, and yet has pillaged European history indiscriminately (an alternative and less euphoric view of architectural hyper-eclecticism, in what is for this purpose analogous Los Angeles, is provided by Davis 1990). The iconography of the Strip is therefore redolent of traditionalism, in this and in its literal vulgarity it is reminiscent of the ordered chaos and imagery of the fairground. There seems in the architecture of post-modernism then a conflation of past and future; a conflation that is also of public and personal spheres. Both forms of conflation acting as means of simplification through stylistic excess.

A consequence of the changes that I have been describing is that style, whether it is of buildings, clothes, foods or whatever, loses the last vestiges of naturalness and becomes radically self-conscious or artificial. This is not in itself a contemporary innovation (there are good reasons for locating it in romanticism, see Rosen and Zerner 1984 in particular the essay 'Realism and the Avantgarde'). My argument is that it has become institutionalised in consumerism and in particular in tourism as a form of consumer leisure. This argument can be clarified by considering one or two implications for the theoretical practice of a discipline as unlikely in this context as archaeology.

There are two points of contact. On the one hand, traditionally, archaeologists 'read' the texts of material culture and use a vocabulary of style to create cultural distinctiveness and coherence. This interpretive exercise, however, need not be confined to the artefacts of dead cultures but can also be used on the material culture of consumer society (see for example the study of beer cans in Britain and Sweden in Shanks and Tilley 1987; see also some of the essays in Hodder 1988). On the other hand, archaeologists have become increasingly involved in the production and management of tourist sites. They have been expected to produce and sustain theme parks of history such as the *Jorvik Viking Centre* at York. This has in its turn had the consequence of raising issues of the authorship of history, and the relationship between performance and audience in a museum. In both respects it is precisely because the data of archaeology are so frequently eclectic, haphazard and authorless that they have come to seem particularly germane to the dramatisation of the present.

The triumph of archaeology is that its practitioners are able to construct convincing accounts, what we can call cultural order, from the random detritus of the subterranean record. This is of course directly analogous to our accounts of the meaning of the Las Vegas Strip. Venturi and Scott Brown see the order of the Strip as difficult:

> It is not the easy, rigid order of the urban renewal project or the fashionable 'total design' of the megastructure . . . . But the order of the Strip *includes*; it includes at all levels, from the mixture of seemingly incongruous land uses to the mixture of seemingly incongruous advertising media plus a system of neo-Organic or neo-Wrightian restaurant motifs in Walnut Formica.
>
> (Venturi and Scott 1972 pp. 52–3 *sic*)

Being inclusive is difficult because it implies contradictions, inconsistencies and polysemy, all qualities welcomed by Venturi and Scott Brown in architectural practice.

The further dimension to utopianism this provides is the recognition that because a landscape is difficult does not mean that it is disordered. The notion of the difficult order in architectural form is in this respect surely analogous to utopian spectacle in social order. The profusion of imagery and meanings may seem chaotic but are always exhilarating. In consumer culture we inhabit a fictive landscape. I do not mean by this that the goods of consumerism are false, artificial and illusory. To say this and this alone is to cling to some distinction between natural and cultural values. The idea of a fictive landscape is that every feature of the world we inhabit is a choice. There is of course a material reality to the landscape but it has lost its intrinsic form. The dramatic order of our cultural landscape is chaotic.

TRAVERSING A FICTIVE LANDSCAPE

In a chapter that is concerned with the framing of entertainment as performance I keep being drawn back to the significance of advertising. The discourse of advertising, as a genre of mass communication, forms a bridge between the subjectivity of consumer culture and the utopian spaces of mass entertainment. I think this is possible because advertising is a genre of literature that has left its generic status behind (like the analogous form of popular music videos which have become equivalently autonomous in that the images do not need to 'illustrate' the songs). One reason is that the 'literary' component in advertising message is becoming increasingly marginalised by other modes of signification. A second reason is that advertising refuses the aura of the work of art. It makes sense only in relation to itself: 'Literature's power is discrete and accretive; advertising's power is aggregate, cumulative – almost, one might say, immanent' (Wicke 1988 p. 175).

The implication of a claim that advertisements transcend the generic character of other forms of performance is that we are led to reconsider the relationship between representation and reality. The illusion of advertising is not that it misleads the audience with unsustainable claims. Rather, the fundamental illusion is the belief that advertising seeks to imbue its subject with distinctiveness. The project of advertising is instead the dramatisation (spectacularisation) of mundane experience. Both because it is no longer governed by external generic conventions and because it is no longer a servant of the phenomenal character of the subject matter: 'advertising speaks about itself in order to narrativize all the relations of and contradictions in the surplus value of capitalist production' (Wicke op. cit. p. 174). The space of its topics is therefore populated with its own interminable narratives, its forms of spectacular excess.

The aura or space of a work of art prior to the development of processes of mass entertainment implied a form of social command. It both framed a claim to distinctiveness and told a story about the relationship between signifiers and signified. This story was itself finite, it was contained within the bounds of the genres of narration. The idea of cultural space combines both the 'place' of performance, the ways in which it commands an audience or congregation, and the controls of social order that are accepted as appropriate for such a place. The consequence of the various modes of dramatisation in a culture of mass entertainment that I have described in this book, is that the boundaries to the space of narrative genres have become unsustainable. They have been subverted by the needs of new forms of collective sociation to find means of representation appropriate to themselves.

The interminable excess of advertising is not explicitly discussed in Raymond Williams' (1975) inaugural lecture on drama in a dramatised society; he is concerned, however, with the implications of the unlimited performance of drama in modernity: 'we have never as a society acted so much or watched so many others acting . . . . It is in our own century, in cinema, in radio and in television, that the audience for drama has gone through a qualitative change' (op. cit. p. 4). The significance of these changes is more than an extension of audiences or new social composition: 'It is that drama, in quite new ways, is built into the rhythms of everyday life' (ibid. p. 5). The process of dramatisation has in complex and mobile cultures burst the bounds of narrative genres. Following a commercial rather than technical logic, illusionistic devices have been liberated from their particular settings and are now employed as personal resources. Drama, particularly spectacular drama, has been naturalised into everyday experience.

I can describe this process as the spectacularisation of everyday life or as the routinisation of spectacular forms. In either case the boundaries or frames of performance are both made more prominent and more arbitrary. This is a process that can offer a radical disruption of the established hierarchies of discourse in social order. The social command inherent in the space of everyday life can be thrown into question. It is, however, only at moments of revolutionary praxis that the enormity of the possibility of disorder becomes visible. Ross (1988 p. 41) argues that the Paris Commune of 1871 was such a spatial event: 'If workers are those who are not allowed to transform the space/time alloted to them, then the lesson of the Commune can be found in its recognition that revolution consists . . . in completely transforming the nature of space/time.' The Communards failed to attack the Bank of France but destroyed the Vendome Column, a militaristic and nationalistic monument, as a: 'refusal of the dominant organization of social space' (op. cit. p. 39).

The basis of this argument is that in de-constructing the hierarchies of conventional discourse, the Communards (as did their heirs in May 1968, see Willener 1972) exposed social space as equivalent to (in Lefebvre's terms – Lefebvre 1971)) everyday life. Social space, it is claimed, mediates between the intentionality of subjective experience and the constraints of institutionalised forms (a dialectic that will be familiar to those who have read Berger and Luckmann (1967) on the social organisation of commonsense). These parallels between space, everyday life and commonsense are only surprising if space is conceived as an autonomous, neutral environment rather than, more positively, as processes of social organisation constituted through practice. Making a connection between revolutionary interruption and the dramatic forms of advertising is not meant to suggest that advertising is a revolutionary practice, but that advertising relativises the organisation of social space in ways that are potentially subversive.

Green's work (1990) on the spectacle of nature, a study of the early years of the development of the city as the space of consumer culture, illustrates the signification (the ways in which we signify) as well as the material inscription of cultural space. It would only be a trivial discovery to find that the countryside or nature has been constructed in contrast to images of urban social forms (certainly not a discovery after Williams' 1973 study of the literary interdependence of countryside and city). Green, however, provocatively situates the structures of perception of nature in the discourses of nineteenth century Paris in urban social relations: 'In other words, there was a *continuum* between the ways the city was consumed and the countryside inhabited' (Green 1990 p. 66 *sic*).

We can go further and say that nature, as it was constituted in metropolitan discourse, is as much a set of means of entertainment or services to be consumed as any range of urban lifestyles: 'Nature has largely to do with leisure and pleasure – tourism, spectacular entertainment, visual refreshment' (op. cit. p. 6). The argument is not just therefore that the space which nature occupies can be used as a resource for forms of dramatic entertainment, but rather that nature is one of the genres of those forms of entertainment. As such it is itself a form of spectacle. This then is one sense of the meaning of cultural space. The physical terrain of a place is re-written or re-formed through guides, maps, pictures and aesthetic values, etc., to become the ground for distinctive forms of social intercourse. The space is inscribed through the multiplicity of forms of enclosure which in their turn entail characteristic forms of use.

The notion of spectacular performance is simultaneously made more signficant, and made arbitrary and relative, by the erosion of boundaries between different forms of space. I have published a study of the staging of three national festivals in the years immediately following the end of the war in 1945 (Chaney 1983B). My initial interest was primarily in how the national broadcasting organisation chose to present festivals as different as the post-war Victory Parade, the Festival of Britain in 1951 (the centenary of the first national festival) and a new Queen's coronation two years later. A number of interesting contrasts emerged but I will focus now on the significance of the development of television as a national medium in the Coronation.

The new medium threw up the unprecedented and unanticipated possibility of redefining public space. Not only did the public at home, although straining to see their tiny television pictures, have, even so, a better view of the ceremony than many in the audience in Westminster Abbey, they were also eventually allowed into (via the television camera) the most mysterious part of the ceremony. This is the moment when the new monarch is re-robed in an almost private ceremony in a chapel appropriately called the Theatre, a ceremony that is a symbolic transformation. (The intrusion of the cameras here also secularised and literally vulgarised a liminal transition in Turner's (1969) terms.)

Some contemporary commentators feared that the cameras might gain access to unintended blunders and slips that would lessen the majesty of established privilege. The more sophisticated realised that the ritual character of monarchy was in any case transformed when the mundane audience gawping over their coffee cups had a more privileged participation than established privilege. The more formal consequence was that the mass audience was brought into a previously undreamt of form of intimate communion with national ritual while at the same time remaining an abstract crowd of anonymous and invisible spectators. This is the crucial transformation of cultural space in forms of mass entertainment and is in itself a new tissue of disciplinary control through vicarious participation for mass publics.

One aspect of the blurring of boundaries to performance is, then, that we are drawn more insistently into dramatisations of our collective identity. Williams sees this as a consequence of becoming anonymous to ourselves, the places in which our social space is inscribed are both familiar and alien:

'I speak for Britain' runs the written line of that miming public figure, . . . we may even say 'Well I'm here and you don't speak for me'. 'Exactly,' the figure replies, with an unruffled confidence in his role, . . . 'you speak for yourself, but I speak for Britain'. 'Where is that?', you may think to ask, looking wonderingly around.

(Williams 1975 p. 15)

I have said earlier that the project of advertising is the dramatisation of mundane experience, and that this is staged in ways that are potentially subversive of the organisation of social space. What dramatisation means here is that the promise of spectacular lifestyles is offered as subjective choice – that dreams can become reality. Identity is not ascribed on this stage but is a personal appropriation and the props and markers of identity are therefore also subjective choices. I have so far accepted that in a culture of mass entertainment, subjective participation has taken the form of that of an audience for a performance. I will conclude by arguing for the possibility of continually engaging with the cultural space of 'audience-ing'.

The inherent necessity of and, further, the claimed social advantages of incessant individual competitive pursuit of limited goods have been a central value of those in power in capitalist social formations. The model of a market has been presented, almost worshipped, as the only effective form of social organisation for the determination of values. Effective is used here in two ways: first, that it provides appropriate incentives for production and distribution; and secondly, that it provides a 'truer' determination of comparative values. In a variety of different discursive guises, a commitment to the 'natural' effectiveness of a market as a model for social organisation has blurred and made indistinguishable the different aspects of citizenship in mass society. The three main aspects of citizenship that have recurred throughout the book have been the roles of consumer, voter and as member of audiences for entertainment. That is, members of ostensibly different forms of sociation – consumers, voters and what we can call entertained-ers – have become members of indistinguishable publics, the same sorts of customers in effectively the same market.

I have so far written of the market as a model for social organisation rather than as a metaphor because it has become so 'naturalised' that it is most frequently presented as a literal account of interactive process. I hope it can be seen that one purpose of my metaphor of the relations of dramatic production has been to point up the equivalently metaphoric status of market imagery. The principal limitation of the market as metaphor is that it treats all goods being traded as functionally equivalent. (There are a number of other limitations which stem from the metaphor being based on an idealisation of the ways in which markets are made and sustained but I do not need to explore these here.)

The metaphor works when we can say that, for example, all the varieties of apples available could be known by any one customer so that her/his choice was adequately informed and their estimate of the pleasure of acquisition was reasonably soundly based. In relation to forms of performance which, as I have said from the beginning, constitute their own reality, such anticipatory knowledge is in principle impossible. (This is true whether one is dealing with a 'performance' such as an ordinary conversation or some more self-conscious staging of a form of representation.) The 'value' of participation/production is part of the ways in which collaboration and subjectivity are interdependently articulated. The value is the possibility of participating in how consciousness or the meaningfulness of social action is constituted (but only in part because cultural forms are historically grounded institutions). Those who would treat the values of creating identity as being of the same order as choosing or consuming an apple, are governed by or seek to impose forms of cultural space in which there is no play.

The inadequacies of the metaphor of the market are not of course purely a matter for social theory. To contest the ways in which the roles of voter, consumer and entertained-er have been scripted is to make a political critique of the organisation of social order. I can in this setting make only some very preliminary notes on the form of the critique implied in this account, although the whole of the book is the basis for a subversive alternative. I will suggest now that if the tissues of disciplinary order are to be subverted through developing the creativity of participation, and the play of narcissism (see Finlay (1991)), then the role of design becomes pivotal in furnishing an alternative language of mass entertainment (and mass consumption and mass politics). Engaging with the design of goods, persons, places and spaces means that their spectacular form is not accepted at face value but made part of a play of meanings.

When I discussed the significance of design earlier in the chapter I argued that design is characteristic of modernity. It is both a consequence of the development of the division of labour and as such an adjunct of mass production, and a central resource for industries of marketing and mass distribution. In this dual role, design directly parallels the functions filled by the notion of formula in mass entertainment. It has been argued that in order to organise the industrial production of culture, something equivalent to a formula is necessary to programme the tastes of anonymous audiences and guarantee predictability (Cawelti 1976). Recurrent features to a number of different narratives also facilitate critical discussion of characteristic formulaic genres (Cawelti and Rosenberg 1987), and can be seen to be providing stable reassurance for mass audiences.

Similarly, I do not think it is stretching terms too far to argue that the cast list of figures in public life, stars, personalities and celebrities, act as representatives of a repertoire of design. Their personalities are marketing strategies designed to mobilise the interest and sympathy of a variety of different types of audience. This is a cynical use of marketing in that it seems that a politics of social policy has been supplanted by a politics of personality. In practice it is not as simple as that, as deeply ideological policies can and do masquerade behind personas of consensus and ordinariness. It does seem, though, that incompetence or the pursuit of bigoted sectional interest are not as disabling in the pursuit of political popularity as a failure to command a symbolic repertoire of trustworthiness that is equivalent to a formula or a design.

The inadequacies of design as it is fashioned in the self-consciously knowing sophistication of the advertising industry are that, as a marketing resource in mass production and distribution, design symbolically re-orders space with imagery. The trappings of individualising lifestyles are tacked on to quite functional machineries for the production of shoddy objects. The order of cultural space is celebrated as difficult or chaotic (and thus paradoxically as simplifying) through spectacular excess.

The idea of design can, however, be taken over for a promise of creative hedonism. In seeking goods and services that are made with respect and without exploitation we practically re-write the forms of social space. I noted in the previous discussion of design that William Morris had emphasised its potential as social critique. He argued that design should be more than features of style; it can and should articulate a way of working (what we can call a form of life). An authentic way of working is accomplished through the twin elements of a truth to materials, and through an emphasis upon 'authority' in production and in use.

It may seem absurd to seek a truth to materials when I have accepted that in late modern culture signifiers have become up-rooted. There are no natural meanings and the materials of design, the goods, persons, places and spaces of our culture, are irredeemably subject to dramatic irony. Truth to materials in this context does not mean an attempt to recapture the past, particularly if that were taken to mean further inventions of traditions. The phrase is used here to conjure the idea that the order of cultural space is generated by, and consistent with, the form of life, that is the multiplicity of projects which use and inform that space.

The notion of authority in relation to design I take from Bristol's (1985) account of popular cultural traditions in early-modern theatrical forms. He is paraphrasing Bakhtin when he argues that authority is a quality of:

> one who conceives and brings to completion even the humblest social initiative or artistic project. In this sense, authority is not a special talent or the exclusive privilege of a small minority of great statesmen or artists, but is, on the contrary, initially dispersed among all men and women with basic linguistic competence.
>
> (Bristol op. cit. p. 22)

The history of art, and in particular theatrical art, has been the expropriation of authority to become the privilege of authors. It may well be that in the terms of Foucault's (1984) influential essay we have witnessed the death of the author in modernity, but that does not mean that we have recaptured the space for authority.

(It is of course not coincidental that an emphasis upon truth to materials became one of the creeds of high modernism, and in particular a focal concern of Bauhaus modernism – a set of design practices that are radically different (to put it no more strongly) from those of Morris. This is not the place to attempt to trace this cultural history. It is, however, important to note that at least one critic of the Bauhaus 'clerisy' ('to use an old term for an intelligentsia with clerical presumptions', Wolfe 1983 p. 18), treats them as an élite who created an aesthetics of social engineering, and locates their failure in the way they expropriated authority from popular use to a vanguard intelligentsia.)

I have no wish to contribute to the by now voluminous literature which has attempted to capture Morris for either medievalism or Marxism or some variant of either or both. But, even so, it is not fanciful in the light of a subsequent politics of the physical grounding of human society to see his concern with meaningful expression through a respect for the means of representation as a precursor of the holism of Green politics: "'Art is man's *embodied* expression of interest in the life of man; it springs from man's pleasure in his life;" . . . Again, he speaks of "the sense of beauty in the external world, of interest in the life of man as drama, and the desire of communicating this'" (quoted in Thompson 1977 p. 656, emphasis added). I infer from this that design, as a way of working, offers the opportunity of what I have called a practical aesthetics.

The work we have at hand, as members of publics for lifestyles, political projects and forms of entertainment, is clearly not physical as in Morris' idealisation of craftsmanship. This does not mean that it cannot be governed by his command of a truth to materials. The enjoyment of design is the same as the pleasure to be derived from a landscape. Some landscapes are designed by individuals but most are fashioned by implicit collaboration in the use of shape, colour, texture and materials in pursuit of practical projects through generations. Some landscapes are spectacular while others persuade through the quiet accumulation of detail. These differences do not create a hierarchy of value. The context for evaluating the ways in which social projects are fashioned through form is always whether there has been exploitation of materials or producers and users. In these ways we can politicise the organisation of social space.

We cannot ascetically repudiate the cultural forms of tourism, leisure and lifestyles; they can, however, be imbued with mundane authority. The 'space(s)' for the ambiguous collectivities of mass society is/are marked out by what is at best a difficult order, but this does not mean that we have lost the power to reflexively dramatise our experience: 'Life-planning in respect of the body is hence not necessarily narcissistic, but a normal part of post-traditional social environments. Like other aspects of the reflexivity of self-identity, body-planning is more often an engagement with the outside world than a defensive withdrawal from it' (Giddens 1991 p. 178). It may well be that there is a 'threat' of promiscuous interpretation (see the essay by Pratt (1986) on this threat to literary theory) but that leads only to the *promise* of the politicisation of the production of meaning.

6

CONCLUSION: POPULAR
AND CULTURE

A history of collective life, whether it is constrained by a national framework or not, has to engage with a notion of the popular. What this means is that although the popular seems to be a fundamental descriptive resource, a historian of collective life should at some point have to consider what sorts of things a notion of the popular might be trying to describe and display. (This account is not meant to contradict or supersede previous discussions of different uses of the popular, such as in Chapter 3; here the same material is re-organised for a different purpose. This is therefore a deliberate re-mixing.)

The term 'the popular' clearly points to some element of social life, such as music or newspapers or customs, which is enjoyed or practised or celebrated by ordinary members of society: 'In relation to cultural forms, however, the term "popular" commonly refers to a particular mode of address identified within the text as presumed to appeal to the "common people"' (Shiach 1989 p. 28). It is reasonably widespread in its occurrence, and there is an implication that participation is unlikely to be restricted to those possessing distinctive qualities. Even if the popular is frequently understood by implied contrast to some other social or cultural forms, such as high or élite or informed groups or whatever, the nature of the contrast is not generally problematic. Indeed the popular in its ordinariness, literally its vulgarity, is self-evidently available and meaningful.

Despite all this, I shall argue that there are two main organising perspectives underlying uses of the popular. Disentangling them will serve three purposes: first, it will help to clarify some incompatibilities in the literature on popular culture; second, it will lead to some further reflections on the concept of culture; and, third, it will help to pull together some points I have been trying to make about ways of talking about ourselves in contemporary culture. The two perspectives I shall distinguish can be labelled, on the one hand, a vernacular approach and, on the other, an interventionist approach. I shall describe and illustrate each in turn and then consider the implications of the distinction.

The grounds of the distinction are that the vernacular conception is fundamentally descriptive in its strategy while the interventionist approach depends upon distinctions made in the course of an analysis. The latter approach is therefore dependent upon the plausibility of an interpretive account which uses structural contrasts. The former depends for its reasonableness upon the self-evident appropriateness of the terms used. I am aware that I have used this distinction between descriptive and analytic concepts before, then in relation to a distinction between play and leisure. In repeating the contrast I do not intend to imply that the pair of terms play and leisure in any sense parallels the pair of terms vernacular and interventionist senses of the popular. What is paralleled is the implied difference within each pair. In order to introduce the difference in uses of the popular I shall review what I mean by the distinction between play and leisure.

Leisure describes a category of things people do. The boundaries of the category are not given by the sorts of things concerned (what people do for their leisure is obviously a potentially infinite list), but by the ways in which they come to be involved. That is, by the expectations they bring to the activity concerned and by the reciprocity of perspectives shared with those who 'stage' that activity for the do-ers who are their potential customers or audience. In contrast, play refers not to an activity but a relationship between those participating (how it is done). The boundaries of the category are therefore given by the boundaries to those relationships. Play is structural in that it is articulated through the differences between the doing and other forms of doing – most frequently expressed as a contrast between play and reality. Play is therefore given in its own performance, it is literally made up as it goes along, and so it can only be understood in its own terms. It is a representation but only a representation of itself.

The vernacular approach to popular culture (and culture can be replaced by a variety of terms such as custom or festivity) takes a set of collective activities as naturally occurring features of the life of a community. These activities will include rituals, carnivals, fairs, sports, rough amusements and gossip. There are characteristic forms to these activities which persist through generations and form part of the distinctive repertoire or identity of the community. And it is important to recognise that the community in early modern Europe is not a homogeneous entity but is patterned by occupational communities and regional diversity (see the discussion in Burke 1978, especially Part 1).

The persistence of these forms is both a display of the conservatism of popular tradition and a central means through which the community renews itself as a stable entity with characteristic values. The last point leads from forms to functions – the stubborn traditionalism of communal life lends itself to being read as serving social purposes:

> Though it [carnival] is a festive and primarily symbolic activity, it has immediate pragmatic aims, most immediately that of objectifying a collective determination to conserve the authority of the community to set its own standards of behavior and social discipline, and to enforce these standards by appropriate means.
>
> (Bristol 1985 p. 52)

There is in this sort of statement a clear slide towards postulating a form of collective autonomy for the popular (thereby providing a distinctive subject matter for historians of collective life, something which is quite different from the accumulated actions of individuals). One consequence of being able to detect a social concept through an account of the functions it is able to serve or provide, is that it provides for the possibility of conflict between this and another cultural 'programme' within the same society. Thus Bristol is able to say that a problem for popular culture has been 'the degree to which that culture retained any degree of independent initiative, and the ability of that culture to articulate and carry out its own partisan agenda in the face of a powerfully organised hegemony' (op. cit. p. 7). This move from function to ideology has obviously been central to those accounts which have sought to equate popular in urban-industrial societies with proletarian or working-class culture.

A second consequence stems from the fact that the 'aims' or 'programme' of vernacular culture implicit in oral tradition are anonymous and not associated with authoritative texts, and are ephemeral in their enactment if not their social function. The 'texts' of vernacular culture are not generally preserved in the several canons of cultural tradition but have been lost in the anonymity of the forms of life they celebrate. It has therefore been easy to slide from the spontaneity of the popular tradition to a use of notions like natural and authentic and organic with which to characterise the popular as opposed to the 'artificiality' of intellectual culture. This sense of an opposition between nature and culture has been particularly prevalent by those who have celebrated folk forms as a version of popular culture.

Interestingly, while this organicism has lent itself to the populism of the radical right (as in the blood and soil of Nazism), and the centrality of conflict noted in the previous paragraph has been the basis of left populism (as in the Proletkult of the early years of Soviet Russia), they have frequently become indistinguishable in aesthetic practice in a common style of heroic naturalism. A further implication of these two consequences is that a vernacular view of popular culture is not confined to medievalism but is equally flourishing in modern societies, particularly as in examples such as Nuttall and Carmichael's (1977) celebration of bawdy vulgarity.

The alternative approach to a sense of the popular, what I have called an interventionist account, does not have a completely different set of 'data' but feeds from the same instances of cultural conflict and difference. Indeed, the need for intervention derives above all else from a recognition of cultural difference – from a self-consciousness in the use of culture: 'Basically "the popular" has always been "the other"' (Shiach 1989 p. 31). In her study of the discourse of the popular, Shiach shows that the use of a notion of the popular as an alternative culture is a development of the fracturing of social order. That is, that during the course of the late eighteenth and early nineteenth centuries as it began to seem necessary and appropriate to use a language of class to formulate the nature of social order, so the term popular began to gain currency.

The basis of this new use was a recognition that how 'they', and less frequently 'we', did things was other than the norms of secular, rational and liberal publics. There were therefore grounds for intervention (see Bailey 1978 for a study of those who sought to impose an agenda of rational recreation), protection, recovery and recording. Amongst those who promoted this new concern with popular cultural forms, there were often interesting contrasts drawn between a folk peasantry who were seen to be needing to be rescued from oblivion, although improved through bowdlerisation for public consumption and an urban proletariat who needed to be civilised (cf. Burke op. cit. 1978 Chapter 1 and Colls 1977). Both forms of intervention were frequently part of a nationalist programme, and could easily be adapted to a socialist romanticisation of a class culture.

It should come as no surprise to be reminded that the period of the invention of the popular is also, as Williams (1958) argued years ago, the period of the major transformation in the meaning of culture (see also Williams 1981). Changing from a predominant meaning of managed growth or cultivation to our sense of a way of life characteristic of, and unique to, a social entity such as a community. It is consistent with the developing uses of popular and culture that under the mantle of a romantic search for authenticity and national identity, painters, poets, folk-song collectors and composers would seek to record and literally re-create indigenous cultural and particularly musical traditions. (It is amusing that in the early twentieth century, nationalist composers seeking inspiration from folk music should sometimes use their discoveries for modernist innovations which have lost them a popular audience (Weber 1990).) This sense of popular as something 'other' is frequently consistent with popular as proletarian. It is not therefore that the phenomena necessarily differ between the two approaches, but that the interventionist account is rooted in relativism.

The significance of this is that popular and culture are seen to be indexically grounded in the emergent language of the social. They are part of that repertoire of classifying and recording and representational practices which is the armoury of the social order of mass society. There are by now a huge number of studies on representational practices as diverse as medicine, photography, criminology and sexuality to name only a few. I have used the metaphor of dramatic performance to illustrate how these practices can both constitute and intervene in the construction of modernity. More generally, my account is one example of the use of one of the analytic disciplines, such as anthropology, sociology and history etc., which have been developed as self-conscious theorisations of the language of the social.

The popular, then, can be used in its vernacular sense to describe pre-modern social practice, but it is taking a term from modernity to use it in a different structure of relationships. The popular is not a natural, transparent, term of description; it is a weapon in a variety of struggles to cope with the crippling unease of a recognition that there are limitations to *any and all* way(s) of talking about ourselves. The history of collective life is not a continuous landscape under the harmonious sun of a universal language.

I said at the beginning of the chapter that to raise any questions about how we use the notion of the popular is, necessarily, to call into question the broader idea of culture. The reason for this is that they are interdependent foundation stones in the edifice of social discourse. Culture has been an invaluable synthesising resource in pioneering studies of customs and beliefs other than those shared within the milieu of academic discourse (a clear sense of the creative power of a vocabulary of culture is given in Wagner 1981). Culture is an agent of imperialism bringing diversity under the benevolent gaze of an intellectual bureaucratic apparatus but it also provides a worm to burrow into the foundations of that structure. Culture is a sorceror's apprentice that once commissioned can never be stopped. In conjunction with the closely-related concepts of nation, language and community we find that any attempt to set up norms of identification can and will be undermined by a re-ordering of the markers of distinction. Thus struggles for emancipation from within our culture have involved an insistence that perspectives deriving from gendered, sexual, ethnic, and religious identities cannot be recuperated within a dominant homogeneity.

The balkanisation of identity is, as I have said, true of concepts of collectivity in general and not just of culture. In addressing what is necessary for a history of collective life it will be helpful to consider a recent theoretical reconsideration of community. Community, like the countryside and public order, is one of those things we always used to have and which seem to have been made impossible by recent developments in modernity. And yet, while mourning its loss, it is frequently used as a term of collective identification (for example, the Catholic community in Northern Ireland), and it grounds a sense of the patterning of social life. Cohen (1985) has therefore suggested that although we cannot define communities externally – through a set of markers – we can let a practical use of community emerge through the boundaries used by those involved to mark off communities one from another. These boundaries may be physical barriers but even then are also, and more importantly, symbolic repertoires or repositories of meaning, so that 'culture – the community as experienced by its members – does not consist in social structure or in "the doing" of social behaviour. It inheres, rather, in "the thinking" about it' (Cohen op. cit. p. 98 *sic*).

For any particular example, tracing the contours of a community involves a sensitivity to ethnographic detail. The community as a resource for social action is marked out through relationships at two

194

levels. First, through contrasts and discriminations with other communities so that any symbolic markers of affiliation are working in dynamic tension with other modes of signification. And, secondly, through relationships within a community. The very fragmentation of moral authority that has been taken to be the criterion of the loss of *gemeinschaft* has also meant that we are members of a multiplicity of only unevenly overlapping communities. The variety of ways in which we can use the symbolic repertoire of any particular communal identity: 'provides the range within which individuality is recognizable. It continuously transforms the reality of difference into the appearance of similarity with such efficacy that people can still invest the "community" with ideological integrity' (Cohen op. cit. p. 21). In another later paper Cohen (1986 p. 12) phrases what seems to me to be the same point as 'that *differences* of meaning are the norm, even though they may be masked by the *appearance* of convergence'.

To the extent that the boundaries of affiliation (and I am using community to stand for the greater range of collective identities) are seen as the framework of social order, and these boundaries are things to think with, as Levi-Strauss has described myths, then social order is a resource for mundane reasoning. The forms of social order are both a network of significations and the simultaneous possibility of constraint and creativity. Cohen has suggested that a view of the structures of social formations as being composed of abstract signifiers has only become possible in very recent years – with the emergence of mass society. In contrast, one of my purposes in this book has been to argue that the languages of collectivity and subjectivity that I have summarised as the dramatisation of modernity have been spread through a much longer period of development. Although it is sometimes helpful to refer to certain aspects or processes as post-modern, the idea of a radical break between modernity and its successor need not be sustained.

It may seem paradoxical that as a concluding coda I say that we can now begin to describe and comment upon the performances or fictions of our collective life, what Horne has called 'The great drama, endlessly playing, . . . that of maintaining definitions of the nation and its social order' (Home 1986 p. 21). I have not restricted the theme of this drama to the nation alone, but instead of considering how communities of social order are played in detail, I have tried to show how they are dependent upon the relations of dramatic production. The distinction I have drawn is between the ways in which the vocabulary of 'the public culture' is inscribed in the spaces and places, the monuments and museums of our collective fictions, and the modes of apprehension and articulation of that vocabulary.

It is tempting to use the grammarians' distinction between competence and performance to describe the difference I seek to make but inappropriate (I would in any case prefer Hymes' (1971) sense of cultural rather than linguistic competence). The metaphor of language carries too much baggage (if I can mix metaphors). We need a hybrid combination of ways of seeing with ways of speaking to give an adequate sense of the constitutive reflexivity of modes of communal affiliation. It is only on the basis of how social order is staged that we can begin to see through the performances of public culture.

This is in some ways a difficult idea as the performances of public culture are not meant to be seen through. They are symbolic mirrors, we look at in order to see heightened reflections of ourselves, they are what Handelman has called a substantive medium of public consciousness: 'Public events are conveyances . . . [they] mediate persons into collective abstractions' (Handelman 1990 p. 15). The problem is that the process of mediation is not innocent; it works to deny inequalities of access to not only the production of public events but also to the interpretive frameworks within which those events are staged. The structures of relationships, through which roles of producer and audience are distributed, and inherited within élite groups, are disguised or naturalised through a number of strategies:

> Fascism was flagrantly and programmatically theatrical, in its rallies, art, architecture, military exhibition . . . . Our military displays are few, our politicians unspectacular and dark-suited, our rituals so ordinary they may easily pass for normal encounters.

> (Inglis 1988 p. 219)

I take the burden of Inglis' witty contrast to be that it is not theatricality that is illusory, we are only too well aware of the artifice of performance in public event. The trick that has to be turned (as Phillip Elliott (1980) put in relation to the ritualisation of outsiders), is to make the form of performance seem reasonable and appropriate. The problem of 'seeing through' processes of mediation is not to unmask the puppet-master holding the strings of performance, but to uncover ourselves – if not as puppets, then as acquiescent performers in dramas over which we lack control. The politicisation of the production of meaning would 'In the long run . . . change our way of doing both political theory and politics. It would be . . . to return the study of narratives (and symbolic actions treated as narratives) to the centre of the human sciences' (Inglis op. cit. p. 223).

Although I am impressed by Inglis' account it seems to me that he takes the spectacularity of modernity too much at face value. The events and performances of public culture are the phenomena any analysis begins with; they are the spectacles of social order. It is, however, too easy to be swayed by their verisimilitude, to assume that we have all become transfixed in their *trompe-l'oeil*. The processions, ceremonies, entertainments, trials, services, resorts and narrativity of public drama insistently affirm collective abstractions. But as popular culture they are caught within a contradiction, a disabling consciousness of their own limitations. To go back to the popular as a form of collective life I have to pose the question of why the spectacular forms of public drama are not more effective. Why our rulers as we ourselves cannot recreate the certainties of faith as collectivity rather than as individuals.

In order to provide an answer to these questions I shall turn to a study by Naomi Ritter (1989). She is concerned with the attractions of popular spectacle for artists. More specifically, she asks about the persistence of clown and circus imagery in cultural forms that are not oriented towards a popular audience. Ritter provides three main types of explanation that I believe can be adapted to illuminate the artistry of popular experience. The three types of explanation are, first, that in feeling themselves rejected or derided in a commercial culture (what Klingender (1972) has called a climate of cashbox aesthetics), artists have developed an affinity with other 'outsiders', principally popular entertainers. Following on from some points made in the previous chapter, I would say that the persistent distrust of the rationality of modernity has led to a countervailing affection for the irrational or foolish in popular entertainment.

The second type of explanation is that the clown offers the possibility of transcendence. As a type of holy fool or child-like innocent the entertainer can offer a charismatic redemption that speaks to otherwise inaccessible insights. This is a tempting possibility for artists who see themselves in opposition to bureaucratic rationality. Finally, popular entertainment, and particularly entertainment based in traditional forms, can be seen as primitive. But rather than this being a term of contempt it captures an authentic naturalism, a feeling that the sophistication of urban modernism has become irredeemably artificial. And so modernist artists have turned to popular forms particularly elements of ritual and style in order to retrieve the vitality of primitivism. Through a fascinating tour of examples Ritter is able to exemplify these points of interchange between the innovations of an intelligentsia and models of popular entertainment encapsulated in forms of spectacle.

I say models of popular entertainment because Ritter is concerned with how versions of the popular have been used in artistic practice. I believe that we can with advantage turn the direction of this approach around and point to the use of 'artistic' ideas in the vulgarity of popular culture. It is not difficult to find; indeed all the forms of popular entertainment discussed in these chapters have been saturated with examples of the themes of a distrust of rationality, a sympathy for a sense of transcendance through innocence, and an acceptance of the release from constraint in primitivism (all of them encapsulated in the tragic jouissance of Tommy Cooper). These themes are not articulated through a meta-discourse concerned with representation but are inherent in the spectacular's recognition of its own staging.

The popular, as a category of collective life, is, as I have said, grounded in the limitations of social description. The spectacular forms of popular entertainment are perennially a simultaneous celebration and yet denial of those limitations. This means that the irony of dramaturgy does not have to be seen to be restricted to the plays of authors but is inherent in the play of representing ourselves to ourselves.

REFERENCES

Alexander, J.C. (ed.) (1988) *Durheimian Sociology: Cultural Studies*, Cambridge University Press, London.

Allison, D. (1989) Photography and the mass market, in C. Ford (ed.) op. cit.

Alloula, M. (1986) *The Colonial Harem*, Minnesota University Press, Minneapolis, MN.

Altick, R.D. (1978) *The Shows of London*, Harvard University Press, Cambridge, MA.

Anderson, B. (1983) *Imagined Communities*, Verso, London.

Anglo, S. (1969) *Spectacle, Pageantry and Early Tudor Policy*, Oxford University Press, London.

Appleton, W.W. (1974) *Madame Vestris and the London Stage*, Columbia University Press, New York, NY.

Arscott, C. and Pollock, G. (1988) The partial view, in J. Wolff and J. Seed (eds) *The Culture of Capital*, Manchester University Press, Manchester.

Aston, M. (1988) *England's Iconoclasts*, Oxford University Press, Oxford.

Atkinson, P. (1990) *The Ethnographic Imagination*, Routledge, London.

Atwell, D. (1980) *Cathedrals of the Movies*, Architectural Press, London.

Babcock, B.A. (1980) Reflexivity: definitions and discriminations, *Semiotica*, Vol. 30 (1/2).

Babcock, B.A. and MacAloon, J. (1987) Victor A. Turner, *Semiotica*, Vol. 65 (1/2).

Bailey, P. (1978) *Leisure and Class in Victorian England*, Routledge and Kegan Paul, London.

—— (1986) *Music Hall*, Open University Press, Milton Keynes.

Baker, M. (1978) *The Rise of the Victorian Actor*, Croom Helm, London.

Bakhtin, M.M. (1968) *Rabelais and his World*, Indiana University Press, Bloomington IN.

Barker, F. (1984) *The Tremulous Private Body*, Methuen, London.

Barker, K. (1977) Bristol at Play 1801–53, in K. Meyer and K. Richards (eds) *Western Popular Theatre*, Methuen, London.

Barnouw, E. (1981) *The Magician and the Cinema*, Oxford University Press, New York, NY.

Barth, G. (1980) *City People*, Oxford University Press, New York, NY.

Barthes, R. (1982) *Camera Lucida*, Cape, London.

Baudrillard, J. (1983) *The Precession of Simulacra*, Semiotexte, New York, NY.

Bauman, R. (1977) *Verbal Art as Performance*, Newbury House, MA.

Baxandall, M. (1972) *Painting and Experience in C15 Italy*, Oxford University Press, New York.

Becker Ohrn, K. (1975) Photoflow of family life, *Folklore Forum*, Vol. 13, pp. 27–36.

Beloff, H. (1985) *Camera Culture*, Basil Blackwell, Oxford.

Benjamin, W. (1973) *Charles Baudelaire*, New Left Books, London.

Bennett, T. *et al.* (eds) (1986) *Popular Culture and Social Relations*, Open University Press, Milton Keynes.

Bennett, T. and Woollacott, J. (1987) *Bond and Beyond: The Political Career of a Popular Hero*, Macmillan, London.

Berger, P.L. and Luckmann, T. (1967) *The Social Construction of Reality*, Allen Lane, London.

Berman, M. (1983) *All that is Solid Melts into Air*, Verso Books, London.

Bommes, M. and Wright, P. (1982) Charms of Residence, in Centre for Contemporary Cultural Studies (eds) *Making Histories*, Hutchinson, London.

Bonham-Carter, V. (1978) *Authors by Profession*, Vol. 1. Society of Authors, London.

Booth, M.R. (1965) *English Melodrama*, Jenkins, London.

—— (1979) Spectacle as production style on the English stage. *Theatre Quarterly*, Vol. 8(32).

—— (1981) *Victorian Spectacular Theatre*, Routledge and Kegan Paul, London.

Bordwell, D. *et al.* (1985) *The Classical Hollywood Cinema*, Routledge and Kegan Paul, London.

Borsay, P. (1984) All the Town's a Stage in P. Clark (ed.) *The Transformation of English Provincial Towns*, Hutchinson, London.

—— (1989) *The English Urban Renaissance*, Clarendon Press, Oxford.

Bourdieu, P. (1984) *Distinction*, Routledge and Kegan Paul, London.

Bowlby, R. (1985) *Just Looking: Consumer Culture in Dreiser, Gissing and Zola*, Methuen, London.

Bowles, P. (1982) *The Spider's House*, Black Sparrow Press, Santa Barbara, CA.

Bradbury, M. and McFarlane, J. (eds) (1976) *Modernism 1890–1930*, Penguin Books, London.

Braive, M.F. (1966) *The Era of the Photograph*, Thames and Hudson, London.

Brandt, B. (1983) *London in the Thirties*, Gordon Fraser, London.

Brantlinger, P. (1983) *Bread and Circuses*, Cornell University Press, Ithaca, NY.

Briggs, A. (1973) The human aggregate, in H.J. Dyos and M. Wolfe (eds): *The Victorian City*, Routledge and Kegan Paul, London.

Brisset, D. and Edgley, C. (eds) (1990) *Life as Theater: A Dramaturgical Source Book*, 2nd edn. Aldine de Gruyter, New York, NY.

Bristol, M.D. (1985) *Carnival and Theatre*, Methuen, London.

Brody, H. (1986) *Maps and Dreams*, Faber and Faber, London.

Brooks, P. (1973) The melodramatic imagination, in D. Thorburn and G. Hartman (eds) *Romanticism*, Basic Books, New York.

Brown, R.H. (1977) *A Poetic for Sociology*, Cambridge University Press, London

—— (1987) *Society as Text*, Chicago University Press, Chicago, IL.

Bruner J. (1987) Life as narrative, *Social Research*, Vol. 54(1).

Bryson, N. (1983) *Vision and Painting*, Macmillan, London.

Buckland, G. (1974) *Reality Recorded*, David and Charles, Devon.

Burgin, V. (ed.) (1982) *Thinking Photography*, Macmillan, London.

Burke, P. (1978) *Popular Culture in Early Modern Europe*, Temple Smith, London.

Burns, E. (1972) *Theatricality*, Longman, London.

Burns, T. (1977A) *The BBC: Public Institution and Private World*, Macmillan, London.

—— (1977B) The organisation of public opinion, in J. Curran *et al.* (eds) op. cit.

Campbell, C. (1987) *The Romantic Ethic and the Spirit of Modern Consumerism*, Blackwell, Oxford.

Cannadine, D. (1981) War and death, grief and mourning in modern Britain, in J. Whaley (ed.) *Mirrors of Mortality*, Europa, London.

—— (1983) The context, performance and meaning of ritual, in E. Hobsbawm and T. Ranger (eds) op. cit.

Carey, J.W. (ed.) (1988) *Media Myths and Narratives*, Sage, London.

Carrithers, M. *et al.* (eds) (1985) *The Category of the Person*, Cambridge University Press, London.

Cawelti, J.G. (1976) *Adventure, Mystery and Romance*, Chicago University Press, Chicago, IL.

Cawelti, J.G. and Rosenberg, B. (1987) *The Spy Story*, Chicago University Press, Chicago, IL.

Chalfen, R. (1980) Tourist photography, *AfterImage* (Summer).

—— (1981) Redundant imagery, *Journal of American Culture*, Vol. 4(1).

Chambers, I. (1986) *Popular Culture: The Metropolitan Experience*, Methuen, London.

Chanan, N. (1980) *The Dream that Kicks*, Routledge, London.

Chaney, D. (1972) *Processes of Mass Communication*, Macmillan, London.

—— (1977) Fictions in mass entertainment, in J. Curran *et al.* (eds) op. cit.

—— (1979) *Fictions and Ceremonies*, Edward Arnold, London.

—— (1981A) Public opinion and social change, in E. Katz and T. Szecsko (eds) op. cit.

—— (1981B) The public eye of documentary, in T. McCormack (ed.) *Studies in Communications*, Vol. 1. JAI Press, Greenwich, CN.

—— (1983A) A symbolic mirror of ourselves, *Media, Culture and Society*, Vol. 5(2).

—— (1983B) The department store as cultural form *Theory, Culture and Society*, Vol. 1(3).

—— (1987A) The symbolic form of ritual in mass communication, in P. Golding *et al.* (eds) op. cit.

—— (1987B) Audience research and the BBC in the 1930s, in J. Curran *et al.* (eds) op. cit.

—— (1990A) Subtopia in Gateshead: the MetroCentre as cultural form, *Theory, Culture and Society*, Vol. 7(4).

—— (1990B) Popular: culture and discourse, *History of the Human Sciences*, Vol. 3(3).

Chaney, D. and Chaney, J. (1979) The audience for mass leisure, in H. Fischer and S. Melnik (eds) *Entertainment*, Hastings House, New York, NY.

Chaney, D. and Pickering, M. (1986) Authorship in documentary in J. Corner (ed.) *Documentary and the Mass Media*, Arnold, London.

Clark, T.J. (1985) *The Painting of Modern Life*, Thames and Hudson, London.

Clarke, J. and Critcher, C. (1985) *The Devil Makes Work: Leisure in Capitalist Britain*, Macmillan, London.

Clifford, J. (1986) Introduction: partial truths, in J. Clifford and G. Marcus (eds) op. cit.

Clifford, J. and Marcus, G. (eds) (1986) *Writing Culture*, University of California Press, London.

Clifford, J. (1988) *The Predicament of Culture*, Harvard University Press, Cambridge MS.

Cockburn, M.M. (1981) Constituting Theatricality, PhD Thesis, University of Durham.

Coe, B. (1989) The Rollfilm revolution, in C. Ford op. cit.

Cohen, A.P. (1985) *The Symbolic Construction of Community*, Tavistock, London.

—— (1986) Of symbols and boundaries, in A.P. Cohen (ed.) *Symbolising Boundaries*, Manchester University Press, Manchester.

Cohen, S. and Taylor, L. (1976) *Escape Attempts*, Allen Lane, London.

Collins, R. *et al.* (eds) (1986) *Media, Culture and Society*, Sage, London.

Collins, R. (1988) Theoretical continuities in Goffman's work, in P. Drew and A. Wootton (eds) *Erving Goffman*, Polity Press, Cambridge.

Colls, R. (1977) *The Collier's Lament*, Croom Helm, London.

—— (1986) Englishness and the political culture, in R. Colls and P. Dodds (eds) op. cit.

Colls, R. and Dodd, P. (eds) (1986) *Englishness: Politics and Culture*, Croom Helm, London.

Connerton, P. (1989) *How Societies Remember*, Cambridge University Press, London.

Conrad, P. (1984) *The Art of the City*, Oxford University Press, New York, NY.

Corner, J. (ed.) (1986) *Documentary and the Mass Media*, Edward Arnold, London.

Cowan, A.B. (1978) Popular Entertainment in London, PhD Thesis, Washington University.

Cowling, M. (1989) *The Artist as Anthropologist*, Cambridge University Press, London.

Crapanzo, V. (1986) Hermes' dilemma, in J. Clifford and G. Marcus op. cit.

Curran, J. *et al.* (eds) (1977) *Mass Communication and Society*, Edward Arnold, London.

—— (1987) *Impacts and Influences*, Methuen, London.

Dahlgren, P. (1981) TV news and the suppression of reflexivity, in Katz and Szecsko (eds) op. cit.

Daniel, P. *et al.* (1987) *Official Images: New Deal Photography*, Smithsonian Institution Press, Washington.

Darnton, R. (1975) Writing news and telling stories, *Daedalus*, Vol. 104(1).

Daunton, M.J. (1983) Public place and private space, in D. Fraser and A. Sutcliffe (eds) *The Pursuit of Urban History*, Edward Arnold, London.

Davey, P. (1980) *Arts and Crafts Architecture: The Search for Earthly Paradise*, Architectural Press, London.

Davidoff, L. and Hall, C. (1987) *Family Fortunes*, Hutchinson, London.

Davis, M. (1990) *City of Quartz: Excavating the Future in Los Angeles*, Verso, London.

Davis, N.Z. (1975) *Society and Culture in Early Modern France*, Stanford University Press, CA.

Davison, P. (1982A) *Popular Appeal in English Drama to 1850*, Macmillan, London.

—— (1982B) *Contemporary Drama and the Popular Dramatic Dramatic Tradition in England*, Macmillan, London.

Dayan, D. and Katz, E. (1988) Articulating consensus: the ritual and rhetoric of media events, in T.C. Alexander (ed.) op. cit.

Debord, G. (1970) *Society of the Spectacle*, Black and Red Press, Detroit, IL

Dellheim, C. (1982) *The Face of the Past*, Cambridge University Press, London.

Dodds, P. (1986) Englishness and the national culture, in R. Colls and P. Dodds (eds) op. cit.

Donajgrodzki, A.P. (1977) *Social Control in Nineteenth Century Britain*, Croom Helm, London.

Doone, V. (1943) *This Other Eden*, Bodley Head, London.

Douglas, M. (1987) *How Institutions Think*, Routledge and Kegan Paul, London.

Duby, G. (1981) *The Age of the Cathedrals*, Croom Helm, London.

Dyer, R. (1979) *Stars*, British Film Institute, London.

—— (1987) *Heavenly Bodies: Film Stars and Society*, Macmillan, London.

Dyos, H.J. (1973) A guide to the streets of Victorian London in D. Cannadine and D. Reeder (eds) *Exploring the Urban Past*, Cambridge University Press, London.

Eidsvik, C. (1978) *Cineliteracy*, Random House, New York, NY.

Eisenstein, E.L. (1969) The advent of printing and the problem of the Renaissance, *Past and Present*, Vol. 45.

Elias, N. (1978) *The Civilising Process. Vol.1: The History of Manners*, Basil Blackwell, Oxford.

—— (1982) *The Civilising Process*, Vol. 2: *State Formation and Civilization*, Basil Blackwell, Oxford.

Elias, N. and Dunning, E. (1986) *The Quest for Excitement*, Basil Blackwell, Oxford.

Elliott, P. (1980) Press performance as political ritual, in H. Christian (ed.) *The Sociology of Journalism and the Press*, Sociological Review Monograph 29, Keele, Staffs.

Ericson, R.V. *et al.* (1989) *Negotiating Control: A Study of News Sources*, Open University Press, Milton Keynes.

Evans, R. (1982) *The Fabrication of Virtue*, Cambridge University Press, London.

Ewan, S. and Ewen, E. (1982) *Channels of Desire*, McGraw-Hill, New York.

Ewen, S. (1976) *Captains of Consciousness*, McGraw-Hill, New York.

—— (1990) *All Consuming Images: The Politics of Style in Contemporary Culture*, Harper Collins, London.

Faust, B. (1980) *Women, Sex and Pornography*, Melbourne House, London.

Featherstone, M. (ed.) (1988) *Postmodernism*, Sage, London.

—— (1990) *Consumer Culture and Postmodernism*, Sage, London.

Featherstone, M. and Hepworth, M. (1983) The mid-life style of 'George and Lynne', *Theory, Culture and Society*, Vol. 1(3).

Febvre, L. and Martin, H-J. (1976) *The Coming of the Book*, New Left Books, London.

Fell, J.L. (1974) *Film and the Narrative Tradition*, Oklahoma University Press, OK.

Finlay, M. (1987) *Powermatics: A Discursive Critique of New Technology*, Routledge and Kegan Paul, London.

—— (1990) *The Potential of Modern Discourse Musil, Peirce and Peturbation*, Indiana University Press, Bloomington, IN.

—— (1991) Re-thinking narcissism, *Free Association*.

Fisher, P. (1975) City matters: city minds, in J. Buckley (ed.) *The Worlds of Victorian Fiction*, Harvard University Press, Cambridge, MA.

Fishman, M. (1980) *Manufacturing the News*, Texas University Press, Austin, TX.

Fiske, J. (1989) *Understanding Popular Culture*, Unwin Hyman, London.

Fiske, J. and Hartley, J. (1978) *Reading Television*, Methuen, London.

Ford, C. (ed.) (1989) *The Story of Popular Photography*, Century, London.

Forsyth, A. (1982) *Buildings for the Age: New Building Types* 1900–39, Her Majesty's Stationery Office, London.

Forty, A. (1986) *Objects of Desire: Design and Society 1750–1980*, Thames and Hudson, London.

Foucault, M. (1977) *Discipline and Punish*, Allen Lane, London.

—— (1980) *Power/Knowledge*, Pantheon, New York.

—— (1984) What is an author?, in P. Rabinow (ed.) *The Foucault Reader*, Penguin, London.

Fox, R.W. and Jackson Lears, T.J. (eds) (1983) *The Culture of Consumption*, Pantheon Books, New York, NY.

Fraser, W.H. (1981) *The Coming of the Mass Market 1850–1914*, Macmillan, London.

Frisby, D. (1988) *Fragments of Modernity*, Polity Press, Cambridge.

Frith, S. (1983) (ed.) The pleasures of the hearth, in *Formations Of Pleasure*, Routledge, London.

Garfinkel, H. (1967) *Studies in Ethnomethodology*, Prentice-Hall, New Jersey.

Garnham, N. (1986) The Media and the Public Sphere, in Golding *et al.* op. cit.

Gay, P. (1984) *The Bourgeois Experience*, Oxford University Press, New York, NY.

Geertz, C. (1972) Deep play: notes on the Balinese cockfight, *Daedalus*, No. 101.

—— (1980) *Negara*, Princeton University Press, Princeton, NJ.

Gershuny, J. and Jones, S. (1987) The Changing Work/Leisure Balance in Britain 1861–84, in J. Horne *et al.* (eds) *Sport, Leisure and Social Relations* Routledge and Kegan Paul, London.

H. Gerth and C. Wright Mills (1954) *Character and Social Structure*, Routledge and Kegan Paul, London.

Giddens, A. (1991) *Modernity and Self-Identity*, Polity Press, Cambridge.

Girouard, M. (1981) *The Return to Camelot*, Yale University Press, London.

—— (1990) *The English Town*, Yale University Press, London.

Gledhill, C. (ed.) (1987) *Home is Where the Heart is*, British Film Institute, London.

Goffman, E. (1971) *Relations in Public*, Harper and Row, New York, NY.

—— (1974) *Frame Analysis*, Peregrine Books, London.

—— (1976) Gender advertisements, *Studies in the Anthropology of Visual Communication*, Vol. 3(2).

—— (1981A) The lecture, *Forms of Talk*, Basil Blackwell, Oxford.

—— (1981b) Radio talk, *Forms of Talk*, Basil Blackwell, Oxford.

Golding, P. (1981) The missing dimensions – news media and the management of social change, in E. Katz and T. Szecsko (eds) op. cit.

Golding, P. *et al.* (eds) (1987) *Communicating Politics*, Leicester University Press, Leicester.

Gouldner, A. (1976) *The Dialectic of Ideology and Technology*, Seabury Press, New York, NY.

Green, N. (1990) *The Spectacle of Nature*, Manchester University Press, Manchester.

Greenhalgh, P. (1988) *Ephemeral Vistas*, Manchester University Press, Manchester.

Grimsted, D. (1968) *Melodrama Unveiled*, Chicago University Press, Chicago, IL.

Habermas, J. (1989) *The Structural Transformation of the Public Sphere*, Polity Press, Cambridge.

Hammerton, E. and Cannadine, D. (1981) Conflict and consensus on a ceremonial occasion, *Historical Journal*, Vol. 24(1).

Handelman, D. (1982) Reflexivity in festival and other cultural events, in M. Douglas (ed.) *Essays in the Sociology of Perception*, Routledge and Kegan Paul, London.

—— (1990) *Models and Mirrors*, Cambridge University Press, London.

Hansen, A. and Murdock, G. (1985) Constructing the crowd, in V. Mosco and J. Wasko (eds) *Popular Culture and Media Events*, Ablex, NJ.

Harrison, M. (1988) *Crowds and History*, Cambridge University Press, London.

Haug, W.F. (1986) *Critique of Commodity Aesthetics*, Polity Press, Cambridge.

Hawkes, T. (1973) *Shakespeare's Talking Animals*, Edward Arnold, London.

Hayden, D. (1976) *Seven American Utopias: The Architecture of Communitarian Socialism 1790–1975* MIT Press, Cambridge, MA.

Hebdige, D. (1979) *Subculture: The Meaning of Style*, Methuen, London.

Heide, R. and Gilman, J. (1979) *Dime-Store Dream Parade: Popular Culture 1925–55*, E.P. Dutton, New York, NY.

Heller, C. (1978) *Broadcasting and Accountability*, BFI Television Monograph 7, London.

Hess, T.B. and Nochlin, L. (eds) (1973) *Woman as Sex Object*, Allen Lane, London.

Hirsch, J. (1981) *Family Photographs*, Oxford University Press, New York, NY.

Hobsbawm, E. (1983) *Mass producing traditions*, in E. Hobsbawm and T. Ranger op. cit.

—— (1990) *Nations and Nationalism Since 1900*, Cambridge University Press, London.

Hobsbawm, E. and Ranger, T. (eds) (1983) *The Invention of Tradition*, Blackwell, Oxford.

Hodder, I. (ed.) (1988) *The Meaning of Things: Material Culture and Symbolic Expression*, Unwin Hyman, London.

Hollier, D. (ed.) (1988) *The College of Sociology (1937–39)*, University of Minnesota Press, Minneapolis, MN.

Hollis, P. (1970) *The Pauper Press*, Oxford University Press, Oxford.

Holt, R. (1989) *Sport and the British*, Clarendon Press, Oxford.

Hoover, S.M. (1988) *Mass Media Religion: Social Sources of the Electronic Church*, Sage, London.

Hopke, L. (1986) Late nineteenth century guidebooks to the city, *Journal of Popular Culture* Vol. 20(2).

Hopkinson, T. (ed.) (1975) *Bert Hardy: Photojournalist*, Gordon Fraser, London.

Horne, D. (1984) *The Great Museum: The Re-presentation of History*, Pluto Press, London.

—— (1986) *The Public Culture*, Pluto Press, London.

Howse, D. (1980) *Greenwich Time and the Discovery of Latitude*, Oxford University Press, Oxford.

Hoy, D.C. (ed.) (1986) *Foucault: A Critical Reader*, Blackwell, Oxford.

Hudson, L. (1982) *Bodies of Knowledge*, Weidenfeld and Nicolson, London.

Hunt, L. (1984) *Politics, Culture and Class in the French Revolution*, California University Press, Berkeley, CA.

Hunter, J.P. (1988) News and new things: contemporaneity and the early English novel, *Critical Inquiry*, Vol. 14(3).

Hymes, D. (1971) Sociolinguistics and the Ethnography of Speaking, in E. Ardener (ed.) *Social Anthropology and Language*, Tavistock Press, London.

Inglis, F. (1988) *Popular Culture and Political Power*, Routledge and Kegan Paul, London.

Irwin, M. (1979) *Picturing: Description and Illusion in the Nineteenth Century Novel*, Allen and Unwin, London.

Ivins, W.M. (1953) *Prints and Visual Communication*, MIT Press, Cambridge, MS.

Jackson Lears, T.J. (1983) From Salvation to self-realization, in R.W. Fox and T.J. Jackson Lears, op. cit.

Jacobs, D.L. (1981) Domestic snapshots, *Journal of American Culture*, Vol. 4(1).

James, L. (1978) *Print and the People 1819–1851*, Peregrine Books, London.

Jencks, C. (1984) *The Language of Post-Modern Architecture*, 4th edn. Academy Editions, London.

Jones, S.G. (1987) *The British Labour Movement and Film*, Routledge, London.

Joyce, P. (1991) *Visions of the People: Industrial England and the Question of Class*, Cambridge University Press, London.

Kahrl, S.J. (1974) *Traditions of English Medieval Drama*, Hutchinson, London.

Katz, E. and Szecsko, T. (eds) (1981) *Mass Media and Social Change*, Sage, London.

Keen, M. (1984) *Chivalry*, Yale University Press, New Haven, NJ.

Kern, S. (1983) *The Culture of Time and Space 1880–1918*, Harvard University Press, Cambridge, MA.

King, A.D. (1981A) A time for space and a space for time, in A.D. King (ed.) op. cit.

King, A.D. (ed.) (1981B) *Buildings and Society*, Routledge and Kegan Paul, London.

King, A.D. (1984) *The Bungalow: the production of a global culture*, Routledge and Kegan Paul, London.

Klapp, O. (1964) *Symbolic Leaders: Public Dramas and Public Men*, Aldine, Chicago, IL.

Klingender, F.D. (1972) *Art and the Industrial Revolution*, Paladin, London.

Kowinski, W.S. (1982) *The Malling of America*, Basic Books, New York.

Kroker, A. *et al.* (1989) *Panic Encyclopedia*, Macmillan, London.

Kumar, K. (1975) Holding the middle ground, *Sociology*, Vol. 9(3).

—— (1991) *Utopianism*, Open University Press, Milton Keynes.

Lacks, C. (1987) Documentary Photography, PhD Thesis, St. Louis University.

Laing, S. (1986) *Representations of Working-Class Life 1957–64*, Macmillan, London.

Lakoff, G. and Johnson, M. (1980) *Metaphors We Live By*, Chicago University Press, Chicago, IL.

Lane, B.M. (1986) Architects in power, in T. Rotberg and T. Robb (eds) *Art and History*, Cambridge University Press, London.

Lane, C. (1981) *The Rites of Rulers*, Cambridge University Press, London.

Lash, S. (1988) Discourse or figure? *Theory, Culture and Society*, Vol. 5(2/3).

Leacroft, R. (1958) The Theatre Royal, Leicester, in *Transactions Leicestershire Archaeological and Historical Society*, Vol. 34.

—— (1973) *The Development of the English Playhouse*, Eyre Methuen, London.

Lee, A.J. (1980) *Origins of the Popular Press in England 1855–1914*, Croom Helm, London.

Lees, A. (1985) *Cities Perceived: Urban Society in European and American Thought*, Manchester University Press, Manchester.

Lefebvre, H. (1971) *Everyday Life in the Modern World*, Allen Lane, The Penguin Press, London.

Leiss, W. *et al.* (1986) *Social Communication in Advertising* Methuen, London.

Lemagny, J-C. and Rouille, A. (eds) (1987) *A History of Photography*, Cambridge University Press, London.

LeMahieu, D.L. (1988) *A Culture for Democracy*, Clarendon Press, Oxford.

Lester, M. (1980) Generating Newsworthiness, *American Sociological Review*, Vol. 45(6).

Levine, D. (ed.) (1971) *Georg Simmel: On Individuality and Social Forms*, University of Chicago Press, Chicago.

Levitas, R. (1990) *The Concept of Utopia*, Prentice-Hall, London.

Leymore, V.L. (1975) *Hidden Myth: Structure and Symbolism in Advertising*, Heinemann, London.

Lohisse, J. (1973) *Anonymous Communication*, Allen and Unwin, London.

Lowe, D. (1982) *The History of Bourgeois Perception*, Harvester Press, Sussex.

Lowenthal, L. (1961) *Literature, Popular Culture and Society*, Prentice-Hall, NJ.

Lurie, A. (1982) *The Language of Clothes*, Heinemann, London.

MacCannell, D. (1976) *The Tourist*, Macmillan, London.

MacCauley, A. (1987) An image of society, in J-C.Lemagny and A. Rouille (eds) op. cit.

McKendrick, N. *et al.* (1982) *The Birth of a Consumer Society*, Europa Books, London.

McLuhan, M. (1964) *Understanding Media: The Extensions of Man*, Routledge and Kegan Paul, London.

McNamara, B. (1974) The scenography of popular entertainment, *Drama Review*, Vol. 18(1).

Maddow, B. (1980) Nude in a social landscape, in C. Sullivan (ed.) op. cit.

Madge, C. and Harrisson, T. (1939) *Britain by Mass-Observation*, Penguin, London.

Manning, F. (ed.) (1983) *The Celebration of Society: Perspectives on Contemporary Cultural Performance*, Bowling Green University Press, OH.

Marchand, R. (1985) *Advertising the American Dream: Making Way for Modernity 1920–1940*, University of California Press, Berkeley, CA.

Marcus, S. (1966) *The Other Victorians*, Weidenfeld and Nicolson, London.

Markus, T.A. (1982) Buildings for the sad, the bad and the mad, in T.A. Markus (ed.) *Order in Space and Society*, Mainstream Press, Edinburgh.

Martin, B. (1981) *A Sociology of Contemporary Cultural Change*, Blackwell, Oxford.

Mason, T.A. (1980) *Association Football and English Society*, Harvester Press, Sussex.

Merton, R. (1949) *Social Theory and Social Structure*, Free Press, New York, NY.

Miller, M.B. (1981) *The Bon Marche: Bourgeois Culture and the Department Store 1869–1920*, Princeton University Press, NJ.

Molotch, H. and Lester, M. (1974) News as purposive behavior, *American Sociological Review*, Vol. 39 (February).

Morgan, E.S. (1988) *Inventing the People*, Norton, New York, NY.

Morris, M. (1988) Things to do with shopping centres, in S. Sheridan (ed.) *Grafts: Feminist Cultural Criticism*, Verso, London.

Mukerji, C. (1983) *From Graven Images: Patterns of Modern Materialism*, Columbia University Press, New York, NY.

Muller, H-P. (1988) Social structure and civil religion, in J.C. Alexander (ed.) op. cit.

Musello, C. (1980) Studying the home mode, *Studies in Visual Communication*, Vol. 6(1).

Musil, R. (1953) *The Man Without Qualities*, Secker and Warburg, London.

Muthesius, S. (1982) *The English Terraced House*, Yale University Press, New Haven, CT.

Neale, S. (1979) Triumph of the will, *Screen*, Vol. 20(1).

—— (1985) *Cinema and Technology*, Macmillan, London.

Needham, G. (1973) Manet's 'Olympia' and pornographic photography, in T.B. Hess and L. Nochlin (eds) op. cit.

Nicholl, A. (1955) *A History of English Drama*, Vol.IV, Cambridge University Press, London.

Nochlin, L. (1972) Eroticism and female imagery in nineteenth century art, in T.B. Hess and L. Nochlin (eds) op. cit.

Nord, D.E. (1988) The city as theater, *Victorian Studies*, Vol. 31(2).

Nuttall, J. and Carmichael, R. (1977) *Common Factors/Vulgar Factions*, Routledge and Kegan Paul, London.

Olsen, D.J. (1986) *The City as a Work of Art*, Yale University Press, New Haven, NJ.

Oosterbaan Martinius, W. (1986) Questions of Style and Taste. *Netherlands Journal of Sociology*, Vol. 22(1).

Orr, J. (1989) *Tragic Drama and Modern Society*, 2nd rev. edn., London, Macmillan.

Orwell, G. (1961) The art of Donald McGill, in *Collected Essays*, Mercury Books, London.

Ovenden, G. and Mendes, P. (1973) *Victorian Erotic Photography*, Academy Editions, London.

Overy, R. (1990) Heralds of modernity: cars and planes from invention to necessity, in M. Teich and R. Porter (eds) op. cit.

Paget, D. (1990) *True Stories? Documentary Drama on Radio, Screen and Stage*, Manchester University Press, Manchester.

Pateman, T. (1975) *Language, Truth and Politics*, Stroud and Pateman, Devon.

Pearson, N. (1982) *The State and the Visual Arts*, Open University Press, London.

Peters, E. (1985) *Torture*, Blackwell, Oxford.

Peterson, L.F. (1987) *The Architectural and Social History of Cooperative Living*, Macmillan, London.

Phillips, J. (1973) *The Reformation of Images*, Berkeley, California University Press, CA.

Pickering, M. and Chaney, D. (1986) Democracy and communication: mass observation 1937–43, *Journal of Communication*, Vol. 36(1).

Plummer, K. (1983) *Documents of Life*, Unwin Hyman, London.

Popkin, J.D. (1989) *News and Politics in the Age of Revolution*, Cornell University Press, London.

Pratt, M.L. (1986) Interpretive strategies/strategic interpretations, in J. Arac (ed.) *Postmodernism and Politics*, Minnesota University Press, Minneapolis, MN.

Pugh, S. (ed.) (1990) *Reading Landscape: Country – City – Capital*, Manchester University Press, Manchester.

Pythian-Adams, C. (1976) Ceremony and the citizen, in P. Clark (ed.) *The Early Modern Town*, Longman, London.

Radway, J. (1987) *Reading the Romance*, Verso, London.

Rahill, F. (1967) *The World of Melodrama*, Pennsylvania State University Press, Pittsburgh, PN.

Rappoport, R. (1980) Concluding comments on ritual and reflexivity, *Semiotica*, Vol. 30(1/2).

Ravetz, A. (1986) *The Government of Space: Town Planning in Modern Society*, Faber and Faber, London.

Ravicz, M.E. (1980) Ephemeral art, *Semiotica*, Vol. 30 (1/2).

Reiss, T.J. (1982) *The Discourse of Modernism*, Cornell University Press, Ithaca, NY.

Reeves, J.L. (1988) Television stardom: a ritual of social typification and individualization, in J.W. Carey (ed.) op. cit.

Rhodes, N. (1980) *Elizabethan Grotesque*, Routledge and Kegan Paul, London.

Richards, J. (1984) *The Age of the Dream Palace*, Routledge, London.

Richter, D.C. (1981) *Riotous Victorians*, Ohio University Press, Athens, OH.

Ritter, N. (1989) *Art as Spectacle: Images of the Entertainer since Romanticism*, University of Missouri Press, Columbia, MO.

Rojek, C. (1985) *Capitalism and Leisure Theory*, Tavistock, London.

Rosen, C. and Zerner, H. (1984) *Romanticism and Realism: The Mythology of Nineteenth Century Art*, Faber and Faber, London.

Rosenau, H. (1959) *The Ideal City in its Architectural Evolution*, Routledge and Kegan Paul, London.

Rosenblum, B. (1978) *Photographers at Work,* Holmes and Meier, New York, NY.

Ross, K. (1990) *The Emergence of Social Space: Rimbaud and the Paris Commune*, Macmillan, London.

Rowe, W. and Schelling, V. (1991) *Memory and Modernity: Popular Culture in Latin America*, Verso, London.

Roy, D. (1971) The Theatre Royal, Hull, in K. Richards and P. Thomson (eds) *Nineteenth Century British Theatre*, Methuen, London.

Rushmer, R. (1990) Reading Newspapers, PhD Thesis, University of Durham.

Samuel, R. (ed.) (1989) *Patriotism*, Vol. 3, Routledge, London.

Sandgruber, R. (1990) The electrical century, in M. Teich and R. Porter (eds) op. cit.

Schechner, R. (1976) Towards a poetics of performance, *Alcheringa*, Vol. 2(2).

Schiller, D. (1981) *Objectivity and the News*, University of Pennsylvania Press, Philadelphia, PN.

Schivelbusch, W. (1988) *Disenchanted Night: The Industrialisation of Light in the Nineteenth Century*, Berg, New York, NY.

Schudson, M. (1978) *Discovering the News*, Basic Books, New York, NY.

—— (1982) The politics of narrative form, *Daedalus*, Vol. 111(4).

—— (1984) *Advertising, The Uneasy Persuasion*, Basic Books, New York.

—— (1989) The Sociology of News Production, *Media, Culture and Society*, Vol. 11(3).

Segal, A. (1970) Censorship, social control and socialization, *British Journal of Sociology*, Vol. 21(1).

Sekula, A. (1983) The traffic in photographs, in B. Buchloh *et al.* (eds) *Modernism and Modernity*, Nova Scotia Press Halifax, Nova Scotia.

—— (1986) The body and the archive, *October*, 39.

Sennett, R. (1976) *The Fall of Public Man*, Knopf, New York, NY.

Shanks, M. and Tilley, C. (1987) *Re-Constructing Archaeology*, Cambridge University Press, London.

Shiach, M. (1989) *Discourse on Popular Culture*, Polity Press, Oxford.

Shields, R. (1990) The 'System of pleasure': liminality and the carnivalesque at Brighton. *Theory, Culture and Society*, Vol. 7(1).

—— (1991) *Places on the Margin*, Routledge, London.

Short, J.R. (1991) *Imagined Country: Society, Culture and Environment*, Routledge, London.

Simmel, G. (1971) The problem of sociology, in D. Levine (ed.) op. cit.

Slater, D. (1983) Marketing mass photography, in H. Davis and P. Walton (eds) *Language, Image, Media*, Basil Blackwell, Oxford.

Smith, O. (1984) *The Politics of Language 1791–1819*, Clarendon Press, Oxford.

Snyder, R.W. (1986) The Voice of the City; Vaudeville and the Formation of Mass Culture in New York Neighbourhoods 1880–1930, PhD Thesis, New York University.

Solomon-Godeau, A. (1986) The legs of the countess, *October*, 39.

Sontag, S. (1978) *On Photography*, Allen Lane, London.

Southern, R. (1952) *Changeable Scenery*, Faber and Faber, London.

Spender, H. and Harrisson, T. (1975) *Britain in the Thirties*, Unicorn Press, London.

Spierenburg, P. (1984) *The Spectacle of Suffering*, Cambridge University Press, London.

Stallybrass, P. and White, A. (1986) *The Politics and Poetics of Transgression*, Methuen, London.

Stange, M. (1989) *Symbols of Ideal Life: Social Documentary Photography in America 1890–1950*, Cambridge University Press, London.

Starkey, D. (1978) Representation through intimacy, in J. Lewis (ed.) *Symbols and Sentiments*, Academic Press, London.

Stedman Jones, G. (1974) Working class culture and working class politics, *Journal of Social History*, Vol.7.

—— (1983) *Languages of Class*, Cambridge University Press, London.

Stilgoe, J.R. (1988) *Borderland*, Yale University Press, New Haven, NJ.

Storch, R.D. (1982) (ed.) *Popular Culture and Custom in Nineteenth Century England*, Croom Helm, London.

Stott, W. (1973) *Documentary Expression and Thirties America*, Oxford University Press, New York.

Strasser, S. (1989) *Satisfaction Guaranteed: The Making of the American Mass Market*, Pantheon Books, New York.

Sullivan, C. (ed.) (1980) *Nude Photographs 1850–1980*, Harper and Row, New York, NY.

Sussex, E. (1975) *The Rise and Fall of British Documentary*, University of California Press, Berkeley, CA.

Tagg, J. (1988) *The Burden of Representation*, Macmillan, London.

Taylor, P. (1986) The semantics of political violence, in P. Golding *et al.* (eds) op. cit.

Taylor, R.R. (1974) *The Word in Stone*, California University Press, London.

Teich, M. and Porter, R. (eds) (1990) *Fin de Siècle and its Legacy*, Cambridge University Press, London.

Thomas, A. (1978) *The Expanding Eye*, Croom Helm, London.

Thomas, K. (1973) *Religion and the Decline of Magic*, Penguin, London.

Thompson, E.P. (1967) Time, work discipline and industrial capitalism, *Past and Present*, 38.

—— (1977) *William Morris: Romantic to Revolutionary*, Merlin Press, London.

Thompson, G. (1983) Carnival and the calculable: consumption and play at Blackpool, *Formations of pleasure*, Routledge and Kegan Paul, London.

Thompson, J.B. (1990) *Ideology and Modern Culture: Critical Social Theory in the Era of Mass Communication*, Polity Press, Cambridge.

Thorne, R. (1980) Places of refreshment, in A.D. King (ed.) op. cit.

Tomlinson, A. and Whannel, P. (eds) (1984) *Five Ring Circus*, Pluto Press, London.

Trachtenberg, A. (1979) Walker Evans' message from the interior, *October*, Vol. 11(1).

—— (1984) Image and ideology: New York in the photographer's eye, *Journal of Urban History*, Vol. 10(4).

Trexler, R.C. (1980) *Public Life in Renaissance Florence*, Academic Press, London.

Tuchman, G. (1978) *Making News*, Free Press, New York.

Turner, B.S. (1984) *The Body and Society*, Basil Blackwell, Oxford.

—— (1990) *Theories of Modernity and Postmodernity*, Sage, London.

Turner, L. and Ash, J. (1975) *The Golden Hordes: International Tourism and the Pleasure Periphery*, Constable, London.

Turner, V. (1969) *The Ritual Process*, Penguin, London.

—— (1974) *Dramas, Fields and Metaphors*, Cornell University Press, Ithaca, NY.

—— (1982) Social dramas and stories about them, in *From Ritual to Theatre*, Performing Arts Journal Publications, New York, NY.

Tydeman, W. (1978) *The Theatre in the Middle Ages*, Cambridge University Press, London.

Urry, J. (1988) Cultural change and contemporary holiday-making, *Theory Culture and Society*, Vol. 5.

—— (1990) *The Tourist Gaze: Leisure and Travel in Contemporary Societies*, Sage, London.

Vardac, A.N. (1949) *Stage to Screen*, Harvard University Press, Cambridge, MA.

Veblen, T. (1925) *The Theory of the Leisure Class*, Allen and Unwin, London.

Venturi, R. and Scott Brown, E. (1972) *Learning from Las Vegas*, MIT Press, Cambridge, MA.

Vicinus, M. (1974) *The Industrial Muse*, Croom Helm, London.

Wagner, R. (1981) *The Invention of Culture*, 2nd rev. edn., University of Chicago Press, Chicago, IL.

Waller, P.J. (1983) *Town, City and Nation*, Oxford University Press, Oxford.

Walters, M. (1978) *The Nude Male*, Penguin, London.

Walvin, J. (1984) *English Urban Life 1776–1851*, Hutchinson, London.

Watney, S. (1982) Making strange: the shattered mirror, in V. Burgin (ed.) op. cit.

Weber, F. (1990) Heroes, meadows and machinery: *fin-de-siècle* music, in M. Teich and R. Porter (eds) op. cit.

Weber, W. (1975) *Music and the Middle Class*, Croom Helm, London.

Wicke, J.A. (1988) *Advertising Fictions*, Columbia University Press, New York, NY.

Wildenbeest, G. (1988) Keeping up with the times, *Netherlands Journal of Sociology*, Vol. 24(2).

Willener, A. (1970) *The Action-Image of Society: on Cultural Politicization*, Tavistock, London.

Williams, J. (1991) Having an away day: English football supporters and the hooligan debate, in J. Williams and S. Wagg (eds) *British Footbal and Social Change*, Leicester University Press, London.

Williams, R. (1958) *Culture and Society*, Chatto and Windus, London.

—— (1973) *The Country and the City*, Chatto and Windus, London.

—— (1974) *Television: Technology and Cultural Form*, Fontana, London.

—— (1975) *Drama in a Dramatised Society*, Cambridge University Press, London.

—— (1981) *Culture*, Fontana, London.

Williams, R.H. (1982) *Dream Worlds: Mass Consumption in Late Nineteenth century France*, California University Press, Berkeley, CA.

Willis, P. (1990) *Common Culture*, Open University Press, Milton Keynes.

Winship, J. (1981) Handling sex, *Media, Culture and Society*, Vol. 3(1).

Wohl, A.S. (1971) The housing of the working classes, in S. Chapman (ed.) *The History of Working Class Housing*, David and Charles, Devon.

Wolfe, T. (1977) *Mauve Gloves and Madmen, Clutter and Vine*, Bantam Books, Toronto.

—— (1983) *From Bauhaus to Our House*, Abacus Books, London.

NAME INDEX

Alexander, J.C. 143
Allison, D. 85
Alloula, M. 97
Altick, R.D. 75
Anderson, B. 68, 114, 135
Anglo, S. 27
Appleton, W.W. 56
Arscott, C. 71
Ash, T. 165
Aston, M. 42
Atkinson, P. 10
Atwell, D. 79, 161

Babcock, B.A. 107
Bailey, P. 57, 192
Baker, M. 52
Bakhtin, M.M. 30, 108, 187
Barker, F. 159
Barker, K. 51
Barnouw, E. 77, 80
Barth, G. 60
Barthes, R. 112
Baudrillard, J. 38
Bauman, R. 17
Baxandall, M. 44
Beloff, H. 91, 105
Benjamin, W. 56, 95
Bennett, T. 61, 137
Berger, P. 9, 182
Berkeley, Busby 56
Berman, M. 32, 89, 175
Bommes, M. 59
Bonham-Carter, V. 51
Booth, M. 54, 55, 75

Bordwell, D. 83
Borsay, P. 28, 46, 47
Bourdieu, P. 39
Bowlby, R. 160
Bowles, P. 22
Bradbury, M. 175
Brady, M. 100
Braive, M.F. 91
Brandt, B. 104
Brantlinger, P. 8, 106
Brecht, B. 10
Briggs, A. 73
Brissett, D. 16
Bristol, M.D. 25, 26, 30, 51, 187, 191
Brody, H. 159
Brooks, P. 77
Brown, R.H. 5, 127
Bruner, J. 135
Bryson, N. 15
Buckland, G. 101
Burgin, V. 91
Burke, P. 29, 60, 191, 192
Burns, E. 18
Burns, T. 117, 124

Campbell, C. 36, 157, 160
Cannadine, D. 20, 68, 69, 92
Carmichael, R. 61, 192
Carrithers, M. *et al.* 159
Cawelti, J.G. 77, 78, 186
Chalfen, R. 92, 103
Chambers, I. 142, 168
Chanan, N. 78, 83

214

Chaney, D. 3, 9, 10, 11, 23, 32, 34, 35, 82, 83, 101, 104, 112, 114, 117, 127, 128, 129, 139, 154, 163, 166, 176, 183
Chaney, J. 35, 166
Clark, T.J. 61, 70, 71, 98, 175
Clarke, J. 162
Clifford, J. 5, 104, 127, 129
Coe, B. 85
Cohen, A.P. 194, 195
Cohen, S. 134
Collins, R. 111, 124
Colls, R. 67, 69, 192
Connerton, P. 44, 108, 138, 139
Conrad, P. 91, 93
Corner, J. 128
Cowan, A.B. 49
Cowling, M. 73
Crapanzo, V. 3
Crichter, C. 162
Curran, J. 118

Dahlgren, P. 131
Daniel, P. *et al.* 104
Darnton, R. 130
Daunton, M. 66
Davey, P. 176
Davidoff, L. 64, 160
Davis, N.Z. 29, 178
Davison, P. 47, 48
Dayan, D. 136
Debord, G. 42
Dellheim, C. 69
Dickens, D. 51
Dodd, P. 69
Donajgrodzki, A.P. 67
Douglas, M. 6, 82, 87, 88
Duby, G. 42
Dunning, E. 67, 149
Dyer, R. 107, 111, 146
Dyos, H.J. 72

Edgley, C. 16
Eidsvik, C. 78
Eisenstein, E.L. 117
Elias, N. 14, 26, 37, 67, 149
Elliott, P. 138, 196
Ericson, R.V. *et al.* 132, 133
Evans, H. 136

Evans, R. 63
Evans, W. 112
Ewen, S. 105, 157
Ewen, S. and E. 158

Faust, B. 97
Featherstone, M. 32, 38, 97, 156, 157, 161, 168
Febvre, L. 117
Fell, J.L. 79
Fields, Gracie 125
Finaly, M. 37, 90, 175
Fisher, P. 72
Fishman, M. 132, 133
Fiske, J. 36, 107, 163
Ford, C. 84
Forsyth, A. 175
Forty, A. 168, 169
Foucault, M. 6, 28, 37, 41
Fox, R.W. 169
Fraser, W.H. 160
Frisby, D. 158
Frith, S. 124, 125

Garfinkel, H. 108
Garnham, N. 118
Gay, P. 63
Geertz, C. 3, 4, 16
Gershuny, J. 163
Gerth, H. 139
Giddens, A. 36, 37, 40, 188
Gilman, T. 168
Girouard, M. 26, 172
Gledhill, C. 77
Goffman, E. 16, 43, 44, 94, 110, 122, 123, 173
Golding, P. 131, 137
Gouldner, A. 118
Green, N. 182
Greenhalgh, P. 70
Grimsted, D. 78

Habermas, J. 117, 118
Hall, K. 64, 160
Hammerton, E. 69
Handelman, D. 3, 18, 19, 29, 107, 109, 196
Hansen, A. 131, 132
Hardy, B. 104

Harlow, Jean 145
Harrison, M. 19, 20
Harrisson, T. 104, 129
Haug, W.F. 156
Hawkes, T. 31
Haydon, D. 176
Hebdige, D. 168
Heide, R. 168
Heller, C. 124
Hepworth, M. 97
Hirsch, J. 82
Hobsbawm, E. 69, 119
Hodder, I. 179
Hollier, D. 130
Hollis, P. 151
Holt, R. 67
Hoover, S.M. 177
Hopke, L. 73
Hopkinson, T. 104
Horne, D. 32, 43, 118, 119, 195
Howse, D. 89
Hoy, D.C. 6
Hudson, L. 98
Huizinga, J. 25
Hunt, L. 20, 115
Hunter, J.P. 160
Hymes, D. 196

Independent, The 98, 138
Inglis, F. 20, 33, 84, 170, 196, 197
Irwin, M. 73
Ivins, W.M. 82

Jacobs, D.L. 82
James, L. 77
Jencks, C. 177
Johnson, M. 5
Jones, G. Stedman 58, 61, 125
Jones, S. 163

Kahrl, S.J. 28
Katz, E. 136
Keen, M. 26
Kern, S. 90, 175
King, A.D. 64
Klapp, O. 134, 143
Klingender, F.D. 197
Kowinski, W.S. 176
Kroker, A. 6

Kumar, K. 135, 175

Lacks, C. 100
Ladurie, E.L. 25
Laing, S. 128
Lakoff, G. 5
Lane, B.M. 172
Lash, S. 112
Leacroft, R. 49, 56
Lears, T.J. Jackson 169, 171
Lee, A.J. 151
Lees, A. 60
Lefebvre, H. 182
Leiss, W. *et al.* 36, 167
LeMahieu, D.L. 120
Lester, M. 135
Levitas, R. 175
Leymore, V.L. 154
Lohisse, J. 117
Lowenthal, L. 144, 146
Luckmann, T. 9, 182

MacCannell, D. 73, 103, 164
MacCauley, A. 101, 103
McFarlane, J. 175
McKendrick, N. *et al.* 158, 160
McLuhan, M. 174
McNamara, B. 52
Maddow, B. 96
Madge, C. 129
Manning, F. 23
Marchand, R. 173
Marcus, G. 104
Marcus, S. 96
Markus, T.A. 63
Martin, B. 168
Martin, H-J. 117
Martin, J. 75
Mason, T.A. 67
Mayakovsky, V. 10
Melville, H. 78
Mendes, P. 96
Merton, R. 145
Miller, M.B. 160
Mills, C. Wright 139
Molotch, H. 135
Morgan, E.S. 114
Morris, M. 141
Morris, W. 169

Mukerji, C. 158, 159
Muller, H-P. 101, 111
Murdock, G. 131, 132
Musello, C. 92
Musil, R. 1, 2
Muthesius, S. 64, 65

Neale, S. 21, 86
Needham, G. 98
Nicholl, A. 51
Nochlin, L. 95
Nord, D.E. 74
Nuttall, J. 61, 192

Ohrn, K. Becker 106
Olsen, D.J. 60, 63
Oosterbaan, W. Martinius 89
Orr, J. 48
Orwell, G. 97
Ovenden, G. 96

Paget, D. 128
Pateman, T. 33
Pearson, N. 168
Peters, E. 41
Peterson, L.F. 176
Phillips, J. 42
Pickering, M. 32, 129
Plummer, K. 10
Pollock, G. 71
Popkin, J.D. 117
Pratt, M.L. 16, 188
Pythian-Adams, C. 27

Rabelais, J-J. 30
Radway, J. 141
Rahill, F. 51
Ranger, T. 69
Rappoport, R. 108
Ravetz, A. 176
Reeves, J.L. 145
Reiss, T.J. 25, 117
Rhodes, N. 40
Richards, J. 125
Ritter, N. 197, 198
Rojek, C. 35
Rosen, C. 178
Rosenau, H. 175
Rosenberg, B. 186

Rosenblum, B. 83
Ross, K. 181
Rowe, W. 20
Roy, D. 49, 50
Rushmer, R. 136

Samuel, R. 120
Schechner, R. 17, 18
Schelling, V. 20
Schiller, D. 131
Schivelbusch, W. 53, 169, 170, 171, 172
Schudson, M. 72, 130, 138, 154
Scott Brown, E. 177, 179
Segal, A. 94
Sekula, A. 88, 98, 99
Sennett, R. 34, 118, 153
Shahn, B. 105
Shanks, M. 173, 179
Shiach, M. 115, 116, 192
Shields, R. 150, 172
Short, J.R. 172
Simmel, G. 1, 60, 158
Slater, D. 85
Smith, K. 145
Smith, O. 115
Snyder, R.W. 57
Solomon-Godeau, A. 96, 97, 98
Sontag, S. 101
Southern, R. 55
Spender, H. 104
Stallybrass, P. 30, 40, 151
Stanfield, Clarkson 75
Stange, M. 101, 102
Starkey, D. 31
Stilgoe, J.R. 64
Storch, R.D. 66
Stott, W. 105, 112, 128
Strasser, S. 171, 173
Sullivan, C. 96
Sussex, E. 102

Tagg, J. 99, 104, 172
Taylor, L. 134
Taylor, R.R. 133
Thatcher, M. 145
Thomas, A. 100
Thomas, K. 25
Thompson, E.P. 89, 188

Thompson, G. 164
Thompson, J. 8, 37, 121, 124, 136
Thorne, R. 74
Tilley, C. 173, 179
Trachtenberg, A. 104
Trexler, R.C. 27
Tuchman, G. 130, 133
Turner, B.S. 32, 41
Turner, L. 165
Turner, V. 18, 183
Tydeman, W. 25, 26

Urry, J. 164, 165

Vardac, A.N. 79
Veblen, T. 168
Venturi, R. 177, 179
Vestris, Mme. 56
Vicinus, M. 58

Wagner, R. 193

Waller, P.J. 59
Walters, M. 95
Walvin, J. 61
Weber, F. 62, 193
White, A. 30, 40, 151
Wicke, J.A. 180
Wildenbeest, G. 89
Willener, A. 181
Williams, J. 121
Williams, R. 33, 124, 141, 181, 182, 184, 193
Williams, R.H. 70
Willis, P. 36, 157
Winship, J. 173
Wohl, A.S. 60
Wolfe, T. 168, 187
Woollacott, J. 137
Wright, P. 59

Zerner, H. 178
Ziegfield, F. 56

SUBJECT INDEX

abstract crowd, 165, 171, 183; disciplining of 149, 155; of the cinema 152

abstract naturalism 97

abstraction 55

acculturation 66

actuality, discourse of 130, 135, 136; imagination of 136

advertisements, cultural form of consumer culture 173

advertising 36, 110, 154; a means of affiliation 173; as a genre of mass communication 180; as articulating the disciplinary codes of the abstract crowd 154; as dramatisation of mundane experience 180, 184; cultural form of representation for consumer goods 166; history of 167

aesthetics, of social engineering 187; discipline of popular culture 170

aesthetic order 32

amateurs 85, 109

American, documentary photography 102; intelligentsia 112

amorphous 68

anachronistic 46

anonymity, the character of modernity 94, 95

anthropology 41, 99, 193

anthropological typologies 73

archaeology 178, 179

architecture, of post-modernism 178

argot 52

aristocracy 68

artificiality 35; of normality 17

artistry, of popular experience 197

audience 2, 17, 47, 48, 52, 56, 65, 70, 83, 103, 117; anonymous 58, 106, 111, 125; as spectators 153; development of 151; disciplining of 8; global 144; mass popular 82, 113, 120, 121; middle class 62; of mass entertainment 149

audience-ing 184; forms of participation 8

audience research, as measure of collective taste 153

auditoria 57

auratic 82, 125

authentic, experience 35; naturalism 198

authenticity 47, 106

authority, in relation to design 187; expropriation of 187; of representation 32

'author' 82, 83, 115

authorship 20, 32, 56, 117

balkanisation of cultural identity 162, 194

Bauhaus, modernism 187

Beamish, social history

re-constructed as entertainment 173
biographical 84, 135
bourgeois 53, 90; theatre 58
bureaucratisation of collective life 99

carnivalesque 67
cataloguing 99
celebrity 111, 143, 145; charisma 144
celebrities as reference points for identification 146
cemeteries 63, 105
censorship 49, 94, 149, 161, 162
ceremony 2, 3, 44, 46, 82, 87, 110
ceremonial 82
ceremonialisation 25, 87, 88, 91
chaos of meaning 149, 161
chaotic, dramatic order of our cultural landscape 179
cinema 34, 47, 50, 52, 55, 83; architecture 161
citizenship 117, 121, 128, 184
city 45, 60, 62, 64, 69, 71; as an increasingly imaginary zone 173; as theatre 74; as tourist attraction 72; centres 7, 68, 73; nineteenth century 60, 64, 65, 67, 68, 70, 71, 73
class and popular, inter-relationship of 66
class culture 61
clown, as in popular spectacle for artists 197
Coliseum 58
collage 32, 33, 129
collective, consciousness 16; character of production 52; experience 16, 113; formations 67; identity 24, 30, 38, 69, 70; identity, dramatisation of 183; identity, institutionalisation of 148; memory 85, 135; performance 21; violence 121
collectivities, of family, gender, race, religion 4; multiplicity of 8
collectivity 13, 24, 42, 70, 119; vernacular of 88

College de Sociologie, Paris 130
collusion, discourse of 142
commercial culture 120, 197; entertainment 8, 45, 48, 78; realism 43, 109
commodities, and distinctions between public and private spheres 160; as arbitrary resources for signification 157; as forms of entertainment 157; cultural status of object or representation 155; symbolic 158
commodity, layers of meaning of 156; and news, inter dependence of 152
common culture 120
commonsense 9
communal, significance 58; discourse 119; imagination 105; integration 125
communalisation, re- 144
communalism 57
Communards 181
communication, anonymous 117; networks 89
communications technology 37
community, as performance 44; of belief 112; of strangers 152; theoretical re-consideration of 194
consensus 13
conservatism 77
consumer culture 8, 35, 97, 121, 142, 145, 156; and mass markets 160; commodities of 155; new forms of dramatisation for public space 161, 172
consumer society, birth of 160
consumer values 157, 161
consumerism 33, 70, 106, 109; as criterion of status 157
construction, metaphor of 10
constructivist formalism 10
contextualising narrative 93
conventions of looking 93; of collective concerns 95
copyright 51
cross-class impersonation 58
cross-cultural 2

cross-disciplinary 10
cross-sex dressing 58
cultural, form 83, 87, 108, 114;
    change 12; conventions 6;
    history 7, 16, 25; imagery 12, 16,
    34; minorities 162; order 43, 74,
    79; performance meanings of
    62; representation 58, 71;
    resources 6; segregation 54;
    space 39, 64, 81, 113, 118, 151,
    182; studies 10; vacuums of
    urbanisation 47
culture, political 47; as a style 10;
    official 56

dandies 22
deconstruction 129
de-construct, the social
    organisation of dramatisation 10
death, rituals of 92
department stores 171; vanguard
    of cultural innovations 160
design, distinctive signifiers of
    goods 168; as alternative
    language of mass entertainment
    185; as social critique 186;
    characteristic of modernity 185;
    creative hedonism 186; of
    figures in public life 186
deviance, symbolic 37
Diorama 76
discipline 66; for audiences of
    mass entertainment 149
discourse, of popular experience
    5, 60; of modernism 25; of
    sexuality and death 63
dislocation, in modernity 88
Disneyland 34
disorder 12, 20, 50
documentary 10, 101, 102, 104,
    128; impulse 100, 102, 103;
    photography 100, 101, 104, 128
drama, as commodity 151;
    aesthetic 18, 19; chivalric 26;
    communal 65; lineaments of
    148; social 18, 19; staged 45, 50;
    transgressive 30
dramatic, agency 110; business 16;
    commonality of identification

152; force 17; metaphor 3, 184;
    performance 3, 18; relations of
    performance 2, 4, 5, 6, 10, 20;
    significance 78; space 59, 162;
    transparency 34; vocabulary 5
dramatisation, forms of 39;
    inclusive 28; of exclusion 28; of
    experience 156; of relationship
    39; of social action 2; of social
    order 5, 31; tactile 30
dramaturgical vocabulary 44
dramaturgy, of the body 41
dream palaces 79

ecology, occupational 88;
    symbolic 88
Egyptian Hall, London 77
electricity, as model for emergent
    industries of mass
    entertainment 170
electronic church 177
elite, cultural form 7;
    institutionalised 116
emblematic 109
enactment 4
Enlightenment 41, 118
enterprise, of a drama 2; staged 3
entertainment, of mass society 3
entrepreneurial 48, 57
epistemic 90
estrangement 105
ethnographic narratives 10
ethnography 17, 107, 127
exclusivity 62, 65
exhibitions 70, 88
existential reality 145

facticity 79, 87, 120
fascism 196
fashions, as adaptations of popular
    drama 9
festival 20
fiction 114, 132
fictions, of collective life 195
fictive, landscape 179, 180
film 78, 79, 83; industry 54; stars 143
fine art, versus design 168
folk 106, 109; forms 192; peasantry
    192

formalisation 122
formalism 26
frame 2; space 122, 123
functionalism 9
funerary cults 92

gothic 54
Great Exhibition 59, 67, 72
Green politics, holism of 188
Greenwich 89

hedonism 97, 161
hegemonic 61
hegemony of conventions 80
heroes, idols of consumption 144;
    anti- 145
heterogeneity, of popular
    experience, 41
heterogeneous, mixing 62, 63
historical consciousness 29
historiography 82
history 193; of collective life 189,
    191, 193, 194
holidays, feature of consumer
    society lifestyles 164; transition
    from crowd to audience 164
Hollywood 75
honour 26, 27
hbhbhrific 99; ethnography 103
Hornor's Colosseum 75
hybrid 124

iconic 33
iconoclasm 42
iconography of sexual titillation
    89, 128, 168
icons, material 42; ritual 112
identity 4, 40; construction 144;
    public 111
ideology, of public culture 121
idolatrous 43
illusions 76, 78, 80; of pleasure, in
    consumer choice 165
imagery, interdependence of 42;
    institutionalised 132
imagin-action, of dreams 70
improvisation 8
inclusive, order of the Las Vegas
    Strip 179

incorporation 66
indexical signs 26
individuality, as root metaphor for
    the collective fictions of
    modernity 159
industrialisation 20
institutionalisation 86, 87, 88
institutional form 4; differentiation
    29
interaction 2, 3, 4
interactional forms 2, 10
interdependence, of knowledge
    and power 6; of market and
    entertainment 9
interpretive resources 5
intertextuality 136
interventionist approach 190, 192
invention, of 'the people' 114
ironic image 134
irony of dramaturgy 198;
    consciousness 108

Jorvic Viking Centre, York 179
journal 108

kingship 116
knowing, different forms of 135
knowledge, forms of 10

landscape, spectacular
    dramatisation 69; fictionalised 9
language, of civilisation 115; class
    61, 62, 65, 67, 68; cultural 59; of
    community 43, 46; of
    imagination in media accounts
    139; of individuality 36; of
    knowing 134; of political
    community 119; of politics 115
late-modern, culture 167; society
    34, 39
late-modernism 32, 33
late-modernity 38, 120
leisure 35, 79, 84, 101, 106, 109,
    116, 162; a characteristic of
    modernity 163; and play 190; as
    adaptations of popular drama 9;
    mobilisation of audiences for
    popular drama 163
Licensing Act of 1737 48

Licensing laws 49
life-style 36, 84, 106, 140
Loch Ness Monster 147
London 60, 73, 75

magic lantern 76
magician 76
Marxism 187
market imagery, metaphoric status
    of 185
marketing, of cultural forms 8;
    metaphor of grand myths for
    modernity 174; of culture 171;
    organisation of 8; parallels
    between consumer goods and
    mass entertainment 170
masquerade 25
mass, advertising 36, 109, 158;
    communication 8, 101, 118, 119,
    128, 141, 142, 157;
    communication, development
    of 154; consumption, hedonistic
    culture of 158; cultural forms
    148; cultural resources 107;
    culture 6, 8, 20, 40, 43, 119;
    distribution networks 70;
    democratic culture 116;
    electorate 113; entertainment 8,
    71, 79, 81, 95, 106, 181;
    entertainment, performances of
    155; international popular
    culture 70; marketing, design
    168; marketing, goods of 171;
    media 117; national culture 106;
    participation 114; photography
    85; politics 8, 115, 120, 137, 139;
    publics 119; society 101, 106,
    121
Mass Observation 32, 129
materialism, modern study of the
    development of 158
media 109, 132, 136; events 136
mediated culture 121
medieval nobility 26
medievalism 187, 192
melodrama 49, 54, 77, 79
melodramatic narrative 74
melodramatist, social 78
membership 4

metaphor 2, 4, 5, 8, 21, 59, 77;
    dramatic 57; generative 5; of
    drama 6; reflexive 6
metaphorical associations 87
metaphors, for forms of interaction
    5
metasocial 3
Metro Centre, Gateshead, a
    utopian zone 176, 177
metropolis 7, 58, 71, 73
metropolitan centres, as 'dream
    worlds' 161
metropolitan city 72, 102, 173;
    centres 68; culture 47, 69, 71,
    81; entertainment 57; society 94
mid-century 61, 67
middle-class 52, 57, 61, 65, 68;
    hegemony 69
modern, Europe 6
modernism 175
modernist aesthetics 177; forms,
    visions of collectivity and
    community 175; high culture 175
modernity 2, 7, 24, 32, 35, 36, 40,
    59, 86, 93, 104, 109, 118, 140; a
    sense of the self 40; changing
    forms of representation 159;
    conditions of social order 88;
    early 40; institutionalisation of
    14; languages of collectivity and
    subjectivity 195; made
    accessible through utopian
    forms 174; paradigmatic
    characteristics of 158
monoliths 63
moral order 47, 149, 150
morality plays 27
multi-national, cultural
    bureaucracies 37, 118
multiple realities 90
municipal authorities 27, 68
Museum of Modern Art 112
music hall 57, 58, 78
musical concerts 62
myth 28, 120, 127, 137

narrative, post-modern 137
nation-state 101, 113, 121
national, character 69;

broadcasting networks 119
nationalism 119
naturalism 47, 48, 55
naturalistic 53
nature, a form of spectacle 182
Nazi, urban and political
    regeneration 172
Nazism 192
networks 4
New Deal 104
news 130, 132, 133; as a form of
    drama 8; as ceremonialisation
    138; as distinct symbolic space
    139; as narrative genre 138; as
    public discourse 131; studies
    130, 131
newspaper 48, 117
nineteenth century 7, 34, 45, 57,
    50, 59, 61, 65, 68, 73, 75, 78, 91,
    115, 149
normative order 32
nostalgia 137
nostalgic communalism 173
nude, female 95; male 95

obscurantism 49
objectification 98
objectivity 51, 131
other, the 115, 192
otherness 37, 97, 116, 147

painting 75
Panorama, Barker's 75
Parisian urban entertainment 61
participation 108; privatised in
    communal forms 177; value of
    184
pastoralism 64
perceptual representation 74
performance 3, 51, 71, 83; as
    dramaturgical metaphor 17;
    commercial 18; in modernity 113
performative character 4
personal experience, show of 96;
    as privatised public drama 35
personalisation, of community 176
personification, significance of 40
phenomenological 136
phenomenology, of theatrical

representation 55
Philistine populism 175
photographic picturing 87; as
    celebration 99; as control 88;
    seeing 105
photographs, art and news 83;
    mass character of 85
photography 101; as first
    spectacular of mass culture 96;
    celebration of mortality 91;
    ethnographic 100
photo-journalism 104
photo-magazine 101
pictorial 55; images 33; language
    21; naturalism 7, 58, 80, 88, 96;
    representation 55; space 81;
    synthesis 74
pictorialism 76, 77, 79
Picture Post 104
picturing, forms of 88; as form of
    control 97; theatricality of 112
play, deep 3, 4; of community 44;
    pragmatic 43
polarisation, polite and popular
    culture 46
political organisation 68;
    spectator, class of 133; violence
    133
politicisation, of the production of
    meaning 188
polymorphous 104
popular, as language of
    exploitation 131; as 'other' as
    proletarian 193; as the form of
    proletarian life 62; government
    114; life 109; newspaper 72,
    152; voice 116, 135
popular culture 59, 60, 84, 120;
    forms of 15, 45, 48; naturalism
    of 175; 'rational recreation' 50;
    understanding of 11; use of
    'artistic' ideas 198
popular experience, 'land-scape
    of' 45
popular photography 81, 82, 84,
    87, 88, 91, 92, 94, 98, 103, 105,
    106, 109, 111
popular press, nineteenth century
    151

popular, the, as a form of
collective life 197, 114, 119, 189;
fracturing of social order 192;
organising perspectives 190
pornographic photography 96, 98
pornography 97
pornotopian 96
post-industrial 32
post-modern 6, 112, 129
post-modernism 32, 38, 177
post-modernity 2
post-traditional 36
power, in social thought 14
pre-industrial village 13
pre-modern 30, 40, 61, 62; social
practice 193
primitivism, vitality of 198
printing 117; first form of mass
communication 159
privatisation 64
privileging, text and author 55
process 107
procession 27, 28
proletariat, their popular culture 7,
191
Proletkult 192
prosaic, naturalism 88
pub 57
public, the 114, 116, 118, 119; as a
rhetorical figure 127
public address 141; discourse 8,
117; events 18, 19; memory 86,
88, 90; relations 102; time 89,
90; voice 122, 123
public consciousness, medium of
196
public culture 118, 121, 129, 131,
133
public drama 2, 3, 18, 19, 20, 21,
26, 33, 35, 36, 37, 56, 68, 82,
104; as a conceptual device and
a metaphor 140
public figures, a vocabulary of
style and manner 146; as
symbolic leaders 143
public life 21, 41, 50, 110, 113, 121;
heroes of 143; participation in 140
public opinion 117, 118, 126, 137,
139

public order, rationality of 93
public service 124; broadcasting
124, 125
public space, changing
de-lineation of 56, 63
public sphere 68, 113; symbolic
character of 147
publics 8, 116, 117, 130, 136, 184,
192; institutionalisation of 139
punks 22

quattrocento perspective 44
Queen's coronation 183

realist aesthetics 31; norms 34
reflexive, accounts of collective
experience 10; participation 108
reflexivity 105, 107, 108; of modes
of communal affiliation 196; of
picturing 7
Reithian 124, 125
relativism, radical 32; abyss at the
edge of 98
religious, authority 116
Renaissance, 117; Florence 27;
reality, representation of 101
reporting, grammar of 134
representation 33, 130; changes in
form of 148
representation, autonomy of 38;
character of 9; rethinking 10
respectable society 66
respectability, as an art form 55
restaurant 73
revisionist 63
revolution 115
revolutionary, society 116
rhetoric of participation 101
riots 131
ritual 2, 19, 23, 24, 30, 46, 82, 87,
91, 105, 108, 110, 119, 127, 190,
196; constitutive form of 44;
secular 112; urban 46
ritualised dramatisation 24
role 17
romance, literature 141
romanticism 55
Royal Academy of Dramatic Arts
52, 75

script 17
secular 9, 111
seeing, ways of 7
self 4, 40, 108, 110
self-conscious, staging 81
self-consciousness, collective 115
self-identity, reflexivity of 188
semantic 133
semiotic instability 38
sensation dramas 54
sensationalism 51, 54
sexual fantasy 96; myth 95
shopping malls, as dilution of
    modernism 176
significance and signification,
    relationship between 156
signification, of cultural space 182
simulacra 43
singing saloon 57
snapshots 92
social action, as performance 17;
    across periods and cultures 158
social, actors 6; body 41, 42;
    consciousness 14; control 7, 67;
    differentiation 64;
    discrimination 62; drama 3, 58,
    133; experience 7, 18, 35; form
    4, 44, 93; identity 18, 87, 90, 98;
    institution 6, 86, 87; intercourse
    7; marginality 52; meaning 71;
    orthodoxy 65; phenomenology
    53; projects 16; realism 22, 55;
    segregation 46, 54, 55; theory 5,
    41
social order 1, 3, 12, 13, 24, 25, 34,
    39, 59, 61, 62, 63, 66, 72, 94,
    113, 115, 131; a resource for
    mundane reasoning 195;
    institutionalisation of 39; in
    transition 45; language of
    control 148
social organisation, of production
    83
social relations carnivalisation of
    150
social space 15; subversive of
    184
sociation 1, 2, 81

society of spectacle 12, 24, 34, 35,
    36, 39, 43, 98; global 39
socio-anthropological 129;
    -structural 61
sociological terminology 16
sociology 193
sophistication, ironic, of popular
    consumerism 168
space, framed 87; as processes of
    social organisation 182; private
    64; redefinition of as defining
    feature of drama 28
spectacle 21, 22; as a form of
    drama 6; of a corporeality 40; of
    performance 39
spectacular, transcendence of
    mundane availability 22;
    articulation of the self 41;
    culture 46; display 36, 39, 42,
    55; dramatisation 7, 22, 24, 27,
    102; pictorialism 58, 76;
    presentation 21; realism 34;
    romantic realism 78; social
    order 23, 24, 26; theatricality 2
spectacular drama 39, 43, 44, 113;
    as naturalised into everyday
    experience 181; as utopian 23
spectacular entertainment,
    changing meaning of 7
spectacular society 6, 12, 24, 25,
    28, 29, 31, 35, 37, 39, 42, 43;
    early-modern 43; local 39
spectatorial 86
spheres, male and female 64;
    public and private 68
spirit world 80
sport 67, 190
squirearchy 68
stage 2, 17; as a machine 56;
    picture-frame 53
staging 17, 55, 57, 81, 122, 198;
    self-conscious 101; tourist
    locals 164
stardom 143
state, as a form of order 13;
    control 48
stereotype 58
street entertainment 57

structural amnesia 137
structural relationship 2
style 105; as key to identity 145; in archaeology 178; institutionalised in consumerism 178; re-writing of the person and self as moral actor 159; secret language of in youth cultures 142
stylisation 77
stylistic communities 38
sub-culture 107
suburb 64, 66
suburban domesticity 37
suburbanism 65
surrealist 129; movement 153
sur-reality 86; symbolic 96
surveillance 37, 84, 93
symbolism, of culture 38; association 93; conventional 89; practices 115
synchronicity 118

tabloid 97
taste, hierarchy of 82; popular 107, 168; publics 67
television 33, 141, 152, 183; as pictorial magazine 152
textual forms 20
theatre 47, 48, 50, 51, 57; as changing type of social space 7; as popular cultural form 7; commercial 48, 58; cultural form of 50; illegitimate 48; institutional respectability 54; of consumption 167; of shopping 162; popular 51, 57; urban 50, 54
Theatres Royal 48, 49
theatrical, art 52; conventions 58; entertainment 52, 56, 59; representation 56; space 53, 55, 57; vernacular 93
theatricality 6; new conventions of 74
theme parks 164
time, mechanised 89; as a commodity 89
torture, history of 41

tourism 35; as adaptations of popular drama 9; as disciplinary codes governing the abstract crowds of mass entertainment 151; mass, leisure of 155; practice of gazing 164
tourist 103, 109, 164; photography 103, 109; post-modern 166
transcendance 197, 198
transformation 29, 31, 39, 77, 117, 135, 142; meaning of culture 193; of leisure and popular entertainment 150; of performer and setting 18; of space 140
transgression, 38; epistemology of 151
transitions 2, 57, 70
transparency of image 85
truth, to materials 187, 188

upper class 65
urban, communities 60; ecology 72; elites 68; entertainment 149; fabric 62; guilds 27; landscape 23, 59, 65, 72; migration 65; proletariat 58, 192; society 45, 68; sophistication 78; space 46, 64
urban culture 10, 60, 68; pre-industrial 46
urban-industrial, society 2, 7, 35, 42, 90, 119, 191; city 57
urbanisation 20, 59, 60, 79, 81
urbanism, as spectacle 71
utopia 174
utopian, forms 9; sociology 153
utopianism, towns 173

variety entertainment 50
verisimilitude 139, 197; of the spectacle 140
vernacular 60, 84, 112; approach to popular culture 190, 193; culture 191
Victorian 55, 56, 58, 63, 66, 80
village society, pre-modern 138
vocabulary, of physical distinction 65; means through which public discourse is spoken 147

voice, public 124, 125, 126
vulgar cultural forms 40
vulgarity 61, 62
voyeurism 94, 110

West End companies 54
'woman's topic' 64
working class, culture 61, 64;
    residential districts 66